DISCURSIVE PSYCHOLOGY

D0859164

INQUIRIES IN SOCIAL CONSTRUCTION

Series editors
Kenneth J. Gergen and John Shotter

This series is designed to facilitate, across discipline and national boundaries, an emergent dialogue within the social sciences which many believe presages a major shift in the western intellectual tradition.

Including among its participants sociologists of science, psychologists, management and communications theorists, cyberneticists, ethnomethodologists, literary theorists, feminists and social historians, it is a dialogue which involves profound challenges to many existing ideas about, for example, the person, selfhood, scientific method and the nature of scientific and everyday knowledge.

It has also given voice to a range of new topics, such as the social construction of personal identities; the role of power in the social making of meanings; rhetoric and narrative in establishing sciences; the centrality of everyday activities; remembering and forgetting as socially constituted activities; reflexivity in method and theorizing. The common thread underlying all these topics is a concern with the processes by which human abilities, experiences, commonsense and scientific knowledge are both *produced in*, and *reproduce* human communities.

Inquiries in Social Construction affords a vehicle for exploring this new consciousness, the problems raised and the implications for society.

Also in this series

DISCURSIVE PSYCHOLOGY

DEREK EDWARDS
and
JONATHAN POTTER

SAGE Publications
London • Newbury Park • New Delhi

© Derek Edwards and Jonathan Potter 1992

First published 1992

All rights reserved. No part of this publication may be
reproduced, stored in a retrieval system, transmitted or
utilized in any form or by any means, electronic,
mechanical, photocopying, recording or otherwise, without
permission in writing from the Publishers.

 SAGE Publications Ltd
6 Bonhill Street
London EC2A 4PU

SAGE Publications Inc
2455 Teller Road
Newbury Park, California 91320

SAGE Publications India Pvt Ltd
32, M-Block Market
Greater Kailash – I
New Delhi 110 048

British Library Cataloguing in Publication Data

A catalogue record for this book is available from the
British Library.

ISBN 0 8039 8442 1
ISBN 0 8039 8443 X pbk

Library of Congress catalog card number 92–50170

Typeset by Mayhew Typesetting, Rhayader, Powys
Printed in Great Britain by Hartnolls Ltd, Bodmin,
Cornwall

Contents

Acknowledgements

This book was undoubtedly shaped by the many hours we spent arguing and thinking with Malcolm Ashmore, Michael Billig, Dave Middleton and Margaret Wetherell. We are particularly grateful to them, finally, for leaving for Leeds, Philadelphia, San Diego and the upstairs study, and letting us get on with it with surprisingly little complaint. All sorts of others have had some intellectual input, and we would pick out Anna Dempsey, Nigel Edley, Mike Gane, Ros Gill from the Loughborough Discourse and Rhetoric Group, and Charles Antaki, John Bowers, Paul Drew and Rob Wooffitt for assorted theoretical input. We are also grateful to the journal editors and referees who provided the opportunity for plenty of rethinking and kept us mindful of the social structure of psychology. Finally, Sue Jones at Sage has been a terrific editor, and we would like to thank series editors John Shotter and Ken Gergen for encouragement and numerous helpful suggestions.

We are grateful to Steve Bell for permission to reproduce the cartoons (originally published in the *Guardian*) as Box 6, and to John Wiley & Sons, Ltd for permission to reproduce some parts of chapters 2, 3 and 5 from *Applied Cognitive Psychology* (1992, in press) and from the *European Journal of Social Psychology*, 20 (1990).

Introduction

The writing of this book coincided almost exactly with the Gulf War of 1990–91. Having spent some months wondering whether there was a book in what we were doing, planning and arguing, we started the job of writing soon after the Iraqi invasion in August. The last chapter was completed as the first pictures of the devastation wrought on the fleeing Iraqi troops (if we may so describe those events for now) started to appear on television. We were particularly struck by the way that what we were writing about psychology could be applied to the versions of the Gulf War that were made available in a torrent of media coverage. The events that took place were, to us, inextricable from their various constructions, each of which allowed for inferences about motives and morality, about strategy and politics. Yet, despite a recent emphasis on naturalism and ecological validity, the perspectives from mainstream psychology which might have been drawn upon to make some sense of these processes offered little even to begin this task.

The psychology of memory has little to say about the way versions of what happened in the recent and more distant past played a part in legitimating and sustaining the war. The psychology of attribution (everyday causal reasoning) has scant regard for the way versions of events are actively put together to bolster particular causal stories and undermine others. For many psychologists, particularly those with a primary concern with capacities and processes, these questions are simply uninteresting, and indeed may stretch their definition of what a proper, or a scientific, psychology should look like. This book is not meant to undermine what we see as entirely reasonable theoretical and empirical concerns. We would not want it to be read as yet another negative attack on traditional psychological work. Nevertheless, it will become clear in the course of this book that the kind of reconceptualizing that we are arguing for, in how conversational and textual materials are dealt with, has profound implications for the conceptualization and practice of traditional psychological approaches.

This book is designed to accomplish three sorts of tasks. First of all, it outlines a new model of how some central psychological phenomena are related in participants' discourse. Our hope is that this model can provide a fertile scheme for interpreting and making sense of a wide range of types of psychological talk. The second task is to illustrate, through an extended set of related analyses, the type of analytical work that underpins discursive psychology. A major feature of such analysis, and something which may seem relatively unfamiliar to psychologists, is its close attention to the fine detail of talk and texts. The third and final task is to develop a critical contrast to the perceptual and cognitivist assumptions that currently underlie much psychological work. The book is organized as an extended argument with perceptual-cognitivism in the guise of memory research and the social psychology of causal attribution. We will elaborate on the first two of these tasks before going on to describe the argument of the individual chapters. Elaboration of the third task makes up the substance of Chapter 1.

A model of discursive action

Although the analyses presented in the course of this book have their own specific focuses, they are meant to provide a cumulative picture of the interrelation among key concepts of discursive psychology. We have tried to explicate this interrelation in terms of a 'discursive action model'. This is a scheme which will be described more fully in Chapter 7, when the analytical bases for all the steps in the argument are in place. Nevertheless, it will be useful to give a bald overview of some of its central points here as a frame for understanding some of the detail of later chapters.

The focus of discursive psychology is the action orientation of talk and writing. For both participants and analysts, the primary issue is the social actions, or interactional work, being done in the discourse. But rather than focusing on the usual concerns of social interactional analyses, such as the way social and intergroup relationships are conducted (through forms of address, speech accommodation and so on), or how 'speech acts' might be identified, the major concern in this book is epistemological. We are concerned with the nature of knowledge, cognition and reality: with how events are described and explained, how factual reports are constructed, how cognitive states are attributed. These are defined as discursive topics, things people topicalize or orientate themselves to, or imply, in their discourse. And rather than seeing such discursive constructions as expressions of speakers' underlying cognitive states, they are examined in the context of their occurrence as situated and occasioned constructions whose precise nature makes sense, to participants and analysts alike, in terms of the social actions those descriptions accomplish. So, within the model, remembering is understood as the situated production of versions of past events, while attributions are the inferences that these versions make available, and that participants *treat as* implied.

One of our central arguments is with the treatment of descriptive discourse in perceptual-cognitivism. In particular, we argue against the common assumption that participants' use of ostensibly descriptive discourse is a sign of 'objectivity', or a sign that more 'psychological' considerations are irrelevant. The problem with this is that it misses the fact that, in everyday discourse, descriptions and reports are often drawn on *precisely* when there is a sensitive or controversial issue at stake (Drew, 1984; Pomerantz, 1984b). Indeed, we suggest that reports and descriptions may be used to manage what, for participants in natural settings, is often a crucial dilemma: the dilemma of presenting factual reports while being treated as having a stake in some specific version of events or some practical outcome. The recipients of such reports may well, in turn, respond to them accordingly, as designed to manage that dilemma. So, by offering a report rather than, say, directly making an accusation, speakers do not ensure a certain interactional outcome, but seek to garner the accountability of 'just telling it how it is'.

Once it is established that participants conduct important psychological business via reports and descriptions, then a novel analytical realm is brought to the fore. This is the realm of fact construction: the sorts of everyday procedures that are drawn on to make any particular version appear credible and difficult to undermine. The major significance of these sorts of procedures can be seen once the central role of reports in managing the dilemma of interest is recognized. Given that reports are commonly a way of performing delicate and psychologically problematic actions, and given that they are often received in precisely this way, then it is important for people to sustain them as factual, disinterested versions. One of the major analytical tasks of discursive psychology is the identification of participants' techniques that help to generate this factuality.

The use of description to manage the dilemma of stake through performing actions in a variety of indirect ways suggests a further analytical focus for discursive psychology, and that is the rhetorical construction of factual versions. One of the features of descriptions or reports being proffered in situations of dispute is that they are typically contrasting versions. That is, they are typically organized to undermine or reject an alternative that may be either explicit or implicit. This has, in turn, a further important analytical implication; that rather than trying to explicate the nature of some factual account through considering its relation to an external 'reality' as defined by the analyst, it can be more fruitful to consider its relation to versions that participants treat as alternative.

The final major feature of the model is its emphasis on the centrality of *accountability* for making sense of participants' discourse. Psychologists have paid close and systematic attention to one level of accountability, specifically where people attribute responsibility for events. This is the major focus of attribution theory. There is a second level of accountability, however, that has hardly been attended to at all, and that is the accountability of the speaker who is producing the report, or the description of the world, from which the causal inferences are supposed to be drawn. Again, once we let go of the objective reality of particular descriptions of events, and consider everyday reportings as parts of discursive actions of different kinds, then we would expect accountability to be a pervasive feature. Indeed, we take issue strongly with the idea of 'mere description' that somehow lies outside the realm of human accountability. Furthermore, we attempt to show that these two levels of accountability have a complex pattern of interrelation. For example, we address the way in which a report of past events, which formulates or implies accountability for those events, can be constructed and deployed to manage issues of accountability in the current interactions being performed in talking. Similarly, characterizations of current actions being performed in speaking may make inferences available about responsibility in the reported events. These rather condensed and schematic themes will be fleshed out in specific analyses in the book's main chapters.

Analysis, detail and rejection of the blurred picture

Although the number of studies of participants' discourse is growing fast in psychology, they are still relatively few and fragmented. For this reason we have chosen to illustrate this combined theoretical and analytical approach through a sustained set of studies of similar materials: public political controversies. A feature of these analyses is a concern with textual detail that is, perhaps, unusual in psychology. Part of the reason for this general lack of concern may be some widespread but usually implicit theoretical assumptions about the nature of discourse.

The area where psychology *has* been closely concerned with the details of naturally occurring language are those of speech production and reception. Here speech errors and minutely fine elements of speech sounds are used to throw light on basic psychological and physiological mechanisms. But it is as if these sorts of phenomena relate to a psychological realm beyond, or below, everyday human practices. This fits too, of course, with the classic psychoanalytical approach to speech errors which treats them as surface manifestations of unconscious processes. However, when psychologists are dealing with talk in terms of its meaning for participants, then two sorts of routes to abstraction are typically taken.

One of these routes, classically associated with Chomsky, is to treat actual linguistic performance – talk with all its timing, intonation and so-called errors – as simply too messy and disorderly to be addressed. The solution is the study of linguistic competence, the supposed ideal grammatical organization that underlies the chaotic realization of actual speech. In a more recent guise this sort of idealization and abstraction from actual speech appears in much computationally based research on cognitive processes.

The other route is more widespread where language *per se* is not the topic of research, but is the medium for consideration of some other topic such as memory or causal attribution. Here, abstraction from the detail of everyday talk is generally achieved in two ways which we can class as *restriction* and *gross categorization* (see Potter and Wetherell, 1987: 39–41). 'Restriction' effectively prevents any participant's natural discourse from entering into consideration through allowing only a highly circumscribed set of 'responses' to count as data. The 'subject' has to tick boxes, circle words, recall or recognize stretches of text, rank a set of options provided by the experimenter, and so on. The fact that researchers attempt to restrict responses in this way does not mean that participants are unable to accomplish a variety of subtle semiotic feats within this limited universe; but it nevertheless makes such feats easy to ignore. And on the whole that is precisely what is done with them.

Although 'restriction' has been widespread in psychology as a way of managing the complexity of natural language materials, there has recently been a recognition, encouraged by a range of critics of research methodology (for example, Gergen, 1978; Harré, 1979), that much is lost by taking this approach. Not only does it heavily predefine what are to count as data, it also prevents the use of natural language materials collected outside the laboratory or survey. The typical response to this, for naturally occurring discourse, has been to draw on some form of content analysis.

In principle, content analysis is a theoretically neutral method; you define precisely some category that you are interested in, and then do a frequency count. The subsequent figures can then be manipulated statistically to reveal various patterns and potential causal processes. However, it is precisely its reliance on the production of decontextualized definitions of segments of talk which marks its inadequacy for dealing with the richness and complexity of discursive materials. By way of such 'gross categorization' techniques the detailed designs of turns of talk can be submerged into general summary statistics. The ideal effect is like a blurred picture which reveals the general forms, but obscures the confusing detail.

Ultimately, the fault lies neither with researchers using restriction procedures nor with the gross categorization of content; it is more fundamentally with the conceptualization of discourse that sees it as a (rather messy) pathway to cognition. The analyses that are developed in this book take a very different perspective, under-, pinned by the discursive action model, which views what would traditionally be seen as the mess or the fine detail as crucially important for the sense of the activities being performed in the talk. This is a principle derived from conversation analysis in which, from its inception, it was established that even the finest levels of conversational detail, every speech error, pause, overlap and lexical correction, might be there as a 'designed' or consequential feature of social action (Sacks, 1964; cf. Schegloff, 1989; Wooffitt, 1990). We pursue this principle in the analyses below. Some readers, particularly some psychologist readers, we suspect, may think that we have taken it too far. However, we hope to make the case as strongly as possible that psychologists should be in the business of tracking down the detail.

Political discourse and the consensus assumptions of psychology

In the course of the different chapters we consider talk and writing from a variety of different sources, including courtroom cross-examinations, everyday telephone conversations, newspaper reports, television interviews, the Iran–Contra hearings and Watergate testimony. Because of its immediacy and significance we also felt impelled to consider some examples of Gulf War discourse. Our most detailed focus, however, is on two sets of materials from British political life. The first relates to a controversial press briefing where a number of journalists claimed they were told by a government minister, who then denied it, that a controversial change in benefits for the elderly was about to be made. The second concerns the motive for Chancellor Lawson's highly damaging resignation.

In each case, these materials provide an excellent opportunity for developing the main themes of the discursive action model which we are offering as a centrepiece of discursive psychology. They also cover events which, in their type if not their specifics, are widely familiar, and we hope that readers will find these materials both intrinsically interesting and of such a type that they can make an informed judgement about the adequacy of our analysis.

It could be argued that we have chosen, in public political discourse, an easy arena in which to consider the operation of interest management, fact construction and accountability: a soft test of discursive psychology. Surely, it could be argued, these phenomena should be expected here and that hardly proves that they appear, or at least appear in the same way, in ordinary discourse or in other realms. There is some cogency to this argument, and we shall certainly not erect a case that analysis of public political discourse should replace analyses of other materials, particularly everyday talk, which elsewhere we also have analysed. Nevertheless, there are important shortcomings and assumptions to the 'soft test' argument.

First of all, we would question the intuition that public political discourse is self-evidently a softer case for the study of fact construction and accountability. For example, one of its features – and this contrasts with everyday talk – is that there is a variety of public records (for example, *Hansard*, media reporting) in which politicians' claims can be checked and tested. Everyday interaction is conducted in situations which are bereft of these kinds of records and, for the most part, outside the gaze of expert commentators and critics. In this sense, public political discourse is a *hard* case; processes are likely to be easier to demonstrate in everyday settings where such checks are rarely available, and talk is more 'naively' produced, more open perhaps in its artifices.

Secondly, we do try in the course of the different chapters to show how the insights that we have developed from a study of public political discourse can help make sense of features of different sorts of discourse, including everyday talk. Without claiming that the specific organizations will be the same in these contexts, the analytical benefits from working with this material can make it an excellent starting point, and have helped generate insights into the subtleties of ordinary talk.

There is a third and more general point which relates again to the assumptions widely taken for granted in current psychological practice. Memory and attribution research have overwhelmingly attempted to produce a psychology of people trying their best, in a disinterested manner, to remember events or adduce causal responsibility. The assumption is that if we start with these artificial situations, where the cognitive processes work in an abstract or unimpeded manner, then it might be possible later to add in the effects of stake, conflict or rhetoric. What we see here is the way psychology has built its own presupposed model of the person, and indeed society, deep into the heart of its own methods (cf. Moscovici, 1972). Why is it that consensus and disinterest should be the norm, the baseline, while conflict and stake are secondary, something *parasitic* (Derrida, 1977a) on the norm? That is not an empirical finding. It has certainly not been discovered by any experiment. So, by taking public political discourse, and, moreover, concentrating much of our interest on conflictual situations involving activities of blaming and excusing, we are deliberately working to invert this basic assumption.

An overview of the book

Chapter 1 contrasts discursive and cognitivist positions in psychology. This sets the scene, noting a recent convergence of interest in cognitive and social psychology, on the study of everyday situations and discourse. We discuss basic issues such as reductionism, and the role of perceptual assumptions in cognitivism, as well as providing a brief overview of the basic features of a discourse-based approach. A contrast is drawn between cognitivist approaches to language, where texts, sentences and descriptions are taken as depictions of an externally given world, or as realizations of underlying cognitive representations of that world; and the discursive approach where versions of events, things, people and so on, are studied and theorized primarily in terms of how those versions are *constructed in an occasioned manner to accomplish social actions*. This re-orientation has the effect of bringing together the usually disparate topics of memory (event representation) and attribution (causal explanations).

   Following this, Chapters 2 and 3 focus specifically on the development of a discursive approach to memory. Chapter 2 addresses Ulric Neisser's well-known study of John Dean's memory, in which he discusses Dean's crucial testimony to the Watergate investigating committee. We argue that Neisser's treatment of Dean's testimony, as evidence of the workings of memory, fails to do justice to how that testimony is constructed to accomplish particular interactional tasks. Phenomena that Neisser categorizes as the workings of different kinds of memory, are re-interpreted as features of discourse. We also raise here the problems of truth and error, as analyst's criteria for participants' rememberings, and examine how Neisser accounts for Dean's errors in terms of the workings of his personality. This notion of personality as providing an explanatory basis for erroneous cognitions, and for causal attributions, is a theme that we take up in later chapters. We also draw attention in Chapter 2 to another recurrent theme: the importance of specific descriptions in event reportings, and how they imply the kinds of causal explanations that are the topic of attribution theory.

Chapter 3 takes up some of the points raised and explores them in a set of our own materials, which provide further evidence of the 'action-orientated' nature of discursive remembering. We also explore further the way assumptions about truth and error in cognitively based memory research are rendered problematical when dealing with people's talk in natural contexts. 'What really happened' is the potentially contentious business of discourse about past events, such that it makes analytical sense to treat it as an outcome of, rather than an input to, how people construct versions of events in talk. The psychologist's privileged position of being able to define, over the heads of participants, the true nature of events has proved a powerful one in experimental studies, but it is a position that can also be illusory (there is no single, definitive version of everyday events), and risks losing sight of what is real for participants themselves. It focuses attention on objective truth and error, and underestimates the constructive, occasioned and rhetorically designed nature of how events are ordinarily described.

If Chapters 2 and 3 show that discursive remembering can be understood as the construction of versions which form the basis of actions, the next two chapters examine the converse of this idea, looking at the way attributions (considered as social actions) can be generated by versions. This reflects one of the main points of the book which is that, in terms of discursive practices, memory and attribution are two sides of the same coin: making reports in talk or text (discursive remembering) is one principal way of accomplishing blamings, mitigations and other sorts of responsibility (everyday causal attributions).

In Chapter 4, recent work in attribution theory which has started to address the role of language is critically reviewed, including studies that deal with attributional reasoning as features of grammar and semantics. While these studies provide useful insights into the kinds of lexical resources that are available for event description, they offer a highly constrained and sometimes tautological model of how people explain events. Other recent approaches are welcomed for offering a more 'conversational' basis for attributional explanations, but again these tend to be idealizations of conversational practices, appealing, for example, to Grice's well-known maxims for conversational coherence rather than to the details of actual talk. We argue that, despite their overt emphasis on natural discourse, both these approaches retain an inappropriate cognitivist meta-theory of mental processes, and ignore crucial features of everyday explanations such as the importance of descriptions as 'interested versions' of events.

In Chapter 5 the importance of discursively situated descriptions is argued further, as we show how one of the central elements in traditional attribution theory, the notion of consensus information, can be reworked in terms of a discursive approach. Rather than having attributional reasoning following automatically from perceptually derived event information, discursive psychology focuses on how events are *constructively described* in ways that, *for participants*, imply particular causal accounts. We show how it is necessary to examine the details and sequential placing of specific accounts in order to see how the process works, how attributional inferences are generated by event descriptions within communicative activities. Discursive psychology reworks the notions of consensus or consistency across events, as discursive claims or achievements, constructed or undermined via an identifiable set of rhetorical devices, and as performing further social action and rhetoric *through* being constructed or demolished.

Chapter 6 follows up the implications of these reworkings of memory and attribution through a discussion of what is involved in the analysis of fact construction (descriptive discourse). It also illustrates the way further psychological notions of *role* and *personality* can be understood as resources for performing particular activities in discourse. As well as providing grounds for cognitive error accounting, and for undermining versions and causal implications provided by other people, we show how particular versions of role and personality can be constructed to work in explanatory opposition to each other, as well as demonstrating the descriptive work necessary to establish particular actions as being due to one or the other. So Chapter 6 brings together, via empirical materials, the constructive discourse of event reporting, fact and error, causal explanation, and role versus trait descriptions. These are shown to work off each other, having to be *constructed as* fact/role and so on, and put to work in a mutually implicative manner in the discursive accomplishment of social actions. It is a central feature of discursive psychology that it treats both external reality and mental states as participants' concerns: not as psychologically prior phenomena, as inputs or explanations of talk's content, but rather as phenomena that are themselves open to constructive description and implication, by participants, as parts of discursive actions.

The final chapter then integrates the various strands and outlines that we have called a 'discursive action model', relating questions of action, fact and interest, and accountability. In addition, it overviews the methods of fact construction in lay discourse that have been documented in the course of the book. Readers may find it useful to cross-refer to this while they are reading other chapters.

Overall, the book is designed not just to present an argument for a discourse-based approach to psychological phenomena, but to introduce some of the main concerns and concepts from that approach in a relatively systematic manner. To assist with this aim, the text is interrupted every so often with boxes which highlight or set aside particular notions or concerns, and develop them further, or differently, than would have been possible in the main text. A number of these boxes address the reflexive questions which inevitably arise when writing a text full of reports, descriptions and explanations which is all about the very status of reports, descriptions and explanations. That is, we have tried in a small way to face up to the consequences of our theory for our own practice. Undoubtedly, we have been too timid here; but we hope to have illustrated some of the questions that this approach provokes for the practice of academic psychology itself.

Finally, some comment is in order about the book's title, *Discursive Psychology*. In the past we have often referred to this kind of perspective as discourse analysis. This has undoubted benefits in highlighting links with other work in sociology and linguistics. However, it also had the unfortunate consequence that it is sometimes treated as a method only, a technique something on a par with an experiment or a questionnaire, which are methods that have been generated from within the framework of variables, effects and responses presupposed by most of traditional and modern psychology. Discursive psychology is a term designed partly to indicate that there is more than a methodological shift at work; there is some fairly radical theoretical rethinking. In this particular book, however, it implies more than that, for it marks a reconstruction of topics that are in the heartland of current psychology: memory and attribution. Before we start that reconstruction, however, we need to consider what it is that marks out a cognitivist approach in psychology.

1

The Social and the Cognitive

The questions 'what happened?' and 'why?' are fundamental ones in a whole range of everyday and institutional settings. They form the centrepiece of science and education as well as everyday talk about friends and relations. Courtrooms and hairdressing salons are places where questions of fact and motivation are explored and judgements pronounced. The central argument of this book can be summarized in two points. First, the particular compartmentalization of psychology, which has placed the 'what happened?' question in the sub-field of cognitive psychology (in the guise of memory research) and the 'why?' question in the sub-field of social psychology (in the guise of attribution research), has left psychology with, at best, a fragmented understanding of human affairs. Secondly, in both cognitive and social psychology, understanding of everyday practices has been deformed by a combination of methodological prescription and a failure to theorize language as the primary mode of social activity.

This argument will be developed in a number of different directions in the course of the book. In this first chapter our goal is to set the scene in a number of ways. First, we shall introduce the ideas of cognitivism and perceptualism and illustrate how their central assumptions have underpinned research on memory and attribution. Secondly, we shall provide an overview of a 'discourse and rhetoric' approach, a discursive psychology, which provides our own theoretical context and informs the more specific analyses that are provided in subsequent chapters. At the same time we shall introduce the idea of courtrooms, legal settings and the adversarial process which recurs throughout the book as a theme or motif. Formal disputations and cross-examinations offer a meeting place for cognitive psychology and studies of everyday discourse, throwing into relief limitations in psychological work and possibilities in discourse analysis.

Converging on discourse

Cognitive and social psychology are usually thought of as separate enterprises. They are dealt with in separate textbooks, or separate chapters of introductory textbooks, separate topics in under-graduate degree courses, separate academic journals. Where a relationship exists, social psychology is the derivative element. Cognitive psychology occupies the mainstream, in its own histories having slain the behaviourist beast and taken its place as psychology's foundational enterprise (Gardner, 1985; Johnson-Laird, 1988). The central topics are perception, memory, language and mental representation, knowledge and reasoning. Social and developmental psychologies have generally followed in its wake, particularly in North America and Britain, defining their problems and issues as cognitive ones, while re-asserting their own older cognitive roots in the work of thinkers such as Jean Piaget and Fritz Heider. Social psychology has largely become the study of social cognition, of how individuals perceive, categorize, interpret the social world, represent it mentally, make inferences about it, explain it causally, such that the social lives of individuals flow from how they perceive, hypothesize or reason about each other (Eiser, 1986; Fiske and Taylor, 1984; Forgas, 1981).

We shall refer to this explanatory strategy, of claiming for the cognitive processes of individuals the central role in shaping perception and action for social and developmental as well as mainstream psychology, as 'cognitivism' (cf. Costall and Still, 1987; Coulter, 1983). In doing so we are not wanting to suggest that there is one coherent theory subscribed to by all. Nevertheless, along with its basic strategy, there tend to be grouped a range of methodological assumptions and practices, a number of inspirational and exemplary studies, a body of taken-for-granted theory and a network of more or less formal groupings and social institutions. For this reason, our arguments will have to be developed on a number of different levels, and part of our task is to make taken-for-granted assumptions and implicit practices explicit, and show how they help structure the content of cognitivist explanation.

There are signs that the separated but derivative co-existence of social and cognitive psychology may be breaking down, and not merely because they share a cognitivist perspective. These signs are, first, a new desire to move outside artificial laboratory settings and into the 'ecological' settings in which people normally think, act and live their real lives. Secondly, and related to this movement to the natural, is an increasing concern with discourse. Of course, these are not entirely new developments. The psychological investigation of behaviour in natural settings has a pedigree older than computational models of mind (for example, Barker, 1968), although this was hampered by some of the most naively positivist thinking that psychology has produced.

Language has enjoyed a central importance in cognitivist psychology since its modern inception. Chomsky's (1959) clinical destruction of Skinner's treatise *Verbal Behavior*, and his own promotion of generative linguistics, are celebrated events in the birth of the 'cognitive revolution' (Gardner, 1985). However, this emphasis on language is a very different one from our own concern with discourse. For Chomsky, and the cognitive psychology he helped to spawn, language is a mental abstraction, knowledge of rules of syntax; it is explicitly not a social practice, not everyday talk. The psychological study of everyday talk was buried along with operant conditioning as a misguided pursuit for the new psychology of language.

Just as social psychology has taken on board many of the major assumptions and concerns of the cognitive revolution, there are signs that cognitive psychologists are themselves becoming more interested in the social and cultural. Notably, however, it is not social psychology as it is narrowly understood (as a sub-discipline of psychology) that they are looking to. There are at least three broad areas of work which are currently informing cognitive psychology that derive from the wider social and human sciences.

First, there is renewed interest in cognition as socially and culturally embedded, distributed between people, rooted not only in mental processes and computational inferences, but also in an externally given and real world of physical objects, artefacts and cultural practices (for example, Lave, 1988; Middleton and Edwards, 1990a; Neisser, 1982; Norman, 1988; Rogoff and Lave, 1984). Gibson's influential and non-cognitivist 'ecological optics' has also provided a spur to revised models of how cognitive processes might operate in a real world of objects and events (Gibson, 1979; Neisser, 1976).

Secondly, for some researchers, Vygotsky's developmental psychology (Vygotsky, 1987) has become the focal point for a new emphasis on language as a cultural medium for thought and action, embedded in everyday social practices (Cole, 1988; Edwards and Mercer, 1987; Edwards and Middleton, 1988; Lave, 1988; LCHC, 1983; Scribner and Cole, 1981; Wertsch, 1985). Some of this work has chosen to focus upon the study of naturally occurring discourse and text, though this is not a defining characteristic of work in the Vygotskian tradition. This treatment of cognitive processes as having to be studied within their cultural settings relates also to cognitive anthropological developments, such as proposals concerning how 'cultural meaning systems' are mentally represented (D'Andrade, 1981). Cognitive and linguistic development are viewed as a form of cultural apprenticeship and socialization

(Lave, 1990; Ochs and Schieffelin, 1984), and the birth, or perhaps resurrection, of 'cultural psychology' has been announced (Cole, 1990; Stigler et al., 1990).

Thirdly, and finally, there has been an increased interest in language as discourse. Cognitive psychology's interest in discourse derives from text-orientated linguistics, and from linguistic psychology (Grice, 1975; Searle, 1969; cf. Kintsch and Van Dijk, 1978; Winograd and Flores, 1986). On the whole this development has been quite independent of both social psychology and the study of ordinary talk, although there have been very recent attempts to utilize conversation analysis to model human–computer interaction (Luff et al., 1990; but see Button, 1990; Oldman and Drucker, 1985).

Taken together, these developments point to a convergence of interest in cognitive and social psychology and, furthermore, they move research concerns towards the study of everyday activity and discourse; that is, to concerns that we agree should be placed closer to centre stage. However, it is important to note that currently, at least, all of these developments remain peripheral to the mainstream cognitive pursuit, which remains the wedding of experimental cognitive psychology to neural and computational models of brain and mind (Johnson-Laird, 1988).

It is discourse, not language, which has to be the unifying theme for these recent developments. Broadly, discourse is to be treated as a social practice which can be studied as a real-world phenomenon rather than a theoretical abstraction. Later in this book we will explore some of the different senses in which the notion of discourse as a social practice can be understood and we shall have cause to distinguish our argument from some of the above. However, for the moment the important point we wish to emphasize is the convergence on the idea that discourse is central to interaction and cognition.

Discourse as topic or pathway to cognition

One of our themes will be the problem of treating everyday discourse as a route to cognition. That is, we shall question the idea that talk and text can be directly mapped onto underlying cognitive representations of knowledge and reasoning. A growing body of work has highlighted the pitfalls of treating everyday discourse as a pathway to cognition. To take one example, several studies have highlighted problems with cognitive interpretations of the notion of attitudes. These illustrate variations in attitude talk which are very difficult to reconcile with the notion that it is a reflection of an underlying cognitive entity (Billig, 1988a; Potter and Wetherell, 1987, 1988) and suggest that attitude talk is better seen as orientated to various sorts of activities (Billig, 1987, 1989a, 1991, 1992a; Condor, 1988; Potter and Wetherell, 1988; Smith, 1987; Wetherell and Potter, forthcoming).

Part of the difficulty with any translation from talk to cognition is that the concerns of the psychologist may also be the topics of ordinary talk; what was seen, remembered, understood? The talk displays how people define and pursue such topics, how they are deployed and resolved, how they are argued, claimed and avoided, and how they are formulated within conversational activities such as assigning or avoiding or mitigating blame. Participants' concerns for what happened and how to describe it are subjugated not to the disinterested pursuit of truth, but to the contingencies of practical action. Put another way, the epistemologies of our everyday discourse are organized around adequacy and usefulness rather than validity and correctness.

The consequence of starting to recognize this is that discourse becomes a topic of study in its own right (cf. Garfinkel, 1967; Zimmerman and Pollner, 1970). That is, conversational remembering ceases to be of interest merely because it might be a route to underlying cognitive processes; rather the organization and functions of such talk become the issue (Edwards and Middleton, 1986a). This means that conversation can not become simply another subject area, another textbook chapter to be placed alongside memory, reasoning, and such. For, as we shall show, topicalizing discourse, rather than using it as a pathway to memories and attributions, cuts across the conventional (though still controversial) pigeon-holings of cognitive psychology to reveal a quite different order of processes at work.

As we shall try to demonstrate in detail, participants' conversational versions of events (memories, descriptions, formulations) are constructed to do communicative, interactional work. A memory is not a mere recalling, isolated and serene, but is related to communicative actions and interests. Versions of mind, of thought and error, inference and reason, are constructed and implied in order to bolster or undermine versions of events, to accuse or criticize, blame or excuse and so on. In discourse, cognition and reality are subjugated to rhetoric. One of the problems with much traditional cognitive research is that it has attempted to study memory, say, as a phenomenon thoroughly permeated by linguistic representations and effects, but disembodied from any real discursive context.

Discursive psychology is concerned to bring these otherwise

contextual and peripheral phenomena into analytical focus. It is not designed to reveal the linguistic structuring of text and talk; nor is its aim to trawl talk for what it tells us about underlying cognitions. Instead, its focus is on how discourse accomplishes and is a part of social practices. This does not mean, however, that it is not addressing issues of everyday conception and reasoning; the point is that these things turn out to be rather different from what we might have expected had we merely stepped from the cognitive laboratory, carrying all of its cognitivist findings and assumptions with us, to see if we could identify cognition at work in the world (cf. the insights of Cole et al., 1978).

What we find in everyday talk is indeed a rich seam of concern about truth and error, mind and reality, memory and perception, knowledge and inference. But it is not a case of 'ordinary people' sitting around discussing such abstractions in some kind of folk psychological seminar, nor of their producing samples of speech which allow the cognitive researcher to unmask the underlying processes that produce them. What happens is that people casually and routinely construct formulations of such things (perception, knowledge, inference and so on) as part of everyday discursive practices, such as describing and reporting interesting events, making plans and arrangements, coordinating actions, accounting for errors and absences, accusing, excusing and blaming, refusing invitations, and so on.

So, our argument in brief is that the relationship between cognition and language has been a major and definitional concern of cognitive psychology. Recent developments have moved towards studying cognitive phenomena as real-world phenomena, and this necessarily involves dealing not with isolated and invented experimental texts, but with naturally occurring discourse. But when we study such discourse, rather than discovering in it how people represent, understand and remember events, what we find are an indefinitely variable range of situated versions and stories, accounts and glosses, descriptions and formulations, the best sense of which is achieved by examining them for their pragmatic placing and interactional orientation. Studying everyday discourse undermines the effort to apply laboratory findings to worldly practices, and encourages a reappraisal of the relations between language and cognition.

The study of such discursive actions is plainly not a straightforward substitute for cognitive and social psychology. But nor is it irrelevant to those pursuits. First of all, it is precisely these kinds of everyday discursive practices that social and cognitive psychology must at some point have to try to explain. Secondly, any 'application' of theories developed by traditional social and cognitive psychology to natural settings will be required to have some detailed understanding of the social and cognitive setting so that the experimentally defined variables can be tied in to naturalistic features. Thirdly, and perhaps most importantly, as we will show in later chapters, the examination of everyday discourse has strong implications for the adequacy of prevailing psychological approaches.

Reductionism

Discussions of the relationship between the social and the cognitive are often attempts to reduce one to the other. On the social, cultural or discursive side, it may be claimed that the phenomena of thought and reasoning, of mind and memory, are best understood as culturally formed, socially shaped and defined, constituted in talk and text, and so on. Cognitive processes, on this view, are not the springs of human sense and action, however much our everyday concepts of mind may get to be refined by experimental psychology and cognitive science. Rather, they are ideas generated within cultures, conceptions of sense, action and motive that people invent to mediate their dealings with each other, to engage in social forms of life. This line of argument is familiar, in one form or another, in the work of social constructionist writers such as Gergen (1982), Harré (1979, 1983), Moscovici (1984), Sampson (1988) and Shotter (1984).

Proponents of cognitivism can counter that not only do individuals perceive, reason and make sense of the world without having to talk to anybody else about it, but also that none of those social, communicative kinds of representation are possible without the presumption of individual minds designed to grasp, analyse and take part in such practices. Whatever can be done socially needs a set of individuals with the cognitive machinery and competence to take part. Culture itself can be conceived as the outcome of a biologically based human nature, the realization of an essentially human mode of thought and action. So no amount of demonstration of the cultural basis of human thought and action need make the slightest difference to a cognitivist position. Of course, it is in the nature of orthodoxies that proponents of the 'cognitivist paradigm' only rarely have to make explicit the foundations of their position and its virtues over alternatives.

Clearly, an approach to cognition and social cognition like ours, which has its theoretical and methodological foundations in the study of discourse, is likely to feel most at home on the social-cultural side of the fence. Various rhetorical strategies suggest themselves to uphold the virtues of this theoretical territory. For example, we could develop the reductionist argument in favour of the discursive organization of cognition, or we could argue for a kind of parcelling up of the field, a division of academic labour where some topics are best studied from one perspective, some from another. Another option might be to argue a developmental line, borrowed from Piaget or Vygotsky perhaps, such that the higher, cultural forms of cognition are later developments that build upon earlier, more primitive individual ones. All these moves have their proponents, and at times we have made them ourselves.

However, it is not our intention in this book to develop these sorts of arguments. Here we intended to bracket, or set aside, the issue of reductionism and origins in favour of an orientation to method and analysis. That is, our concern will be to examine how participants in talk address the kinds of concerns that cognitive and social psychologists have raised. Of course, the interest for psychologists then lies in what such studies may imply for prevailing models of cognition and social life.

Perceptualism, memory and attribution

Within some kinds of cognitivism there resides another basic assumption which it is important to tease out before we start. We shall call this 'perceptualism'. The significance of this is that while cognition remains the central concern, it needs some kind of perceptual input to root it in reality. The perennial problem posed for cognitive theories, at least as far as the apprehension of reality is concerned, is how, for all the machinations of our cognitive apparatuses, we manage most of the time to see the world as it is, or to be effectively 'right' in our understandings of it, and of each other (Neisser, 1976). It is no use having mental operations which code, select, infer, transform and distort the world, if they leave us wallowing in fantasy and distortion, unable effectively to act, react and generally survive in the world. It is doubtful that we could have evolved as mere confabulists and dreamers. Perceptualism is one favoured solution to this problem; it has it that cognitive representations are perceptually based, and that perception is basically realistic.

The central importance of perceptualism can be illustrated if we take as an example one kind of mental structure that has been proposed for cognitive, social and developmental psychology: the 'schema'. This is a hypothetical cognitive organization whose role is to make sense of experience and guide action (for example,

Bartlett, 1932; Mandler, 1984; Piaget, 1970). In modern cognitive theory, which includes the pursuit of artificial intelligence, it is not the distorting effects of schemas that is emphasized, not the fascinating ways in which they help us understand the cultural workings of mind (Bartlett) or the eccentric cognitions of children (Piaget), but rather, how they help people in everyday settings (members of exotic cultures and children included) to see the world for what it is. So, a schema is 'a spatially and/or temporally organized cognitive structure in which the parts are connected on the basis of contiguities that have been experienced in time or space' (Mandler, 1979: 263).

Schema theories include the notion of cognitive 'scripts' (Schank, 1982; Schank and Abelson, 1977). Scripts are mental representations of routinely structured social occasions such as going to a restaurant or visiting the dentist. According to one influential account, scripts 'are *derived from concrete experience of events* and thus represent "how the world works". Nonetheless, they are very much *abstractions of experienced reality*' (Nelson, 1986: 8; emphasis added). It is not our ambition here to criticize schema or script theories, but merely to note their pervasive application across the great psychological divides – developmental, social and cognitive psychology – and also the strong reliance in modern schema theories upon an ontologically given, and more or less correctly perceived, external world.

Perceptualism is also a strong feature of 'ecological' psychology which, as we have noted, promotes the importance of studying and theorizing about cognition in terms of how it operates within a context of action and perception in the real world. The term derives from the work of J.J. Gibson (1966, 1979) for whom the perceptual apprehension of the real world remained the central issue even throughout the halcyon days of cognitive psychology (the 1960s and 1970s). For Gibson, information about the world does not have to be heavily 'processed' by some inner cognitive machinery, but is available to the senses in the patterning of light, sound and so on, that reaches them, and merely has to be 'picked up'.

Our interest here is not in Gibson's perceptual theory itself, but in its influence upon cognitive psychology, and in particular upon the influential work of Ulric Neisser. Neisser (1967) had initially been at the forefront of the very cognitive orthodoxy against which Gibson argued. But as a colleague of Gibson's at Cornell University, Neisser too saw the light. Convinced of the virtues of perceptualism, Neisser (1976) set out to promote an integration of Gibson and his earlier cognitivism in which, in a 'perceptual cycle', cognitive schemas were subject to the available patterning of sensory input, while actively guiding what that input would be, through the actions of looking and attending to things.

As a consequence of this new interest in perception and action in the real world, and dissatisfied with the limited and artificial products of laboratory-based cognitive psychology, Neisser and others (Shaw and Bransford, 1977) have promoted the development of an 'ecological' cognitive psychology. One of the consequences of this movement is a growing concern for locating cognitive processes in the context of real-world activities. Memory, for example, is understood as open to study as an everyday activity, rooted not in the procedures and materials of the laboratory, the word lists and prose passages given to subjects to recall, but in the contexts of everyday life, where people remember things that matter to them, spontaneously and for their own reasons (Neisser, 1982). For example, recent developments of this concern for memory in everyday life include studies of 'autobiographical memory' and of 'prospective remembering' (see Cohen, 1989).

Within the 'ecological' tradition, what people remember can be studied as a function of the context of action and perception in which the remembering occurs. One of the major sources for a study of everyday remembering is discourse; indeed, specially invented textual materials have played a large part in laboratory studies of memory since Bartlett (1932; cf. Bransford, 1979). Naturally occurring conversations, and texts such as diaries, records and so on, are perhaps a preferable and rich source of materials to be analysed for how they embody the workings of memory. But, of course, conversational and textual materials lend themselves to other kinds of analysis. They have a life of their own, as discourses, which may interfere with the psychologist's desire to find in them the workings of mind. It is one of our aims in this book to pursue the implications of the analysis of discourse for the study of memory, and especially for the assumption that ecological psychology brings to such an enterprise, that cognition can be grounded in reality via some kind of perceptualism.

While Bartlett's (1932) pioneering study of remembering was explicitly an exercise in both cognitive and social psychology, the modern study of 'social cognition' displays scant concern for the social basis of memory (notwithstanding work on 'social representations', see McKinlay et al., 1992; Moscovici, 1984). The species of social cognition we shall focus on here is attribution theory, which is the largely experimental study of how people provide causal explanations for their own and other people's behaviour.

Box 1   *Straw men and corn dollies*

'Is there such a thing as *cognitivism*? And if there is does it look like your description? Isn't what you have done simply producing a *straw man* that can be knocked down?'

The notion of a straw man is an interesting one. The idea is that a version of some argument, position or tradition is produced in such a way that it is easy to rebut; the straw man is erected because it can be demolished much more easily than the real one. The very notion of a straw man points to what we suggest is a common feature of argumentation; that people construct versions of the world to fit with the production of specific activities. You produce a version of a theory which makes it seem weak and therefore facilitate criticism. In later chapters we show this process at work in political argument where the version of 'what went on' is designed to fit particular activities, such as blamings, compliments and rebuttals. To this extent, then, the accusation that we are producing a straw man is already buying into something of the theoretical perspective that we are developing.

There is another sense, however, in which we see the notion of straw man as problematic. The reason for this is that it implies an *actual man* lying behind the straw one. That is, it presupposes a version that is somehow versionless; an utterance that is not occasioned but lies completely outside of context; an account of a position which is definitive, timeless and true. As people who have been touched by the insights of the later Wittgenstein and ethnomethodology we reject such essentialism. For example, one of the points made by a wide range of studies of scientific discourse is that the content of particular theories and the allegiance of particular scientists is a remarkably flexible phenomenon, made out differently from setting to setting (Gilbert and Mulkay, 1984; Myers, 1990; Potter, 1988b; Yearley, 1984). Looked at another way, there is no essential Platonic nature to cognitivism that accounts can capture more or less exactly; rather cognitivism is constituted out of such accounts. Such general versions of disciplines are useful sense-making devices for textbooks and provide a shorthand for theoretical dispute. In science everyone is in the business of weaving diverse sets of ideas and practices into corn dollies that can be fitted to the different contexts at hand.

Of course, the straw man accusation can draw attention to deficiencies and unwarranted simplifications. And here we hope that our simplifications are indeed warranted and there is not too much deficiency in our argument. Our version of cognitivism is certainly rhetorical: it is designed to draw attention to the limits and blind-spots of a wide range of research. We would also point to the fact that the straw man argument is itself a rhetorical device. It is a commonplace technique of rebuttal which can occasion a reworking of the nature of a theory or position to provide new rhetorical flesh in contrast to the old straw.

Of course, all this in turn could be a straw man version of the straw man argument (Ashmore, 1989).

Not only is this a central topic in social cognition, but it also shares several important features with developments in the cognitive mainstream. One of these is perceptualism.

Attribution theory emerged from the study of person perception, and the classic treatments of attributional reasoning are more or less explicitly studies of perception (Shaver, 1983). For example, Michotte's (1963) work on the perception of causation through viewing a film of moving objects has been cited as a forerunner of the psychological study of causality (Hewstone, 1989); and Heider's (1944) first important writing on attribution is explicitly framed as concerned with social perception and phenomenal causality. The same kind of cognitive process, in which the regularities of experience are abstracted into schemas, can be found in attribution work as in studies of general cognition and memory. In Kelley's (1967) influential model, for example, events in the world are subjected to a kind of cognitive analysis of covariance (the ANOVA model), in which the regularities of experience (defined in terms of the variables of consistency, distinctiveness and consensus) are abstracted to provide the explanation of newly observed events. The assumed perceptual basis of the process resembles that of schema theories. Thus, 'It is assumed that the perceiver typically starts with the overt action of another; this is the grist for his cognitive mill' (Jones and Davis, 1965: 222). The basic point, then, is that the study of how people provide causal explanations for human conduct has been generally understood as an exercise in cognitive psychology thoroughly grounded in perceptualism (cf. Billig, 1985, on perceptual versus rhetorical approaches in social psychology).

In parallel to the 'ecological' movement in cognitive psychology, the experimental study of causal attributions has also taken some recent steps towards the enticing realities of everyday talk and texts. Recent approaches have begun to address the kinds of attributions that people may ordinarily and spontaneously make, rather than those required by laboratory procedures for invented scenarios (for example, Antaki, 1988; Harvey et al., 1990). Nevertheless, the pursuit of the everyday and real is almost exclusively, just as it was in the older laboratory studies (McArthur, 1972), a study of linguistic responses to textual materials (although these textual materials have often been treated as stand-ins for some perceived world). Operationally at least, as for much of the study of memory, the study of causal attributions is a study of talk and text.

The new developments in attribution theory seek to replace artificial texts with real, or more realistic, ones, and even to study attributions as a phenomenon of everyday conversation. As with ecological studies of memory, however, we shall show that the study of attributions in everyday talk and text runs into serious and similar problems. There is, potentially, a clash between the conceptual (cognitivist) apparatus that psychologists bring with them, and the action-orientated nature of everyday discourse. Once again, as we shall argue, the examination of discourse for what it tells us about cognition turns out to be no simple matter. But rather than retreating to the laboratory and the manipulation of artificial textual materials, we shall argue that attention to ordinary discourse is indeed a rewarding step, though one which forces a radical reappraisal of cognitivism itself.

Memory, attribution and an adversarial motif

As we have noted at the start of this chapter, one of the consequences of moving to a discourse analytical position is that it cuts across conventional categories of psychology; categories such as those which divide memory and causal attribution into separate sub-fields. From a discursive perspective these topics, suitably reconceptualized, can be seen as closely related. People blend notions of thought and reality, fact and reason, cause and account, when they talk. This is not because they are confused but because they live in a world orientated to action (Heritage, 1984). In this practical world versions of past events are developed in the context of causal accounting, which is meshed in to broader activity sequences to do with issues like blame and praise, making arrangements and resolving disputes. The past is reconstructed according to the functional concerns of the present – and it is here that the analysis of discourse has much to say to the study of cognition. Our choice of memory and attribution as themes for subsequent chapters, then, reflects the reorganization of cognitive topics that a study of discourse requires. However, it also has the secondary benefit of tackling topics that are respectively the very epitome of cognitive and social psychology, and as such are familiar markers on which to lay out our reconceptualization.

When we come to examine these traditional topics of psychological study from very different sub-fields, one of the striking things is the very similar basic assumptions they hold about human thought and action. In both cases, there is a strongly perceptual cognitivism at work, with apprehensions of reality based in schematic abstractions of the regularities of experience. The cognitive psychologies of causal attribution and textual remembering are both concerned with how people apprehend and understand the world, in terms of facts and causal inferences. In the psychology of memory, causal inferences play a major part in mediating the act of remembering; people forget the precise factual details of what they read or hear, in favour of a version of events that is strongly influenced by plausible connections, inferences and causal links. On the other hand, when people make causal attributions they do so on the basis of given factual information about what people are described as having done. In this sense, memory and attribution research can be seen as mirror images of one another. Fact and inference are the essential concerns of studies of remembering and of attribution, and as we shall see, they are also central and pervasive issues for discourse analysis.

We shall concentrate on specific developments in the psychology of memory and attribution, rather than overviews of those entire fields. These specific developments are the ones we have discussed, the move towards studying cognitive processes in real-world contexts and, in particular, towards the study of cognition in discourse. We shall take as points of departure for our own analytical work, Neisser's (1981) study of John Dean's testimony to the Watergate Committee, and recent developments of linguistically based and 'conversational' approaches to attribution (for example, Au, 1986; Hilton, 1990).

The advantage of taking up these particular studies is that they appear to meet us half-way. While retaining cognitivist perspectives, they represent efforts to deal with the phenomena of talk and text. While stronger contrasts could be drawn with more conventional studies of memory and attribution, we wish to avoid the futility of arguing that people who study one kind of phenomenon ought really to be studying another. As we have stated, it is not our intention (here, at least) to argue that cognitivism is wrong. Indeed, it is self-evidently a viable and productive basis for theory and research. Rather, while welcoming the turn to natural contexts and discourse, we shall argue that it is a movement which calls for a far more radical shift in method and theory, and a greater reconceptualization of the nature of everyday cognition and discourse, than has been recognized.

It is a feature of the John Dean case, and one that we shall emphasize, that it takes place in the context of a kind of courtroom. Dean provides his written testimony as a witness in a hearing, and produces his spoken testimony under cross-examination. The versions of events he produces are ones that attend not only to issues of what really happened, how good his memory is or how his memory works, but also to such attributional issues as who was responsible for what, who was to blame, and so on – issues in which he himself was implicated. This adversarial context is an admirably appropriate one for a study of issues of memory and attribution. It has been noted (Edwards and Middleton, 1986a) that if the experimental psychology of memory has any kind of parallel in real-life settings, it is likely to be those where a dispassionate effort at full and accurate recall is asked for. And, on the face of it, legal settings, where people are called upon to provide evidence, offer excellent examples of this. Indeed, experimental studies of eye-witness testimony are another notable feature of recent moves towards dealing with real-world issues (for example, Lloyd-Bostock and Clifford, 1983). Closer to the adversarial setting of cross-examination, attribution theorists have derived insight from Hart and Honoré's (1985) analysis of causal reasoning in the legal process, and have used this as a basis for a generalized conversational model of causal attribution (Hilton, 1990; Turnbull and Slugoski, 1988).

Legal settings are rich 'ecological' sources for a study of how factual reports, rememberings, attributions and causal explanations are constructed as parts of situated talk. Apart from their clear relevance to the study of memory and attribution, they have also been the focus of concerted work in conversation analysis (for example, Atkinson, 1978; Atkinson and Drew, 1979; Drew, 1978, 1985, 1990; Halkowski, 1990; Linell and Jönsson, 1989; Molotch and Boden, 1985; Pomerantz, 1987). This makes the courtroom or, let us say, more broadly, the notion of bearing witness under cross-examination, of a conversationally embedded, dialogical pursuit of truth and interest, of cause and account, a useful motif for this book. It may appeal to forward-looking cognitive psychologists as the kind of setting which, because of its rigour in the treatment of fact and evidence, and its social organization, offers a useful half-way stage between laboratory and world, where laboratory findings might be expected to have some applicability. It appeals to discursive psychology for similar reasons, in that it enables that applicability to be examined, in ways directly relevant to issues in the psychology of memory and attribution, while also providing for the kinds of rhetorical organizations, interests and conflicts that are the stuff of mundane talk.

It is important to stress that we are not proposing a new model of the person, as lawyer, to replace 'man the scientist', the computer, the white rat. It will be instead a kind of ecological and metaphorical motif; an anchor point for our argument and exposition, and a setting for examining situated talk. Its advantage, again, is that it is not one of our own invention. Not only are courtrooms real-world contexts, but ecologically relevant studies of memory, attribution, conversation and rhetoric have usefully been there before us.

Discourse analysis: a preliminary account

Fuller introduction to the principles and methods of discourse analysis can be found later in this volume and also elsewhere (Potter et al., 1990; Potter and Wetherell, 1987; Wetherell and Potter, 1988). We shall restrict ourselves here to a brief overview, and to distinguishing our approach from other enterprises that go by similar names. Nevertheless, the following account, together with the specific analyses provided in later chapters will convey many of its essential features.

Discourse analysis, as used here, is a functionally orientated approach to the analysis of talk and text. As it has been carried out up to now it has been overwhelmingly qualitative. However, quantification *per se* is not frowned upon for theoretical reasons; rather, it is the sorts of 'operationalizations' that typically underpin quantification in psychology, and the sorts of theoretical concerns that they mask, that are rejected. Its most immediate origins are in the sociology of scientific knowledge (Ashmore, 1989; Gilbert and Mulkay, 1984; Potter and Mulkay, 1985), and applications of that to social psychology (Potter, 1984, 1987, 1988a,b; Potter and Wetherell, 1987, 1988). These in turn had their origins in linguistic philosophy, where problems of knowledge had been reworked as problems of language and, specifically, as problems that could be fruitfully recast in terms of language *use* (Austin, 1962; Wittgenstein, 1953). Alongside these developments, semiotics and later post-structuralism and postmodernism in cultural and literary theory were focusing attention upon the constructed and active nature of texts (Barthes, 1974; Derrida, 1977b; Shapiro, 1988), and also, therefore, on the sense of 'reality' which they produce (Atkinson, 1990; Todorov, 1968).

Elsewhere in the social sciences, speech act theories (Grice, 1975; Searle, 1969) and ethnomethodology (Garfinkel, 1967; Heritage, 1984) were developing functional approaches to language and the detailed practices of everyday social life. Again, language emerges as a reality-constituting practice, such that the mapping of descriptions onto a cognitive or worldly reality is made complicated and interesting, by the indefinitely many ways in which it might be done. Versions of events, of memories, facts and causes, for example, are therefore to be examined for their nature as versions (texts), and in terms of the specific contexts of situated action for which they are constructed. An important part of this new attention to the detail of language and social life took shape in the growth of conversation analysis (for example, Atkinson and Heritage, 1984a; Button and Lee, 1987; Levinson, 1983; Sacks et al., 1974) in which the analysis of carefully transcribed conversations reveals the highly organized nature of ordinary talk as sequential social action.

It is not the case that you could simply add all these influences together and get discourse analysis. They do not fit together in that way and, indeed, are sometimes to be found in open conflict. What distinguishes discourse analysis in the sense that we have developed it in psychology is the following:

1   Discourse analysis deals with naturally occurring talk and text, including interview transcripts understood in this way (cf. Potter and Mulkay, 1985; Potter and Wetherell, 1989). This separates it from most of speech act theory and analysis, and from most of experimental psychology's dealings with textual materials, as well as providing for a somewhat wider set of concerns and materials than those addressed by conversation analysis.

2   Discourse analysis is concerned with the content of talk, its subject matter and with its social rather than linguistic organization. This distinguishes it from linguistic studies of text grammar, cohesion and so on, which have the typical goal of providing content-free schemes.

3   Discourse analysis has a triple concern with action, construction and variability (Potter and Wetherell, 1987). In saying and writing things, people perform social actions. The specific features of these actions are a product of constructing talk and text out of a range of styles, linguistic resources and rhetorical devices. Part of the interest of analysis is in this constructive process. Since talk and text are action orientated, versions are likely to show variability according to the different interactional contexts they are constructed to serve. Variation in accounts provides another important lever for discourse analytical work, revealing the situated and functional character of versions.

4   One of the central features of discourse analysis is its concern with the rhetorical (argumentative) organization of everyday talk and thought (Billig, 1987; McCloskey, 1985; Simons, 1989a). One of the major features of rhetorical analysis is the demonstration of how, in order to understand the nature and function of any version of events, we need to consider whatever real or potential alternative version it may be designed to counter (for example, Billig, 1988a, 1989b).

5   A final feature of discourse analysis has been its concern with

the ostensibly 'cognitive' issues of reality and mind. This reflects its origins in the sociology of scientific knowledge and in the reworking of psychological categories such as attitudes, learning, memory and so on. Discourse analysis is particularly concerned with examining discourse for how cognitive issues of knowledge and belief, fact and error, truth and explanation, are dealt with (Edwards, 1991, 1992a,b; Edwards et al., 1992; Edwards and Mercer, 1987; Potter et al., 1991; Potter and Halliday, 1990). It is a further development of these issues here which leads us to move beyond talking merely of discourse analysis and start to describe the enterprise as a 'discursive psychology'.

This is a very schematic overview of the principal features of discourse analysis. In the next chapter we will start to put flesh on these bones through a critical reading of recent ecological work in memory and, in particular, Neisser's study of John Dean's testimony.

2

Ulric Neisser's Memory

In a plea for ecologically situated studies of memory, Ulric Neisser (one of the founders of modern cognitive psychology) was able in 1978 to comment that 'If X is an interesting or socially significant aspect of memory, then psychologists have hardly ever studied X.' While clearly designed for its shock value, this statement not only annoyed many experimental psychologists, but encouraged others to extend their interests beyond laboratory settings, and into the sorts of rememberings – the Xs – that occur 'naturally', such as everyday involuntary recall, prospective remembering, autobiographical memory, conversational remembering, memory for faces and so on (see, for example, Cohen, 1989; and the collections of Gruneberg et al., 1978; Gruneberg and Morris, 1979; Harris and Morris, 1984; Neisser and Winograd, 1988). While the move to natural settings recommends itself to many on grounds of the pursuit of ecological validity and application, Neisser's shift to the ecological is, as we noted in Chapter 1, part of a more specific theoretical orientation towards a Gibsonian, perceptually based psychology of cognition.

This movement to consider rememberings as a feature of ecology has inevitably brought the analyst into closer contact with everyday discourse, in contrast to the kinds of decontextualized and invented sentences and passages typically used in laboratory studies of memory (we shall have more to say about this in Chapter 4). Although the term 'ecology', through its historical links with the study of biological systems in natural habitats, summons up ideas about the physical settings in which remembering takes place, what we find in the natural settings peopled by humans is very often, of course, people talking to each other. Furthermore, the experimental cognitive psychology of memory has itself been very largely concerned with linguistic materials, with memory for words, sentences and texts, and with language-based theories of how memory works (semantic memory, scripts, text and story grammars and so on). So, an ecological approach is very frequently going to involve some sort of study of discourse (although it is not always conceived in this way). Yet this presents special problems. Our argument throughout this book is that everyday discourse has dynamics of its own which render its status as evidence of under-lying cognitive processes highly problematic. And our response to this argument is to press the virtues of an alternative approach which analyses discourse and to discover how notions of mind and reality are constituted in the course of situated actions.

Our goal here is not to provide a comprehensive overview or critique of either traditional or recent studies of memory. Our concern is, rather, to explore in a more positive way the implications of studying everyday remembering through its embodiment in ordinary discourse – but in a way that takes discourse seriously. While laboratory studies are often heavily concerned with language, the contrasts between those studies and analyses of everyday discourse are already very obvious, and do not need to be laboured here. But even the more recent, naturalistically orientated studies tend to treat linguistic materials as resources for studying the cognitive workings of memory, their purpose quite clearly being to extend and test laboratory models and findings in real-world contexts (Cohen, 1989). We can illustrate this with the conceptualization of texts in so-called 'autobiographical' memory research.

Some studies of autobiographical memory have taken diary records, sometimes the analyst's own records specially made for the purpose (Linton, 1982; Wagenaar, 1986), or else experimental participants' diaries are used (Rubin, 1982). In Wagenaar's study, for example, events over a six-year period were systematically recorded under the headings of who, what, where and when. These records then serve as criteria for accuracy of recall. Little account is taken of diaries *as texts* – what they ordinarily are, how they ordinarily come to be written, how they might ordinarily work as *sequentially coherent* and *socially interested constructions* of events (see, for example, Weisner's 1991 study of the diaries of Mario Cuomo). For the psychologists of real-world memory, diaries (if they can properly be called that) serve merely as records of significant real-life events that can be used to measure event memory. Indeed, it is not always clear what these are studies *of*: memory for events, or for diary entries, or perhaps memory for events mediated by such textual records. Event records are treated as equivalent both to events themselves, and to mental representations of events; language is treated as a window on the world, and on the mind. In analysis, and sometimes also in their initial writing, those events/records are immediately decontextualized and, for example, coded into event–person–time categories, for cued recall, losing whatever narrative sense and continuity those events might have had as entries in diaries.

We are not suggesting that these studies are not important, that they tell us nothing about the workings of memory, although it is not immediately clear what they do tell us about the workings of memory (Cohen, 1989). Rather, we are pointing up a sharp contrast between them and what we are calling discursive psychology. It is a matter of how to approach, use, analyse and theorize about discourse. We suggest that diary-based studies of autobiographical memory have displayed scant regard for the nature of diaries or, more widely, for relations between discourse and knowledge, or discourse and the world, or for discourse *per se*. Rather, they continue to deal with language in just the same way as experimental studies of memory always have, as a transparent medium for studying relations between cognition and reality. These ostensibly 'real-world' studies look at the world through the laboratory window.

Rather than attempting a general review of ecologically situated studies, we propose to concentrate upon one important example, which is Neisser's (1981) study of John Dean's testimony to the Watergate investigative committee concerning President Nixon's involvement in illegal activities designed to undermine political opponents. This study recommends itself for several reasons. These include its intrinsic interest and clarity, and the fact that it represents the work of a leading proponent of the new cognitive-ecological approach. It also deals centrally and qualitatively with extended discourse – Dean's spoken and written testimony – and, moreover, with discourse that was widely reported, televised and published, and which commanded at the time of its occurrence a massive popular interest. Further, it is discourse which occurs within a legal setting of testimony and cross-examination. This makes for a useful basis of comparison with the other materials we shall be examining, as well as combining with public interest in the events, to provide for the existence of other and contrasting kinds of textual analysis of materials from the same source.

A final and notable feature of Neisser's study is that he presents relatively large segments of his source material and thus makes his interpretations much more explicit than is common in cognitive work dealing with discourse. In the majority of studies of naturalistic remembering (and, indeed, attribution, as we shall see in Chapter 4) the analyst's most basic interpretations are hidden behind various kinds of under-explicated numerical codings and practices of 'text trawling' which allow a full evaluation of only the more superficial aspects, both of the studies and of the materials they are based on. Neisser's study of Dean is selected precisely because it represents as close a study as we can find to the kinds of materials, concerns and methods of discourse analysis, while still retaining an explanatory base in the cognitive workings of mind. It therefore offers the most relevant and fruitful basis for critical attention, and for the development of a more thorough-going discursive psychology of remembering.

John Dean's testimony

Neisser's (1981) analysis of Dean's testimony was founded upon the availability not only of his actual testimony to the Watergate committee, but also of subsequently published transcripts of some of the original conversations between Dean, Nixon and other White House figures. The availability of both the testimony and of the original conversations was crucial to Neisser's analysis. They capture important features of the kind of experimental controls that keep many psychologists in the laboratory: the ability to map output (rememberings) onto input (perceptual experience), and thus to infer the cognitive machinations that intervene between them. In this case, the rememberings appear in Dean's responses to examination, while the transcript of the original conversation is taken as a record of what would have been experienced by the participants at the time.

Neisser adopts a functional as well as cognitive view of Dean's remembering. He draws attention not only to its cognitive aspects, but makes further sense of those patterns by reference to personal goals such as Dean's concern to tell the truth, and his desire to display himself in a favourable light. In keeping with the major thrust of ecological psychology, Neisser studies the testimony for its accuracy rather than for its inadequacies. In this chapter we will be concerned both with Neisser's functionalism, along with its blind-spots, and with the issue of veridicality and how this is assessed. Our argument is that in its construction of function and accuracy Neisser's approach fails to take proper account of the nature of discourse itself and, specifically, its pragmatic organization.

We suggest that in any account of conversational remembering, what is required is not merely an extension of traditional cognitive concerns into real-world settings, but a re-focusing of attention upon the dynamics of social action and, in particular, of discourse. Despite the introduction of a limited, formalized version of discourse pragmatics, in some approaches to knowledge representation, such as in the study of question-answering (Graesser and Black, 1985; Lehnert, 1978), there has as yet been little attempt to deal either with naturally occurring conversational discourse (as

Bekerian, 1987, notes; see also Levinson, 1983: 305–6, on the indeterminacy of naturally occurring question–answer pairs), nor with the issues of participants' truth construction, and the experimenter's unacknowledged role in that process.

Studies of memory have invariably begun from some unquestioned notion of what really happened – an undisputed record or version of original events, that can be taken to represent the original experience (for the subjects), and also (for the psychologist) the essential criterion of what is remembered, forgotten, inferred, distorted and so on. Without this prior knowledge of the 'truth', the traditional psychology of memory cannot proceed. As we have noted, it is precisely the publication of tape transcripts of meetings in the Oval Office which afforded the opportunity for Neisser's study. We shall explore some of the problems that arise from this assumption – that the truth of events can, and must, be pre-established in this way as a necessary condition for the study of remembering (cf. Edwards and Middleton, 1986a, 1987, on studying remembering without knowledge of 'input').

It is important at the outset that we make clear the basis upon which we are subjecting Neisser's paper to close scrutiny. It is not out of any disregard, either for Neisser's work in general, nor for the Dean paper in particular. On the contrary, we perceive this work to represent a significant and welcome departure from earlier, laboratory-based and information-processing studies, and to have mapped out many of the important issues that confront the relocation of cognitive issues in the context of real-world activities. It is precisely because of the significance and value of Neisser's work that it merits close attention. Moreover, in pursuing the discourse-analytic perspective, and in addressing notions of truth, veridicality, accuracy of accounts and how these things can be analysed as discursive accomplishments, we inevitably raise issues of how cognitive psychology, or any other study of remembering, constructs truths of its own. Psychology's construction of truths (evidence, models, theory) about remembering is intimately involved in how truth and memory are defined operationally in the analysis of subjects' rememberings. So Neisser's paper itself becomes a proper subject for study, just as in other spheres analysts of discourse and social action have studied the construction of scientific knowledge (for example, Gilbert and Mulkay, 1984; Latour, 1987; see Woolgar, 1988a, for a summary of the field). It is one of the most significant features of the discourse-analytic approach that the same methodology that reveals how ordinary persons construct versions of reality can be turned upon science itself.

John Dean was the key witness in the Watergate hearings. He had provided in his opening written statement, and again under cross-examination, detailed accounts of conversations in the Oval Office of the White House between himself, President Nixon and various high-ranking White House officials. It was Dean's evidence that was seen as most damning and central to the outcome of the hearing against Nixon. The subsequent publication of selected transcripts of some of those conversations was seen as providing an opportunity to examine the accuracy of Dean's testimony. Neisser's concern was with what an analysis of Dean's testimony could tell us about the workings of his memory, and about memory in general. In particular, he set out to show that there was a sense in which Dean could be accurate, while apparently mis-remembering virtually all of the important details.

In Neisser's analysis, not only did Dean mis-remember the details of time, place and conversation, he also frequently mis-remembered even the *gist* of what happened and what was said. Despite this, 'there is usually a deeper level at which he is right. He gave an accurate portrayal of the real situation, of the actual characters and commitments of the people he knew, and of the events that lay behind the conversations he was trying to remember' (Neisser, 1981: 4). Neisser's 'deeper level' of accuracy is the third of a three-part distinction he draws among kinds of accurate recall. These are: (a) 'verbatim recall' or 'literal memory'; (b) 'gist'; and (c) so-called 'repisodic memory', in which Dean 'extracted the common themes that remained invariant across many conversations and many experiences, and then incorporated those themes in his testimony' (Neisser, 1981: 20). Unlike Bartlett's (1932) story reconstructions, confabulated and altered across many re-tellings, 'repisodic' memory is recall distilled from many different but related experiences, in which some significant essence of the truth of things remains, despite all sorts of inaccuracies of detail and circumstance. This third type, 'repisodic memory' has not been taken up with enthusiasm in laboratory-based studies of memory; however, this is hardly surprising because it does not fit easily into the usual methodological constraints – it involves persons having to go through a long time-series of personally significant experiences, and all this without the knowledge that they will be called upon to construct a painstaking account of it all later. As such, it poses a serious challenge to the ingenuity of any committed experimentalist.

Neisser's concern with delineating various 'levels' of accurate recall can be seen as part of the broader attempt to establish an 'ecological psychology of memory' (cf. Neisser, 1976, 1982, 1988).

While the constructivist, information-processing approach to cognition has emphasized forgetting – the distortions, confabulations and general unreliability which results when memories are schematically assembled in some kind of cognitive processor (Alba and Hasher, 1983) – the ecological perspective seeks to emphasize memory's veridicality: true remembering is something like abstracting the nature of the world from invariances in the flow of the subject's visual field. Neisser's point is that if we look at 'gist' and 'repisodic' remembering in this context they can be seen as ways of getting it right about the past.

Let us begin with Neisser's three-part distinction: (a) verbatim recall; (b) gist and (c) repisodic memory. Each can be considered as a kind of text. Our central point here is that what counts as 'getting it right' is highly problematic for each of these categories of remembering.

Verbatim recall

This is the kind of recall that is conventionally taken as unproblematically accurate and without distortion, the successful achievement of rote memorization. Rote learning has found itself out of favour in psychological laboratories during the reign of distortion-orientated information-processing and schema approaches. Neisser points out (1982: 17; cf. Rubin, 1977) that in spite of this neglect, verbatim recall plays an important part in many people's everyday lives, in so far as people might rehearse and remember the Lord's Prayer, the National Anthem, songs and poetry and so on.

However, these sorts of achievements are notable for the special nature of the social-discursive contexts deemed appropriate for their production. The repeated performance of a prayer or a poem is just that – the speaker reproduces her own performance on each occasion. The distinctive feature of these materials is that they are designed for repetition, such that, in each case, there is some normatively agreed standard with which any particular rendition can be compared. The situation is quite different with natural dialogue such as that occurring between Nixon and Dean in the Oval Office. It is tempting to imagine that such a dialogue could be rendered to look like the script of a play, such that this could provide a neutral criterion for assessing the accuracy of Dean's version. However, a brief examination of the debate among linguists and conversation analysts about the transcription of talk quickly shows the weakness of that idea. Transcriptions are always highly conventionalized versions of talk, in which the level and content of the encoding of speech depends crucially upon, and develops alongside, the analytical insights that are revealed by it (for example, Atkinson and Heritage, 1984b; Cook, 1990; see also our appendix on transcription). The general point is that our familiarity with standard orthography gives the idea of assessing verbatim recall a deceptive simplicity which is misleading in practice, where our criteria will be contingent upon the context and purpose of our study.

In addition, pragmatic analyses of speakers' reportings of verbatim versus gist versions of other people's speech (that is, direct and indirect quotation) point to an interesting patterning of everyday talk that is not reflected in analyses that restrict themselves to considerations of recall accuracy. Speakers may choose to quote speech indirectly *as* gist, or directly *as* verbatim recall, according to such considerations as 'footing' (Goffman, 1979; Levinson, 1988; see Chapter 7). That is, whatever they may otherwise imply about memory, verbatim and gist reportings are options for speakers to choose, so as to associate themselves more or less directly with the reported speaker. They provide opportunities for acting as intermediary or spokesperson, and for constructive formulations of what was said, or indeed for displaying oneself as possessing a rather acute and veridical recall of otherwise doubtful or questioned events (Wooffitt, 1991). While such studies may not tell us what speakers are *able* to remember, their relevance to the study of memory increases as our interest shifts to ecological settings in which remembering is studied as an actual and contextualized activity.

Recall of gist
One of the central difficulties with the idea of assessing the accuracy of gist is that in ordinary conversation what may be taken as an adequate or accurate gist is, on any particular occasion, and for the participants involved, a disputable matter. Its adequacy will depend upon the communicative context in which the speaker is called upon to produce it. In the context of a psychological experiment, this contingency of gist upon communicative considerations is usually amongst those features of everyday talk that are controlled out of the study. What counts as gist is resolved by fiat, by the experimenter, as part of the methodology. A piece of text is analysed for its case-grammatical event structure, story or script structure (Rumelhart, 1975; Schank and Abelson, 1977; Thorndyke, 1977), or is subdivided in advance into a set of 'idea units' (Bransford and Johnson, 1972), or of 'propositions' (Kintsch and Van Dijk, 1978), and the experimenter then counts up how many of these units a subject manages to recall. In all of these approaches, gist figures as an abstracted, context-free summary of

Box 2 *Losing one's footing*

The notion of *footing* was introduced by Goffman (1981) to characterize conversational practices such as that where the current speaker is reporting another's speech. He makes a contrast between the *animator*, the current speaker who is doing the talking, and the *composer*, the person who originally made up the words. And he notes that a further distinction is needed between the *composer* and *origin* of the viewpoint; for example, a political speech-writer may write words to express ideas for a leader. At the same time Goffman distinguished a range of different reception roles: for example, *addressed* versus *unaddressed* recipient, *overhearer* versus *eavesdropper*. Levinson (1988) has extended and systematized this typology to include a range of further options. He also notes the way in which some languages grammatically mark particular sorts of footing; for instance, they may mark the source as second-hand yet not specific to one individual.

Such concerns have been lost in psychology, probably because the predominant methods of research predefine footing to such an extent that it does not need to be explicitly attended to. For example, the situations studied are overwhelmingly ones where animator, composer and origin are embodied in one individual. However, footing becomes much more important in discursive psychology. It is one of the principal ways in which speakers display the accountability of their utterances; are they themselves responsible for their words or are they passing on the views of others? People can emphasize their distance from a particular attitude or evaluation by sharply making the animator/origin distinction or they can align themselves with it by blurring or ignoring the distinction. An analysis of footing and its management thus becomes an important part of understanding the way discourse is orientated to action.

It is important, nevertheless, to emphasize that these are participants' distinctions; Goffman and Levinson are providing explicit terms for contrasts that are commonplace in everyday talk. Uncritical use of the origin/animator contrast can give the misleading impression that some people are making up their talk from scratch and others are merely citing it or acting as mouthpieces. We would resist this reification of the distinction, on three grounds. First, much of the talk that is marked as merely animated or composed is used by the current speaker to do particular kinds of interactional work (Clayman, 1992; Levinson, 1988). Secondly, much of the talk that people mark themselves as originating is made up of widely shared views, commonplaces of reasoning and more or less standard devices for factual accounting (for example, Billig, 1989a, 1992a; Moscovici, 1984; Wooffitt, 1992). Thirdly, and more fundamentally, one of the important insights of post-structuralist work which is highly pertinent to psychology is that there are major problems with the notion of intention and individual creativity when applied to talk. This is illustrated in the general attack on the priority of authorship in literary studies (Barthes, 1977) and, more specifically, in Derrida's deconstruction of the central categories of speech act theory (Derrida, 1977a,b).

main points or underlying themes. The social-discursive process of defining gist is expropriated by the analyst, who also has to judge whatever alterations and rewordings subjects produce, as legitimate paraphrases, or else as illegitimate distortions or omissions.

In ordinary conversation things are very different. What count as adequate or accurate gists and summaries is a matter for the participants themselves to resolve. And the criteria for doing so will themselves be occasioned and disputable, according to the pragmatic work that the summary is supposed to achieve. That is, a gist is understood according to its suitability for a particular task in context. For example, we can compare the cognitive psychological notion of gist with the conversation analytical notion of 'formulations', which are conversational events where the nature of an earlier sequence of talk is formulated (Heritage and Watson, 1979, 1980; cf. Schegloff, 1972). Typically, such formulations are not neutral summaries but are designed for specific upshots relevant to future actions. For example, Greatbatch (1986) shows the way television interviewers use formulations of what the speaker has just said as a way of packaging critical points without departing from an accountably neutral stance.

This is equally true of institutional contexts. For example, Edwards and Mercer (1989) have analysed the way that summaries of classroom lessons, of activities, findings and conclusions, are used by teachers to reformulate capricious and problematical classroom events according to their originally planned outcomes – in effect, articulating classroom events in terms of what 'ought' to have happened. Others have examined the role of formulations in legal and scientific contexts (Atkinson and Drew, 1979; Yearley, 1986), and have studied how interrogators often 'go back over' testimony with a witness, providing opportunities for developing inconsistencies and counter-versions that might undermine it (Bogen and Lynch, 1989).

Further methodological problems with the notion of 'gist' arise when the 'input' is not, or not all, text to start with. For Dean, for example, the business at issue was not merely recall of talk, but of events, persons present in a room, documents, times and dates and sequences of actions, all to be synthesized into verbal testimony. The cognitive psychology of textual comprehension and memory is full of arguments for intervening processes involving imagery, mental models, causal inferences and so on, even when the task is that of going from textual input to textual output (Bransford, 1979). But once we enter the realm of 'cross-modal' remembering (Edwards and Middleton, 1987), then we are confronted even more clearly with the complex nature of talk as *description*, as transposition between the visual and the verbal, or between thought and language. This is not strictly, or restrictedly, a problem of memory at all. But it has profound implications for any understanding or study of memory that uses textual and discursive representations.

Even when faced with a scene or some events to be described, and the opportunity to do so 'live' as we look, or with the aid of multiple viewings of video recording, it is impossible to define, outside the context of its function or purpose, what would be a definitive version, a proper or sufficient gist, an acceptably finely drawn level of accuracy. Descriptions are in principle indefinitely extendable (Garfinkel, 1967; Heritage, 1984), such that it makes analytical sense to study actual descriptions not in terms of their, correspondence to some real set of events, but in terms of the situated actions they perform, on the occasions of their use. It is to shift our allegiance from the Wittgenstein of the *Tractatus*, looking for the rules of correspondence between propositions and the world, to the Wittgenstein of the *Philosophical Investigations*, looking for the uses of language for constructing truth inside the 'language games' that make up a 'form of life' (Wittgenstein, 1921, 1953).

Clearly, then, it is misleading to talk about accurate gist in any decontextualized way, abstracted from the situated pragmatics of talk. Our analysis will show that Dean's testimony needs to be understood in terms of the pragmatic constraints and objectives of legal discourse, and of the specific occasions of its moment to moment production.

Repisodic memory

This is the type of memory in which Neisser is most interested in the Dean study. He defines it in cognitive terms, as the process of '[extracting] the common themes that remained invariant' – a very familiar sort of cognitive-perceptual process, as we have noted, often favoured in accounts of perceptual learning, pattern recognition, language and concept acquisition, and so on. Our aim is to question the status of 'repisodic memory' as a cognitive process, as an aspect of Dean's thought, and to relocate it as an artefactual category fashioned through Neisser's 'cognitivizing' of Dean's discourse.

The notion of an accurate 'repisodic' memory, which is independent of gist and verbatim recall, is the outcome of a carefully constructed argument. Neisser's very recognition of the phenomenon relies crucially upon his possessing a knowledge of the truth of what 'really happened' in the White House, which is independent of, but comparable with, Dean's testimony. This is not merely a matter of comparing the tape transcripts with Dean's accounts. It is not verbatim recall, nor even gist that is at stake here. What Dean's 'repisodic' memory is claimed to have got right is the *general nature* of Nixon's involvement and culpability in the cover-up of the Watergate conspiracy.

That the tape transcripts afford such an interpretation is not at all as straightforwardly obvious as Neisser makes it appear. Indeed, Nixon himself, in his foreword to the published transcripts, is quoted as claiming that they *contradict* Dean's testimony (Neisser, 1981: 2). Neisser relies upon other sorts of evidence and argument: 'the outcome of those trials vindicated him . . . If history has ever proven anything, it surely proves that Dean remembered those conversations and told the truth about them' (1981: 3). Neisser can assert in advance of analysing his testimony that Dean was right – the historical outcome is taken not only as self-evident, but as proving Dean's mnemonic correctness. However, this seems to be a rather circular way of demonstrating truthfulness. In so far as Dean was a crucial prosecution witness, the outcome of the hearing merely corresponds with the general upshot of Dean's testimony. The verdict was of Nixon's guilt, not of Dean's truth, whether verbatim, gist or repisodic; and it was based on legal criteria, not scientific.

Dean's testimony is taken by Neisser to represent, with minor reservations, the best efforts of a man with a good memory, at accurately recalling the reported events: 'The impression Dean made when he testified – that he had a good memory and was determined to tell the truth, even if only because truth-telling would best serve his own interests – was essentially correct' (Neisser, 1985: 24). Moreover, the correctness of Dean's account is warranted in a very direct fashion by the transcripts: '*The transcript makes it quite clear* that Nixon is fully aware of the coverup . . .' (Neisser, 1981: 9; emphasis added). Note how the transcript itself is presented as the agent of its own interpretation (cf. Kress and Hodge, 1979; Latour, 1987; Mulkay, 1985; Silverman and Torode, 1979), disguising Neisser's own interpretative work in coming to that conclusion. Rather than taking Dean's testimony as a (fairly direct) window upon his memory, we propose that it may be taken instead as a pragmatically designed piece of discourse. It is a series of accounts, occasioned by cross-examination, and orientated towards the avoidance and assigning of blame and mitigation. Seen in this light, features of Dean's testimony are open to new readings. Features that are ostensibly signals of truthfulness and accuracy, the outcome of mnemonic cognitive processes, are revealed as communicative devices that Dean uses for warranting his *claims* to truthfulness and accuracy.

Neisser notes some inaccuracies in Dean's testimony about the meeting with Nixon and Haldeman on 15 September. His examination of the transcript reveals that:

> Nixon did not say any of the things attributed to him here: He didn't ask Dean to sit down, he didn't say Haldeman had kept him posted, he didn't say Dean had done a good job . . . he didn't say anything about Liddy or the indictments. Nor had Dean himself said the things he later describes himself as saying: that he couldn't take credit, that the matter might unravel some day, etc. (Neisser, 1981: 9)

Neisser's principal concern is the extent of Dean's accuracy – how little detail or even gist is correct, while he manages nevertheless to convey the correct impression that Nixon was engaged in, or at least aware of, a cover-up operation. But the pragmatically situated nature of Dean's account is ignored. Both Dean's testimony and the transcript itself were 'just as incriminating' (1981: 9). This word 'incriminating' calls out for further attention, in that it implies a discourse-functional context for Dean's story. For example, Dean presents himself in the following ways:

1   Scrupulously modest and honest (not taking credit for the work of others). Dean: 'I responded that I could not take credit because others had done much more difficult things than I had done' (quoted by Neisser, 1981: 9).
2   Having a particularly good memory. He makes direct claims to this effect: 'anyone who recalls my student years knew that I was very fast at recalling information' (1981: 5), but also supports it indirectly, via the use of vivid descriptive and narrative detail and supposedly direct quotation, all of which serve to bolster his appearance as someone with a virtually direct perceptual access to the original events: 'you know the way there are two chairs at the side of the President's desk . . . on the left-hand chair Mr. Haldeman was sitting' (1981: 11); 'I can very vividly recall that the way he sort of rolled his chair back from his desk and leaned over to Mr. Haldeman and said, "A million dollars is no problem"' (1981: 18). This theme will be further explored in Chapters 3 and 5.
3   Being under the awesome influence and direction of the highest authority in the land (the President of the United States) – as being, therefore, less culpable himself, for his own involvement. Dean rhetorically reiterates Nixon's title, rather than calling him Nixon: 'When you meet with the President of the United States it is a very momentous occasion, and you tend to

remember what the President of the United States says when you have a conversation with him' (Neisser, 1981: 6; cf. Halkowski, 1990).

On this analysis, Dean's testimony can be seen as a pragmatically organized phenomenon and certainly not merely a straightforward window upon the workings of his memory. It is contextually occasioned in terms both of conversational turn-taking (as responses to questions, accusations etc.; cf. Atkinson and Drew, 1979), and also, more broadly, in terms of the business of the hearings – as relevant to determining the extent of various people's complicity and guilt, including his own, as well as his own credibility as a witness. It is likewise a part of Dean's display of 'truthfulness' that he expressed metacognitive disclaimers about accuracy – he was careful to deny verbatim recall, but claimed to remember the gist (Neisser, 1981: 3).

Similar pragmatic use of metacognitive claims and disclaimers can be found in the testimony of Oliver North to the Iran–Contra hearings (Bogen and Lynch, 1989). North is here being questioned about his knowledge of some shipments of anti-tank missiles (he had been accused of selling armaments to Iran in return for money to support the Contra forces' fight against the Sandinista Government of Nicaragua); he is asked if he 'simply would describe for the committee' what his 'understanding and role was in that transaction at the time it happened' (Bogen and Lynch, 1989: 207). Note how the questioner constructs a gloss or expectation for North's testimony, that it should be simple, straightforward and definitive reporting, as if of perceptual experience, 'at the time it happened'. This places North in the position of a straightforward knower of the events in question, a possibly incriminating position from which North had reason to distance himself. North replied:

Ah::m, I'm working without (.) refreshed reca:ll, uh:, let me do: the best I ca::n teh, (1.0) remember ba::ck teh that (.4) period of ti::me. (4.0) I h'd ha:d several meetings: uh with Mister Ledeen?, (1.2) which led to a meetin::g (0.2) or two: (0.6) with two Israeli citizens, (0.2) private citizens (0.8) an' then a subsequent meeting (.) as I reca::ll (1.0) wi::th Mister Ghobanifa/r. (2.0) that in turn led to a meeting with Mister Kimche (1.0) an' I believe all these took pla:ce (0.6) prior to::: (0.6) the September shipment . . .
(Bogen and Lynch, 1989: 207; see our appendix for a list of transcription conventions)

North's response contains some interesting material for a study of discursive remembering. It includes details of persons and events which could, in principle at least, be checked for accuracy against other sources of evidence, and also specific metacognitive formulations about the extent and reliability of his memory. But we can also analyse it as a piece of situated talk. In producing disclaimers about the nature of his memory ('I'm working without (.) refreshed reca:ll, uh:, let me do: the best I ca::n . . .'; 'as I reca::ll . . .'; 'an' I believe'). North attends to the fallibility of his rememberings while simultaneously displaying a concern for truth and accuracy. He displays himself as a cooperative and truth-seeking witness, while also providing for the ability, should counter-evidence or argument go against him, to deny his account in the future. North's testimony is a subtle discursive achievement, the deployment of truth and fallibility as rhetoric, creating 'plausible deniability' (Bogen and Lynch, 1989: 203), a hedge against the undermining of his testimony in cross-examination. The precise construction of his testimony can be examined for the work it does in relation to exactly how it was asked for. North later stresses the accuracy and authority of his testimony: 'My next very specific recollection . . .'. But here he begins by undermining the interrogator's rhetorically dangerous construction of his testimony as 'simple description', accomplishing this in the very act of displaying how hard he is trying to comply with that requirement.

To return to the case of John Dean, then, our argument is that his efforts at remembering are, in analytical practice, indistinguishable from his mode of *accounting*. It is testimony occasioned by cross-examination, studiable for its 'defensive design' (cf. Sacks, cited by Bogen and Lynch, 1989: 211). Dean's version of his 'memory' is operationally an account, rhetorically couched, in which the accuracy of his detailed evidence is warranted with further accounts of his mnemonic methods (what Neisser calls a temporal version of the method of *loci*; 1981: 5), the fact of his self-attributed 'good memory' (quoted by Neisser, 1981: 5), and the metacognitive claim that people do recall important events, such as a conversation with the President of the United States. Where we would disagree with Neisser is in his reading of these pragmatically orientated claims as if they were evidence of the nature of Dean's memory.

Dean cross-examined

The pragmatically formulated nature of Dean's rememberings is clearly displayed when we examine a different study of Dean's testimony carried out by Molotch and Boden (1985). Their concern was entirely different from Neisser's, in that they focused upon the exercise of power in Dean's cross-examination. Further, their choice of data was also different; whereas Neisser concentrated almost exclusively on Dean's testimony to Senator Inouye, Molotch and Boden's topic was Dean's testimony to Senator Gurney. The difference between the two kinds of testimony is startling. Inouye asked Dean relatively open-ended questions and allowed him to give long and elaborate answers without interruption. He also provided the opportunity for Dean to warrant his credibility, by providing the extensive account of his own special memory skills that is discussed by Neisser. Gurney, in contrast, asked many questions which required simple yes/no answers and at times cut Dean off when he tried to elaborate beyond these. His questioning was also noted as being 'hostile', peppered with disagreements and admonishments.

This difference, of course, is not merely incidental. Molotch and Boden chose to focus on Gurney's examination because he was 'Nixon's man' on the committee which examined Dean (Molotch and Boden, 1985: 275). As such, an adversarial relationship was established, with Gurney attempting to discredit Dean's testimony. For others on the Ervin Committee which examined Dean, particularly Democratic Senators such as Inouye, this adversarial relationship did not so clearly obtain. Moreover, Molotch and Boden stress that Dean's actions made him a tempting 'scapegoat' and thus he had considerable personal investment in showing that responsibility lay further up in the White House hierarchy.

The point, then, is that these differences in Dean's testimony need to be understood as an occasioned discursive product that attends to issues of blame (for Nixon) and mitigation (for himself). In Gurney's hostile examination we see Dean's versions criticized, cut off and variously undermined; while in Inouye's sympathetic questioning Dean is given free reign to organize blamings and mitigations (cf. Atkinson and Drew, 1979; Drew, 1990; Pomerantz, 1978; Potter and Wetherell, 1988; Watson, 1978; Wowk, 1984). The difference is graphically illustrated by interchanges specifically on the topic of Dean's memory. As indicated above, Neisser makes much use of Dean's elaborate account to Inouye of his own memory skills and he takes this account to be essentially correct. However, Dean also refers to his memory skills in the course of Gurney's questioning:

> *Dean:* . . . I've told you I'm trying to re<u>call</u>. My mind is not a <u>tape</u> recorder. It <u>does</u> recall (0.3) im<u>pressions</u> of conversations <u>very</u> well, and the impression <u>I</u> had was that he told – the – he told <u>me</u> that Bob had reported to <u>him</u> what I had been doing. That was th– the impression that very //clearly came out.
> *Gurney:* In other words, your – your <u>whole</u> thesis on saying that the

President of the United States knew about Watergate on September 15 is <u>purely</u> an <u>impression</u>, there isn't a <u>single</u> <u>shred</u> of evidence that came out of this meeting.
(Slightly simplified from Molotch and Boden, 1985: 281)

Two things are striking about this passage. First, in this account, which follows a series of turns where he had found difficulty in answering questions and was 'in a bit of trouble' (Molotch and Boden, 1985: 281), Dean finds it useful to emphasize the short-comings of his memory as well as its virtues. As we saw with Oliver North, Dean's occasional metacognitive formulations, and indeed the carefully framed mixture of detail and vagueness, can be studied for the rhetorical work that they perform, in reporting events while displaying a cooperative concern for truth and accuracy, and simultaneously building in some scope for 'plausible deniability'. The disclaimer about being a tape recorder allows Dean to account for various inadequacies in his answers, while the emphasis on the 'gist' quality of remembered impressions allows Dean nevertheless to warrant his essential accuracy. Secondly, while Neisser, and more tacitly Inouye (who does not disagree with Dean's assessment: see the treatment of this option by Bilmes, 1987; Goodwin and Goodwin, 1987; Pomerantz, 1978, 1984a; Sacks, 1987), accept Dean's version, Gurney provides an opposing view. So, rather than displaying a remarkable abstraction of repisodic truth, a capturing of underlying themes and experiences, in Gurney's formulation Dean has provided '<u>purely</u> an <u>impression</u>' and not 'a <u>single</u> <u>shred</u> of evidence' (this passage of talk from Gurney also provides a clear illustration of the point we made above about a gist being constructed for rhetorical purposes). We can start to see, then, the way that Dean's memory accounts are carefully designed to fit the functional discursive context, and that Neisser's reading of them, as revealing the natural workings of memory, is just one of a variety of interpretative possibilities – indeed, the one offered by Dean himself.

Attribution of error: Dean's personality

The substantiation of Dean as essentially (repisodically) a truth-teller requires an account of how he nevertheless got things variably right or wrong. Repisodic memory is defined by Neisser as a characteristic of individual cognitive processing and, correspond-ingly, the account of Dean's truth and error is also framed in terms of individual psychological processes. Neisser notes that Dean's apparently superior (more accurate) recall on 21 March is some-thing that requires an explanation. It was supposedly a set-piece script that Dean had rehearsed, and it had for Dean a basis in his psychological aspirations, in his hopes and fears, and in his efforts at self-presentation: it 'fulfilled Dean's hopes' of giving 'a personal lecture to the President . . . It became John Dean's own story' (Neisser, 1981: 16). Neisser seems close here to providing what we have been arguing for, an account of Dean's conversational rememberings as pragmatically occasioned, but opts instead for a personality-orientated, dispositional account (see Chapter 6, and also Gergen and Davis 1985; Potter et al., 1984; Potter and Wetherell, 1987; Wetherell and Potter, 1989).

Amongst all of Dean's repisodic correctness in assigning blame and duplicity, the one area in which Neisser has it that Dean got things noticeably wrong was in claiming a special role for himself:

> Dean's errors . . . follow, I believe, from Dean's own character and especially from his self-centred assessment of events at the White House. What his testimony really describes is not the September 15 meeting itself but his fantasy of it: the meeting as it should have been, so to speak. (Neisser, 1981: 10)

> His ego got in the way again. (1981: 18)

> His ambition reorganized his recollections . . . A different man in the same position might have observed more dispassionately, reflected on his experiences more thoughtfully, and reported them more accurately. Unfortunately, such traits of character are rare. (1981: 19)

Thus, Dean's account is explicated by Neisser in terms of truth and error, where errors can be attributed to personal biases, which might be eliminated in a more perfect person.

Neisser's form of accounting here is a familiar one. Numerous studies of the argumentation of lay people (Yearley, 1987), of legal personnel (Atkinson, 1978; Pollner, 1987; Yearley, 1985) and in particular of scientists (Gilbert and Mulkay, 1984; McKinlay and Potter, 1987; Mulkay and Gilbert, 1982; Potter, 1984) show that people tend to attribute deviation from what *they perceive* to be the truth to distorting factors such as personality, lack of competence and a variety of social psychological and sociological factors. Put another way, there is seen to be nothing to explain in the case of 'factual' accounts because they simply reflect the way things are; it is only when distortions arise that there is something to explain (Bloor, 1976). This idea is reflected in Neisser's treatment of Dean.

Dean is presented as functionally distorting the truth in favour of his own 'ego', while with regard to the character of Nixon and others, he merely tells the (repisodic) truth. It is this straightforward acceptance of the truth of things, we suggest, that stops

Neisser from coming to grips with the functional orientation of what he takes to be factual accounts. Indeed, Neisser's whole argument is based on the premise that memory can be understood as essentially veridical in a Gibsonian fashion and thus he is forced, by his own rhetoric, into having to discount error in this way, as basically not to do with memory *per se*, but nevertheless produced via the distorting prism of another individual factor such as personality. This is unfortunate for an ecologically situated approach to remembering, since one of its most important points of departure from conventional laboratory studies is precisely that the latter seek to exclude all sorts of interesting and essential features of everyday accounts of past events, as not really 'memory' as such, but extraneous to the intrinsic workings of that faculty. The study of remembering as an everyday practice does not have to adopt the psychology of individuals as its explanatory basis (Edwards and Middleton, 1987). We shall return in Chapter 6 to how personality trait and role attribution are discursively occasioned and constructed.

Our argument, then, is that the study of conversational remembering reveals how recollections are governed by conversational contingencies – the pragmatics of speaking – rather than requiring appeals to the traditional apparatus of mentalistic, dispositional psychology and the truth–error distinction. Dean's presentation of himself as having a good memory, as being unwilling to take credit that belongs to others, as only following the authority of others, as telling the truth, all serve to enhance his reliability as a prosecution witness, to bolster his own disputed version of things and to mitigate his own culpability under cross-examination.

Mundane and courtroom talk

Let us summarize the principal points we have made. First, we have argued that there are major problems with each of Neisser's three kinds of truthful remembering, verbatim, gist and repisodic: there can be no neutral interpretation-free record against which to check claims; what counts as gist is an occasioned phenomenon closely related to the specific concerns and interests of the participants: the overall themes and patterns that are taken to exist are not separable from the rhetorical nature of the different passages of talk. Secondly, we suggested that Dean's accounts of his memory and his displays of memory could themselves be understood as occasioned productions that attend to 'attributional' issues of human cause, motive and explanation for actions: the assignment of guilt to the President, and preventing his own 'scapegoating'. Indeed, Neisser's own version of Dean's performance was seen selectively to reify (read as literal) or ironize (read as functional) Dean's discourse in such a way that the theoretically important notion of repisodic abstraction of real features of the world could be sustained, while certain systematic errors were accounted for as due to flaws in Dean's personality.

It is important to note that both the 'information-processing' and the 'ecological' approaches to mind are subject to the same fundamental problems with regard to what 'really happened'. Both require that the objective world is unproblematically known *by the psychologist*, in some way not open to the subjects, in order for the psychologist to know to what extent the subject, whether perceiving, comprehending or remembering, got it right or not. Both perspectives ask the same question of Dean: what did he get right, and what wrong, measured against the psychologist's privileged access to the truth? Indeed, as we have noted above, one of the features of the natural context of the Watergate hearing is that it, supposedly, allows a detailed comparison of someone's recollection of a set of events with their original experience of those events.

This is similarly a feature of experimental research on eye-witness testimony, and especially the well-known studies of Elizabeth Loftus and her colleagues (for example, Loftus, 1979; Wells and Loftus, 1984). Here, psychological explanation is offered in information-processing terms, based upon a methodology in which the experimenter, often by staging some events to be witnessed, is able to define 'genuine memories' that can be distinguished from the 'distortions' that are promoted by 'post-event information' such as the manipulation of question content (Loftus, 1975; Loftus and Ketcham, 1983; Loftus and Zanni, 1975). 'This paradigm has been adopted by current researchers of eyewitness testimony, and much of their current work is aimed at discovering the conditions under which testimony about complex events is more or less accurate' (Loftus, 1981: 194). The problem for such studies is that, in situations outside the carefully controlled settings and materials that they use, 'what really happened' is not available for simple examination.

It is not merely that in everyday life we do not generally have a video recording to look at, which would, supposedly, solve all possible disputes. It is that even if we did, true versions of events are not simply 'perceivable'. As a wealth of conversational research has documented, and as we will argue in later chapters, reports are constructions, versions, laden with theory and interpretations, pragmatically formulated within conversational contexts. That it is possible to devise simple settings, in which no sensible person would disagree about what really happened, is no basis upon which to argue that psychology should conceive of everyday talk and remembering in that manner. To do so is to ignore the genuine and fundamental problems of both everyday *and scientific* knowledge, where observations, observation terms, data, interpretation and theory and the pragmatics of accounts are all intrinsically bound up with each other (cf. Gilbert and Mulkay, 1984; Heritage, 1984; Hesse, 1974; Pollner, 1987). Indeed, the putative existence of scenarios, for which all sensible people produce the same sorts of accounts, is an interesting notion, also laden with assumption and suggestive of possibilities for empirical investigation, including study of how those kinds of experiments are constructed and carried out, comparisons with courtroom practices, and with scientific and everyday observational description.

But let us remain in court for a moment. There have been a number of detailed examinations of courtroom and other kinds of legal dialogue, carried out from the perspective of conversation analysis (for example, Atkinson and Drew, 1979; Bogen and Lynch, 1989; Drew, 1978, 1990; Halkowski, 1990; Molotch and Boden, 1985; Pomerantz, 1987; Pomerantz and Atkinson, 1984). These studies are concerned to reveal the systematic and highly sequentially sensitive character of the talk, and how it accomplishes a variety of social actions, while drawing upon the same range of devices that are to be found in everyday casual conversation. In doing this, such studies inevitably deal with issues of how participants construct memories (the major basis of testimony), and how they negotiate their causal attributional implications (culpability and innocence, the major business of the court). We can illustrate something of the subtlety of these issues with an example.

The following two extracts of dialogue are from Drew (1990), and our use of them is based on a discussion by Wooffitt (1990: 13–15). Counsel for the defence (C) is cross-examining the main prosecution witness (W), the victim of an alleged rape.

C: [referring to a club where the defendant and the victim met] it's where girls and fellas meet isn't it?
W: People go there.

C: And during the evening, didn't Mr O [the defendant] come over to sit with you?
W: Sat at our table.

Wooffitt points out how C and W produce different and competing, but not contradictory, versions of the two incidents, each of which is 'designed to make available certain inferences to the overhearing jury' (1990: 13). The counsel's choice of the description 'where girls and fellas meet' conveys an impression of the kinds of intentions and expectations that club patrons might have of each other, which are clearly of implied relevance to the alleged offence. For example, 'girls and fellas' not only establishes gender as relevant but, in the specifics of the membership categories used, implies a particular style of relationship (contrast the sense of alternative compatible category descriptions such as 'men and women' and 'girls and boys'). The phrase 'people go there' neutralizes those implications. In a similar way, 'sat at our table' depersonalizes and defamiliarizes the relationship implied in 'came over to sit with you'.

These sorts of materials demonstrate how what is ostensibly mere 'description' of actions and events can be constructed to generate specific implications concerning the speaker/actor's involvement with regard to attributional issues of responsibility and blame (cf. Jefferson, 1985a). A verbal remembering of events is a description. Descriptions can vary in a range of significant ways without their being merely (objectively, obviously) true or false (Schegloff, 1972). In the context of their production in sequences of conversational acts, they display an in-built 'recipient design' (Sacks et al., 1974; Sacks and Schegloff, 1979). Versions are constructed to perform conversational work, via their implications, and the inferences they offer, concerning issues of cause and reason, blame and complicity, and so on.

In conversational remembering, there are indefinitely many ways to describe 'what happened', even discounting categories such as lies and errors, and even those categories are ones that can be flexibly and rhetorically deployed by participants, as we shall show in later chapters. In courtroom cross-examination, of course, such issues are pervasive concerns for all witnesses, accusers and defendants. Establishing the facts is not the indefinite task of establishing any and all possible facts, even concerning the events in question. Such a corpus would be potentially infinite; and long before the task was even started the important issues would be clouded for all in the courtroom. Descriptions are marshalled and facts are produced in so far as they have, or can be seen to have, bearing on specific accounts and narratives. This is so, whether we are dealing with courtroom dialogue or any ordinary conversation. It is a matter of constructing suitable descriptions of events, for the pragmatic business at hand (such as establishing blame). What count as appropriate descriptions, relevant events and proper criteria for them, including criteria apparently outside the current talk (physical evidence, corroborating testimony and so on), are also issues that participants address in talk. One of the central goals of discursive psychology is to explicate this process.

Our discussion of conversational remembering has taken as its starting point Neisser's analysis of John Dean's testimony. This has led to a thematic focus upon adversarial talk, of which the courtroom provides the paradigm example. However, it is important to recognize that any kind of conversation can be examined for how it deals with issues of fact, cognition and inference, and how it manages potentially inferable 'attributions'. An example from a conversation analytical study of an everyday piece of talk will serve to illustrate this.

Reports and attributions

One of the virtues of conversation analysis is that it has started to reveal how issues of reported fact and personal responsibility are frequently at stake for participants. That is, it has started to show how issues that have often been construed in individual psychological terms are a feature of social interaction. For example, a variety of conversational phenomena has been shown to display 'preference structure' (Atkinson and Heritage, 1984b; Sacks, 1987). For certain kinds of actions, such as invitations, requests and offers, the 'preferred' responses are acceptances and compliances. Refusals, rejections, disagreements and such generally display a 'dispreferred' organization; they tend to be linguistically longer, marked by hesitation, by prefacing remarks, and often include the provision of an 'account' for the action.

These 'accounts' (which are generally constructed from some sort of report or description) are interesting for the attributional work they do; for example, they often serve to soften the social implications of activities of refusing, disagreeing and so on. The account typically attends to the kind of negative identity that might be inferred from the action of refusing and attempts to implicate a more positive alternative. Within such accounts we find versions of current, anticipated and past events and, again, these can be examined for how they attend to the attributional problems of doing 'dispreferreds'. They are typically constructions of events that imply good reasons for non-compliance. As Drew (1984: 129) notes, 'instead of saying that they did not or are not going to do something, speakers commonly assert an inability to do it' (see also Heritage, 1984). An event may be reported, then, in the context of a refusal or rejection, in just such a way as to externalize responsibility, to blame circumstances and avoid unfavourable personal attributions. In the following extract, provided by Drew (1984:

138), having been invited on a shopping trip by N, E launches into a lengthy description of the enduring effects of a recent operation on an infected toenail. The report ends thus:

E: . . . and I had to have my <u>foot</u> up on a <u>p</u>illow for two days,
   <u>you</u>know ⌜ and – ·hhhmhh
N: ⌞ Yah?
E: But honey it's gonna be alright I'm sure,
N: Oh I'm <u>sure</u> it's gonna be al<u>ri</u>:ght,
E: Yeuh,
N: <u>Oh</u>:: do:ggone. I ⌜ thought maybe we could ⌝
E: ⌞ I'd <u>like</u> to get   ⌟ some little slippers
   but uh,
(Drew, 1984: 138)

It is not only the analyst who hears the story about the toenail as an account designed to accomplish a rejection of an invitation. As is typical in conversation analytical work, close attention is paid to how participants display their own readings of each other's talk; in this case, the analysis is consonant with N's own reaction to the account displayed in: '<u>Oh</u>:: do:ggone'. For our purposes, the interesting matter is what these sorts of conversational organizations tell us about discursive remembering. They alert us to the ways in which reportings, rememberings, accounts, witnessings and so on occur as parts of social actions. They are constructed with regard to matters such as responsibility and blame, even in ordinary, mundane talk. Courtroom testimony is a special kind of talk, but it is developed from, and draws upon, the resources of mundane talk.

It is a routine feature of conversation, and a special feature of courtroom dialogue, that establishing 'what happened' is done with regard to issues of personal responsibility, such that the psychological categories of memory and attribution have to be seen as intimately connected, even as mutually constitutive. Reportings of events carry their attributional implications with them, and are constructed precisely to do that. Attributional considerations are important criteria for the construction of versions. In the next chapter, we shall enrich these claims via a case study of press reports, where public records, issues of fact and blame, memory for a disputed conversation with a high-ranking politician, and the possibility of an objective record to resolve disputation, offer a useful parallel to the case of John Dean.

3

Chancellor Lawson's Memory

In Chapter 2 we argued for a discourse analytical approach to remembering. We suggested that no single version, nor any collection of actual versions, can be taken as a person's real or definitive memory. Before they can be taken as cognitive representations, accounts of past events need to be examined as pieces of discourse – as contextualized and variable productions that perform pragmatic and rhetorical work. That is, we have tried to show the value of considering remembering as an occasioned discursive activity and therefore as something that can generate considerable confusion for traditional psychological approaches which assume that the path to cognition involves 'stripping off' as much 'interfering' context as possible.

In this chapter we shall develop this argument through a detailed analysis of reportings of a different event, in which similar (Watergate-like) issues of memory, truth and accuracy are at issue. Conducting our own analysis in this way allows us to bring in issues and elements that are unavailable in Neisser's study. Once again, our focus will be upon how notions of a true, original event (the 'facts') are constructed, and upon how distortions and errors – usually those of other people – are accounted for. As the chapter progresses we shall also start to show the way that issues of truth and error become bound up with 'attributional' considerations concerning dispositional and intentional characteristics of persons. This is not at all surprising, of course, because in natural settings when telling stories about past experiences, or when rememberings are demanded, we do not (often) offer phenomenologies of merely conjunctive events but provide tales rich in motivation and replete with assignments of responsibility.

The analysis is again of 'remembering' in a natural context; although, as the last chapter should have made clear, we are now considering 'remembering' as a considerably richer phenomenon than is common in traditional cognitive psychology. The analytical materials are a series of newspaper reports, and parliamentary records, of a controversial press briefing given by the then British Chancellor of the Exchequer, Nigel Lawson. This material has the advantage of being similar in many crucial ways to the John Dean/

Watergate material: disputations of memory and inference about what was really said at a politically sensitive meeting, about the adequacy and accuracy of various versions of those events, the status of various 'objective' records and so on. But, at the same time, it provides additional elements which were missing from the restricted data source that Neisser concentrated on. In particular, it provides for an analysis of the rhetorical context of the event, as well as an opportunity to study processes of event reconstruction occurring over time, which Neisser also clearly recognizes to be an important feature of real-world studies (cf. Bartlett, 1932).

It is worth noting some of the wider reasons we had for focusing on material which might initially seem to be specific to some of the more arcane features of the British political system. First of all, once we start considering remembering and other psychological phenomena, such as attribution and motivation, in terms of their organization in discursive practices we have to pay much more attention than we have done in the past to considering the specifics of content and the detail of sequential context. It is only by doing this that we can start to make clear some of the pragmatic considerations that come into play and how they structure the patterns of discourse.

Given this requirement we elected to focus on disputes over the activities of politicians because they are something that is familiar (with some differences of inflection) in all Western countries. Although some of the customs for political briefings of journalists vary, and although the specific political policies that are the subject of controversy vary, the broader pattern of politicians attempting to manipulate political reporting and of conflicts over the nature and meaning of political acts is a virtually universal one. This provides a second reason for focusing on this material. For, in spite of differences of detail, most readers will have a general competence in making sense of news reporting of politics, and this can assist them in understanding and evaluating our own analysis. In a sense, readers are bringing with them a wide tacit knowledge of context which eases our task of exposition.

Having argued this, we could, nevertheless, have focused on a very different kind of talk, for example that between family members (Billig, 1990; Edwards and Middleton, 1988) or accounts of unworldly experiences (Wooffitt, 1991, 1992). And, in some ways, this talk from outside institutional settings might have been a firmer basis for our argument that the phenomena we are documenting are general features of discourse rather than things specific to the institutional settings of political argument and media reporting. Conversation analysts, for example, have stressed that everyday talk is always the analytical first base (Atkinson and Heritage, 1984a; Heritage, 1984). Nevertheless, we hope that the accessibility and intrinsic interest of the material may make up for any possible limitation on generalizability.

There is one final point to note concerning the use of newspaper and television reporting as a focus for analysis. It might be objected that such materials are not the product of a single individual; instead, they have often been through a complex social and institutionally embedded process involving various different agents in writing and speaking and a number of different levels of refinement and editing. As such, this discourse would be a collective or interactional product. However, we emphasize that this is, at least in part, merely a more explicit example of a pervasive feature of discourse in face-to-face situations (for example, Leudar and Antaki, 1988; Levinson, 1983). Moreover, our concern is not primarily with the natural history of any utterance or text, the processes by which it came to be how it is, but with its rhetorical organization in its specific context of use.

In the course of the chapter we examine: (a) how discourse about what could be used as an arbiter of truth was rhetorically organized; (b) how participants' versions of events were constructed rhetorically, as parts of arguments; (c) how both sides of the dispute maintained the coherence of their positions by a form of error accounting similar to that used by Neisser with respect to Dean.

We should add a word of caution about how we are using the term 'construction'. As we have noted, Neisser has been moving from his early cognitive constructivist position (Neisser, 1967) increasingly towards a position where memories are organized as reflections of the true facts, albeit after a process of repisodic synthesis. The constructivism we are concerned to develop here, however, is of a different kind. Whereas in the cognitive constructivism characteristic of Neisser's earlier work a person's reality is created through the operation of a variety of mental schemata, analysis and synthesis processes and such, in the discursive constructivism we are recommending the constructive processes are to be found in the organization of talk, and in the situated ordinary reasoning it embodies. Indeed, constructivism (or constructionism) has been used in psychology to refer to a variety of different strands of work (Gergen, 1985), not all of which are directly compatible with the argument of this book.

It is important to emphasize that for this kind of naturalistic discourse analytical inquiry we shall need to take a more circumspect position on 'truth' than either the information-processing or the ecological approaches have done. Given our constructivist theoretical position it would be quite inappropriate for us as analysts to legislate as to the truth of the matter; for this is exactly one of the central concerns of the participants' ordinary reasoning. Indeed, as work in the sociology of scientific knowledge has shown, it is vital to maintain a neutral position with respect to what the participants treat as facts, or else their own interests and purposes begin to contaminate the analytical conclusions (Bloor, 1976; Collins, 1981; Mulkay, 1979). As we have argued, this is precisely the issue raised by Neisser's (1981) study, and it is the reason for which that article was given the close critical scrutiny usually reserved for textual 'data'; it is not that it represents a form of psychologizing that is especially worthy of criticism.

Thus in the analysis that follows 'the truth of what really happened' will not be the starting point for analysis, as it was for Neisser; nor will it be the end goal of the analysis. Rather, our concern will be with the discursive practices of reasoning which the participants bring to bear on this concern. In effect, we are moving from a view of people struggling to remember with the aid of their mental faculties to a view of people struggling with one another in their talk and texts over the real nature of events. Truth is what they try to accomplish – our concern is with how these attempts are marshalled, and with their rhetorical organization. We aim to show the essentially contingent and functionally orientated nature of any construction of factuality or 'true versions of events'. That is, just as we have suggested with respect to John Dean, accounts of 'what happened' occur within and as part of communicative activities such as assigning blame, denying responsibility, justifying interpretations, and are therefore variable in a systematic way that is subject to the requirements of those rhetorical activities.

We turn now to the press reports concerning 'Lawsongate'. While a comparison of a scientific report with a set of newspaper reportings may at first seem inappropriate, we intend to show that very similar issues are raised, and are problematic, in both. These issues include: the ways in which contentious versions of 'what really happened' are constructed, the way appeals are made to ostensibly objective criteria for warranting such claims, the use of rhetorical devices in the establishment of claims to accuracy, and the deployment of explanatory devices for accounting for errors in other people's accounts. After a preliminary summary of the dispute between Chancellor Lawson and the journalists, we shall divide our discussion of the press accounts into three main sections, each of which concerns a major issue in the psychology of remembering, and in the case of John Dean's testimony:

(a) dispute over *where* the truth lies; (b) dispute over the *nature* of the truth; (c) dispute over the nature of the *error*.

Lawsongate: a gist

During November 1988, over several weeks, the British press carried a series of reports and discussions of the content of a disputed conversation which had taken place on Friday 4 November between Nigel Lawson, the Chancellor of the Exchequer, and ten journalists from the Sunday newspapers. Sunday newspapers are an established institution in Britain (the oldest is currently celebrating its bicentenary), and have a combined circulation higher than that of daily papers. This meeting was universally characterized as a regular event, one of a series of 'off-the-record' briefings in which senior politicians are able to 'float ideas in the press': forthcoming policies, plans and so forth, to which they do not yet want publicly to commit themselves. It was one of a series of these 'unattributable' briefings called 'lobby journalism', the 'lobby' being the group of journalists. It is important to note that in this setting 'lobby' does not carry its usual connotation of partisan political pressure groups.

Controversy, allegations and counter-allegations, between journalists and the Chancellor, centred around several key issues. The most contentious of these issues concerned what Lawson had said about plans to alter benefits payable to old-age pensioners. The Sunday papers reported that a major and controversial alteration was looming, in which benefits currently payable universally to all pensioners would in future be 'targeted' upon the more needy, through a process of 'means testing' (income assessment), such that some would receive reduced allowances or none at all (this was the controversial point), while others might receive increases. Lawson subsequently (on the following Monday, on radio, television and in parliament) denied that he had said any such thing, claiming at one point that the journalists had got together and their 'fevered imagination' had produced 'a farrago of invention', 'inaccurate, half-baked' accounts which 'bear no relation whatever to what I said' (quotations from *The Times* and the *Guardian*, Tuesday 8 November). The existence of a tape recording of the meeting, itself the subject of later claims and denials, led to whimsical comparisons with Watergate, dubbed 'Lawsongate' (*Observer*, 13 November), and 'a fish and chips version of Nixon's White House Tapes. Expletive deleted' (*Guardian*, 9 November).

We have indicated the main sequence of events in Figure 3.1 for ease of reference and because we wish particularly to stress the

Figure 3.1 *Events following Chancellor Lawson's 'lobby briefing'*

4 November	Lobby briefing between Lawson, press adviser John Gieve and ten Sunday newspaper journalists.
5 November, evening	Independent Television News runs a story claiming similar policy changes to those reported in the next day's papers.
6 November, morning	Sunday newspapers headline changes in benefits to old-age pensioners, and emphasize their controversial nature.
6 November, lunchtime	Barney Heyhoe (former Conservative minister) criticizes on television the reported policy changes.
7 November, morning	Lawson denies the stories on BBC radio.
7 November, evening	Lawson denies stories in a parliamentary response to a 'private notice question' asked by the Leader of the Opposition. Lawson denies stories in a major interview on BBC television.
8–10 November	Numerous articles on the briefing and its contents and speculation about the existence of a tape of the meeting.
13 November, morning	Sunday newspapers report the 'independent corroboration' of their stories by ITN. They run lengthy and detailed stories describing the events in the briefing, their context and the ensuing controversy.
24 November	The Social Security Secretary announces extra benefits for poorer pensioners.
25 November, morning	The newspapers link the benefits to the lobby briefing; e.g. '£200m windfall for old', 'Extra benefits for 2.6 million pensioners rushed through to cover Lawson's means test gaffe' (*Guardian*).

sequential relevance of the different versions of what went on in the briefing. Some features of Figure 3.1 will be discussed in Chapter 5. The analytical materials we have used were derived principally from five newspapers, the *Guardian*, *The Times*, the *Observer*, the *Sunday Mirror*, and *The Sunday Times*, and the official parliamentary record of debates, *Hansard*. These particular papers were chosen because they are for the most part considered to be 'quality' papers (the exception, the *Sunday Mirror*, had its own journalist present at the briefing) and they cover a range of political opinion, with the *Guardian*, the *Sunday Mirror* and the *Observer* usually being identified as somewhat more left or liberal than *The Times* and *The Sunday Times*. The papers were collected each day for a fortnight after the controversial briefing and every article referring to it was collected and photocopied. The decision to concentrate on papers of this kind was not made because we considered the tabloids to be any less interesting or important. Far from it; the tabloids have a combined circulation far in excess of the quality broadsheets, and they provide their own complex and entertaining coverage of politics. Rather, our focus was motivated by the detail and extent of the coverage of the quality papers (often several stories on the topic in the same issue) and by our greater familiarity with the genre which helped us to gain an initial understanding on analytical issues.

Where the truth lies

In this section our goal is to show that the issue of *where* the truth lies, or what *counts* as the factual record, is a live one for participants. Different participants on different occasions made different suggestions as to how the facts could be checked. Moreover, we suggest that it would be wrong to take these suggestions as neutral descriptions of attempts to comprehend, because the descriptions can themselves be understood as embedded features of the rhetorical conflicts being played out between the newspapers and the government representatives.

All parties to the dispute made frequent recourse to the existence of some objective record which might reveal the unequivocal truth about the original events. The most obvious of these was a tape recording of the meeting made by a government official who was also present. Neither the tape recording, nor a transcription of it, have to date materialized in public: 'when Sunday newspaper journalists challenged him [Lawson] to justify his claims by producing a transcript of the interview a further Treasury embarrassment was revealed. The tape recorder used by an official to record the meeting had failed to work properly' (*The Times*, 8 November). The failure or otherwise of the tape recording was a recurring source of controversy. The papers suggested that this recording would vindicate their version of what went on, just as Neisser took the 'presidential transcript' to vindicate Dean, and they offered motivated accounts for its non-appearance; the absent tape 'inevitably . . . fuelled suspicions of a cover-up' (*Observer*, 13 November). Press reports detailed several contradictory Treasury statements to the effect that the tape recorder had malfunctioned so that the tape was blank, that there was a transcript of the recording but it would not be released, that the pause button had been accidentally pressed so that the spools did not turn, that the original tape had been lost, and so on.

Treasury officials and journalists alike offered detailed descriptions to warrant their own versions of what happened. Thus: 'A Treasury spokesman told the *Guardian* on Wednesday that the tape recorder was "a fairly sophisticated machine . . . the light was on but it did not work" . . . The tape was blank, according to the Treasury. The machine was a voice-activated recorder. It did not work properly' (*Guardian*, 11 November). The machine's sophistication appears here not as a warrant for how good it was but, on the contrary, as a plausible basis, offered by the Treasury, for its claimed unreliability or difficulty of operation. As counter-evidence that the recorder *was* working, and that the spools were turning, the journalists offered graphic descriptions, rich in the kind of contextual detail that led Neisser to give such credibility to John Dean: 'At one point I heard a click, and assumed the tape had run out. It was directly in front of me. When I looked to check, the spools were still spinning. The clicking I heard turned out to be Don Macintyre of the *Sunday Telegraph*, seated to my right, chewing a pen top' (*Sunday Mirror*, 13 November). Conflicting claims to the existence, or non-existence, of the tape recording thus varied according to the claimant's pragmatic situation. More interestingly, so also did the ostensibly objective grounds vary upon which those claims were made. It seems that we can best make sense of these accounts by viewing them as not summoning up details of description and of context according to some abstract overall criterion of truth or accuracy, but because of the specific rhetorical work they could sustain (cf. Pomerantz, 1987).

Thus far, the reader might be forgiven for thinking that this dispute only exists because the full verbatim record is missing. Indeed, the logic of the journalists' suspicions about the missing tape seemed to be based on its potential for resolving the dispute. However, if we now go on to examine the dispute about the adequacy of the journalists' notes this assessment seems much less plausible.

Despite the absence of the tape recording, even Lawson appeared willing to grant the existence and reliability of the journalists' detailed shorthand notes. Here *Hansard* quotes his words in parliament: 'The journalists concerned know very well and if they *look in their notebooks* they will see that the stories that appeared in Sunday's newspapers bear *no relation whatever* to what I said' (*Hansard*, 7 November; emphasis added). Chancellor Lawson here remarkably claims the journalists' own records as evidence against their accounts, a rhetorical device that is consistent with his claim that they had 'concocted' their stories for lack of anything more exciting to report, but which runs the obvious risk of being directly contradicted by the journalists themselves. It is also interesting to note how Lawson describes the process of constructing events from written records, as one of simply 'looking' to 'see' what they say. The notion of definitive, unproblematical versions and definitive descriptions, apprehended by mere perception, is clearly deployed here with rhetorical force. It was not to be Lawson's only formulation of the relationship between records and truth, as we shall demonstrate. Meanwhile, the *Guardian* (a daily paper not represented at the lobby briefing) offers its own rationale for Lawson's challenge. The fact that the meeting was to be 'off-the-record' allowed Lawson room for rhetorical manoeuvre: 'So the hacks' notebooks contain only a sketchy summary, not a verbatim note. Mr Lawson was thus on safe ground when he challenged them to back their stories with quotes' (*Guardian*, 9 November). According to the *Guardian*, then, the notion that there existed ten careful and independent sets of detailed shorthand notes was unfounded, as was the simplicity with which such notes could be mapped onto the truth of what happened. In seemingly playing into the journalists' hands by validating the accuracy of their written records, Lawson was able to avoid denying the existence and status of those records while remaining immune from refutation.

Now, the variable status of these shorthand notes, as possibly precise records of what really happened, is particularly interesting. In the other newspapers, and in the *Guardian* itself, we are informed that there existed 'verbatim notes of the Chancellor's words' (*The Sunday Times*, 13 November), taken by '10 fully trained shorthand-writing journalists' (*Guardian*, 9 November). Yet elsewhere, and sometimes in the same article, the *Guardian* casts serious doubts upon the existence and reliability of those detailed records. Rather than trying to sort out a factual from a false version, we can make sense of this variability by considering the pragmatic contexts in which the two accounts occur (cf. Potter and Wetherell, 1987).

The functional orientation of claims for the detailed accuracy of the journalists' notes is straightforward enough. They operate, in the context of criticisms of Lawson, as parts of arguments that support the journalists' versions of events against Lawson's claims for what he said. However, the functional orientation of the *Guardian*'s claim that the journalists had only a sketchy summary is slightly more complex. It becomes clear when we note that this claim is part of a broader critique of the lobby system, with its practice of unattributable press 'leakings' – 'a system from which, chiefly because of the scope which it offers for tendentious manipulation, the Guardian unilaterally withdrew two years ago' (*Guardian*, 11 November). In this version, the very unanimity of the Sunday press reports, which in other contexts was used as a warrant for their truth and accuracy, merely shows up their inadequacy:

> With that perfectly drilled unanimity which the lobby system shares with the Brigade of Guards . . . Two of the so-called heavies [i.e. the 'quality press'] actually gave the story an identical headline . . . the stories underneath were equally similar in content. (*Guardian*, 7 November)

Similarly, and in a clear rhetorical context:

> Because they assumed that the comments were unattributable, the correspondents present did not attempt their usual assiduous verbatim note. Instead they gathered afterwards to ask each other the traditional lobby question: 'What's the story?' . . . The stories duly appeared, with that impressive unanimity which is the dangerous fruit of mass lobby briefings, on Sunday morning. (*Guardian*, 11 November)

So, in one discursive context (criticizing Lawson), we are told about a detailed set of notes carefully taken by ten independent senior journalists, each offering in its record of events a basis of truth sufficiently independent of the journalists' own press stories that they could serve as bench-marks for the accuracy of those same stories. As we have noted, this version was also available for recruitment by Lawson himself. In another discursive context (criticizing the system of lobby journalism), the same notes are characterized as sketchy and incomplete and, in any case, the product of collusion and *post hoc* reconstruction by the journalists concerned. Accounts of whether the notes contained sufficient records of the event clearly vary according to rhetorical context.

Similar variability is observable in Lawson's discourse. Having at first made strong claims that the journalists' reports were fabricated inventions, he subsequently declared 'that the unsourced quotations that had appeared were "absolutely accurate"' (*Guardian*, 11 November). Again, we have what appear to be contradictory versions of events in the discourse of one of its major participants. And, again, rather than concerning ourselves with what the absolute truth might be, we can analyse Lawson's variability in terms of the pragmatics and sequencing of his different accounts.

Lawson's second version, in which the journalists' quotations were accepted as accurate, followed the appearance in the press of detailed narratives of what 'actually' happened in the briefing, rich

---

Box 3   *Who is Nigel Lawson?*

Nigel's position as I said to him is unassailable. He was a very strong person. (Margaret Thatcher on ITV's 'Walden Interview')

He is that rarity in public life, a man who came into politics not out of some general ambition for high office, but in the hope of reaching the one office for which he had sought to qualify himself all his life.

. . . combative, bold, confident in his capacious and fast-moving mind, impatient, funny, difficult, instructive and a much kinder man than he would ever let on.

. . . if he had not got a fight of his own he would cross the street to start one.

His style, his immense intellectual power, justified even the arrogance which so irritated some of his colleagues. (*Daily Telegraph*, 27 October 1989)

[His] heavy physique has been the butt of many jokes about the excesses of the rich under Thatcherism . . .

Mr Lawson, beneath the brash demeanour, was always a fastidious man who never wholly submitted to the indignities and violations which are the price of a successful political career. (*Independent*, 31 October 1989)

. . . he has disdained image building and the careful nurturing of political support. The chief adjective used to describe him is 'arrogant'. (*Independent*, 27 October 1989)

The primary medium within which identities are created and have their currency is not just linguistic but textual: persons are largely ascribed identities according to the manner of their embedding within a discourse . . . In this way cultural texts furnish their 'inhabitants' with the resources for the formation of selves; they lay out an array of enabling potentials, while simultaneously establishing a set of constraining boundaries . . . (Shotter and Gergen, 1989: ix)

(With acknowledgements to Ashmore et al., 1989, ch. 4)

---

in description of surroundings and sequence of dialogue and context. These narratives were themselves framed as responses to Lawson's earlier accusations of wild journalistic inaccuracies ('described . . . as "the most inaccurate, half-baked and irresponsible" he had seen in 10 years', *The Sunday Times*, 13 November). The pragmatic work done by Lawson's apparent volte-face was to maintain his claim to have not mooted means-testing benefits, while conceding the accuracy of the journalists' reports. This was achieved by his switching the issue from what he actually said, to the claim that what he had said had been misunderstood: 'Treasury officials later said that Mr Lawson regarded all the accounts of the briefing given by journalists during the last few days as broadly accurate, though he strongly contested the interpretation given to them' (*The Times*, 10 November).

The upshot of the Chancellor's new statement was of vital importance to the issue of defining what really happened. It now hardly mattered whether there was a direct record of the meeting or not, since the dispute concerned not what was said, but what was meant. That is, despite the dispute about the tape recording which presupposed that it would decide the facts of the matter, here we see the parties agreeing about the words – the 'verbatim truth' – but disagreeing over their interpretation. No longer was the truth, in Lawson's terms, to be discerned merely by 'looking' to 'see' what the journalists' notes said. Perceptualism and constructivism arise here, not as analysts' conflicting approaches to explaining memory and talk, but as participants' own conceptual resources, flexibly deployed in the rhetoric of truth and disputation.

Let us spell this out a little more. Note that it is Lawson, and the *Guardian*, and not the lobby journalists (who still claimed to have a clear record which supported their version) who point up the constructive nature of versions. The point is that participants themselves can do what psychologists do, offering either objective or constructive notions of reality. But here we see these theoretical positions deployed flexibly as options, with participants moving from one version to the other (as both Lawson and the *Guardian* do), as context and pragmatics require (Latour and Woolgar, 1986; Woolgar, 1988a). The reality–construction dichotomy, upon which axis the constructivists and the Gibsonians dispute the real nature of mind, appears here as an everyday rhetorical resource for bolstering different sorts of pragmatic work. 'Realist' common sense is useful when the work to be done is that of claiming knowledge of the unambiguous truth; constructivism comes into its own as a device for undermining that claim in others.

What the truth is

The notion that the epistemological status of 'original events' is problematical is, of course, nothing new to cognitive psychology, at least when it is concerned not with memory, but with comprehension. It has been a commonplace at least since Bartlett (1932; cf. Bransford, 1979) that comprehension and memory are closely linked. Memory is understood to be a function of the comprehensibility of the original experience, and indeed has even been described as a sort of reiteration of the process of comprehension (Schank, 1982). Similarly, models of the comprehension of textual materials are understood to require detailed and well-organized memory components, models of the world, of events, and of how inferences can be made through consultation with those components, in order to enable sense to be made of the text (for example, Bransford, 1979; Winograd, 1972, 1980).

However, the dependence of memory upon comprehension is generally framed as a problem concerning what goes on in the minds of cognizers – whether experimental subjects or simulations. Psychologists themselves appear to be immune from the problem. They have direct access to the experimental 'input', have often invented it themselves, having designed into it some degree of comprehensibility, or of ambiguity, and so on, and can plainly see its meaning: 'In a psychological experiment, it is relatively easy to determine whether what the subject says is true. The experimenter knows what really happened because she staged it in the first place, or because she kept a record with which the subject's report can be compared' (Neisser, 1981: 2). But in everyday conversational remembering, and in the Lawsongate data, it is precisely the status of the original events that is at issue. By removing that issue from experimental study, a major concern of ordinary rememberers is systematically excluded from the great majority of cognitive psychological investigations. The outcome is that the constructive, to-be-achieved nature of that 'original event' cannot be studied. We shall examine now some of the interpretative work that was done in the construction of events in the 'Lawsongate' reports.

The journalists' presentations of what happened at the meeting can be divided into three phases. In the first Sunday reports, which prompted all the controversy and denials, the story was simply one of what an anonymous government minister had revealed about plans to 'target' welfare benefits for the elderly upon the less well-off: 'Means test threat to pensioners . . . "Targeting" would entail switching resources from benefits currently paid to all pensioners . . . and concentrating instead on helping the poorest' (*Observer*, 6 November). This and similar versions of what was said were picked up in the Monday dailies, when Lawson's counter-claims were first being voiced: 'The plan is to divert more resources to the genuinely needy by removing the rights of better-off pensioners to receive such universal benefits as . . .' (*The Times*, 7 November).

The second phase came after Lawson's 'farrago of invention' speech, whereupon the journalists produced detailed narrative accounts of the meeting. It was in these accounts that the journalists first addressed themselves to the fact–interpretation distinction, and the constructive task of justifying the meanings that they had assigned to what the Chancellor had actually said:

> *The Times* contacted several of the journalists present at the meeting and all were adamant that while the Chancellor did not specifically mention the removal of the £10 Christmas bonus, the loss of free prescriptions for pensioners and the introduction of means testing for old people, the meaning was clear. (*The Times*, 7 November)

The major issue for interpretation centred upon the word 'targeting'. Lawson claimed that it was not meant to imply redistribution of resources but, rather, the much less controversial offering of *extra* resources to the poor. In this third phase of reporting the journalists were united in their claim that Lawson had been forced into offering extra cash in order to extricate himself from the embarrassment caused by the original leak: 'Extra benefits for 2.6 million pensioners rushed through to cover Lawson's means test gaffe' (*Guardian*, 25 November). The very notion of a distinction between fact and interpretation, between what was precisely said and what was obviously meant, was originally introduced by Lawson when faced with the detailed rebuffs of his claim that the journalists had misrepresented him: the journalists had got the quotes right, but had drawn the wrong interpretations from his words. In the third phase, the journalists' interpretative work in phase two has become a taken-for-granted background for reverting to a factual account, of what we all know Lawson really said. Let us look at phases two and three.

The journalists happily operated with the distinction Lawson had offered, between what was said and what was meant: 'Guardian political reporters sift through the facts, fancies and furore surrounding the Chancellor's briefing on pensions' (heading in the *Guardian*, 11 November). In this metaphor, facts pre-exist like little objects, which can be sifted through, and separated like wheat from chaff, from those other little objects, the 'fancies' of interpretation. However, the facts in question are not merely the words said, but their meanings. Interpretations have to be made into facts. The journalists' interpretations are presented as what any rational person would be forced to acknowledge, given such powerful warrants as accurate records, independent accounts, vivid memories, contextual plausibility ('logic'), and common knowledge (what everyone knows). And thus the interpretations become indistinguishable from the facts of what was actually said. We do not wish to overburden our text with an extended analysis of these features of the material. Nevertheless, a flavour of this type of warranting is given in the following list of extracts, organized into topics. In each we have emphasized the most significant sections.

Common knowledge
the [press] interpretations of what the Chancellor told the lobby correspondents of Friday *chime in completely with other government moves.* (*The Times*, 8 November)

Any 'practising politician' will tell you never, ever speak of means testing when a euphemism can be used . . . Instead, *1988 Tories speak* of 'accurately targeting needs'.

The meaning of targeting under this government *has never been in any doubt.* (*The Sunday Times*, 13 November)

Context and logic
The main message [that imputed by the journalists] in fact, was in line with earlier ministerial statements on targeting. It was a logical next step . . . (*Guardian*, 8 November)

Discourse context
With his words about child benefit *still ringing in our ears*, Mr Lawson *turned immediately* to the pensioners . . . *As with child benefit*, it sounded as though what he had in mind was . . . switching resources from universal benefits . . . and putting money instead into means-tested payments, targeted on the poorest. Indeed, *the very next question* [on the need to 'educate' his back benchers] reflected that conviction. (*Observer*, 13 November)

Given his previous remarks about child benefit and his observation that most pensioners were now well-off enough to afford the new, means-tested charges for health check-ups, that sentence could only mean one thing. (*The Sunday Times*, 13 November)

I said I was going to write about the changes in pensioners' benefits. I recall using the word 'cuts'. It was another chance for the Treasury to inform me that Lawson had been talking about a new and extra benefit. He [Gieve] didn't do so. (*Sunday Mirror*, 13 November)

We have already discussed other sorts of warrants: appeals to accurate records, independent sources and vivid memories (graphic descriptions of the scene), and shown how they can be viewed as *accomplishments* in the rhetoric of truth-telling. What we have in total, then, is a series of discursive devices through which the journalists were able to justify their claims to having provided true and accurate versions of events, such that the upshot of all their interpretative work is to formulate it as hardly necessary – the conclusions are obvious, the only ones permissible, inherent in the facts, so that the fact–interpretation distinction is once again pragmatically closed down, with the journalists' accounts the only one remaining: 'Targeting (the polite word for means testing) . . .'

(*The Sunday Times*, 13 November); 'It is entirely right that he should not get away with denying what he said, or with calling a dozen journalists liars' (*Guardian*, 15 November). In *The Sunday Times* formulation, 'targeting' is given simply as a direct translation of the term 'means testing' – terms differing only in their politeness conditions. This effectively short-circuits the fact–interpretation altogether, in favour of the journalists' version. The *Guardian* quotation similarly reifies as simple fact, what once had to be carefully established and argued. What Lawson might have meant is now what Lawson actually said. In addition, Lawson's inaccuracy appears in this extract presuppositionally, as given information; it is multiply embedded in layers of presupposition (cf. Wilson, 1990):

(a) interpretation is gone – what he said and meant are the same;
(b) x (to deny what he said) presupposes y (that he said it);
(c) that he should not get away with x (denying what he said) presupposes x and therefore y;
(d) 'it is entirely right that . . .' further embeds the other already nested propositions.

Clearly, we are now a long way from what was previously a painstakingly crafted business for participants, of textual interpretation: from phase two, where the issue of what Lawson may have said and might have meant were at stake.

The phases through which these journalists' versions passed should not be dismissed as merely what might be expected of journalists and politicians. Nor should they be dismissed as having little relevance to psychology's concern with 'real' remembering, or with objective truth. In the ecological settings of ordinary talk, remembering is always an actual, not merely a potential, activity. It takes place within the context of whatever actions the talk is 'designed' for. Furthermore, they are features not only of everyday talk, but also of that ultimate arena in which objective truths are at stake – the construction of scientific knowledge.

Latour (1987) suggests that not only political talk about fact, but also scientific knowledge, can be analysed in terms of 'modalities' of discourse. Established truths are ones that once were contentious, and can later become contentious again. It is a matter of how close a formulation of knowledge is to the conditions of its production:

> We will call *positive modalities* those sentences that lead a statement away from its conditions of production, making it solid enough to render some other consequences necessary. We will call *negative modalities* those sentences that lead a statement in the other direction

towards its conditions of production and that explain in detail why it is solid or weak instead of using it to render some other consequences more necessary. (Latour, 1987: 23)

As with the Lawsongate journalists, matters of fact, once they were challenged, were taken back to the conditions of their production, and warranted or undermined in terms of their evidential basis and plausibility (cf. Pomerantz, 1984b). Graphic and vivid descriptions of contextual events were offered, as warrants for the accuracy of the more contentious elements embedded within them. Furthermore, whether in science, politics or everyday talk, we are dealing with an essentially rhetorical process. Even in the absence of overt argumentation, factual accounts are designed to counter possible alternative versions and refutations (Billig, 1987). In the case of, scientific texts, 'reading the sentences of the paper without imagining the reader's objections is like watching only one player's strokes in the tennis final' (Latour, 1987: 46).

Another feature of scientific discourse, which reflects its basis in ordinary social practices, is the movement between empiricist and constructivist positions. Latour refers to this as the 'two-faced Janus' character of science, and it is reflected in discourse analytical studies of scientists' 'interpretative repertoires' (Gilbert and Mulkay, 1984; Mulkay, 1985; Potter and Wetherell, 1987). In ratcheting facts up and down the scale of modalities, the same scientists will shift between an empiricist vision of scientific knowledge as determined by nature, and a constructivist position in which nature is indistinguishable from knowledge of nature (cf. Woolgar, 1988a), the outcome rather than the determinant of scientific understanding. Again, the process is rhetorically rather than cognitively organized, embedded in textual or discursive practices, with the empiricist repertoire deployed for truth, and the contingent, constructive account reserved for doubt and error. As we noted with Dean and Neisser, these positions are also resources of ordinary talk.

What the error is

One of the features that we noted in Neisser's study is that to accomplish his account of Dean's essential truthfulness he also has to deal with what he presents as Dean's blatant errors. Basically, error posed for Neisser an interpretative problem, for it was not encompassed by his 'repisodic' account of Dean's remembering (cf. Gilbert and Mulkay, 1984; Mulkay and Gilbert, 1982). To maintain the coherence of his explanation, some other principle needs to be invoked, and the distorting prism of Dean's personality, his vanity,

Box 4 *Black boxes, ratchets and facts*

Boxes are metaphors for three relevant things. This 'box' is a container for text set aside from the rest of Chapter 3, a device like a toy cupboard, where side issues or reflexive elaborations can be placed, that might otherwise clutter the main text's floor space. This one is in turn a box about boxes, or black boxes, and there are two sorts of those. One is the familiar metaphor of the subject of psychology, 'human beings and animals as a kind of box with input and output' (Hamlyn, 1990: 8) that cognitive psychology inherited from its critique of behaviourism. We have noted how cognitive psychology deals with memory as a capacity, rather than with remembering as an activity, with characteristics that can be inferred from discrepancies between input and output. It is a conceptual and methodological habit that is carried over once more into ecological studies. That makes it a kind of 'black box' in a third sense discussed by Latour.

Latour (1987) uses the term 'black boxes' as part of an exposition of the nature of scientific knowledge. Any scientific document or discussion, however empirical, technical or theoretical, rests upon a set of earlier findings, methods, aims, conclusions and so on, which can be referred to uncontroversially, or merely cited, or assumed. The growth of scientific knowledge consists in the transfer of contentious ideas and practices into black boxes, as well as the opening of such boxes when provoked by criticism or the promotion of contrary findings.

By citing Latour in this way, we 'black box' Latour, strengthening his case, rendering his own description of scientific knowledge a little more solid, something to be referenced, or cited, as well as reflexively doing that by doing it. There is no need for us to reproduce the detailed warranting and argumentation of the idea, for which Latour's own text required 274 pages. Indeed, to attempt such a task would quickly make all accumulative talk and text impossible. The creation and subversion of 'common knowledge' is a pervasive concern of any discourse (Edwards and Mercer, 1987; Heritage, 1984).

While we have black boxed Latour on black boxing, giving his analysis 'positive modularity' in Latour's own terms (see also Chapter 6), we have done the opposite with Neisser (1981); we have opened the lid to gaze at the workings of this piece of research. Neisser's study of John Dean's testimony is nevertheless available for black boxing. It categorizes phenomena, sets up conceptual distinctions, exemplifies method and reaches conclusions, like all scientific works do, and is citable for any of these things. Indeed, Cohen (1989: 185–7) does precisely this, in a two-page summary of Neisser's study, from which 'two findings emerge most strongly . . . Firstly, recall is strongly influenced by motives, personality, and wishful thinking. Secondly, we need to distinguish several different levels of memory for conversation.' Neisser's study is transformed in Cohen's text into a summarized statement of findings and conclusions, including assimilations into general cognitivist thinking (Dean's false recall that Nixon invited him to sit down is a 'script-based intrusion . . . from an arriving–at–a–meeting script', 1989: 186).

This kind of black boxing, or modularizing, of Neisser's and Latour's work is a commonplace and necessary feature of any scientific (or ordinary) discourse. Our purpose here is to 'draw attention' to it (the perceptual metaphor helps us constitute it as real) as an aspect of the discursive construction of knowledge. Whatever we might do with Neisser's study, whichever direction we choose to ratchet it, up or down the scale of modalities, sealing the box or opening it up for inspection, we inevitably exemplify how scientific knowledge, and everyday knowledge, and ordinary talk, are socially produced, and studiable as discourse and rhetoric.

serves this purpose. While Dean's account of Nixon is offered as repisodically correct, his own role in events is distorted.

There is a close parallel here in the way the Lawsongate journalists used a dispositional account of Lawson's behaviour:

> Yet Mr Lawson, though perhaps a trifle insensitive, is a highly intelligent man. So is there something which might account for the timing of the leak? (*Guardian*, 7 November)

> But while he is clever, he is sometimes too clever by half. He doesn't suffer fools gladly . . . His super-confidence verging on super-arrogance has too often stirred up trouble . . . It was hubris, many [conservatives] will suspect, which got him (and them) into needless trouble this week. (*Guardian*, 9 November)

> . . . an object lesson for *the cavalier Chancellor* to choose his words· more carefully. (*Sunday Mirror*, 13 November; emphasis added)

For Neisser and the journalists alike, truthful accounts need no such explanation. There may indeed be an explanation for why somebody *chooses to tell* the truth – it may be in one's interests to do so (Neisser on Dean): one may be forced to admit certain things when presented with overwhelming evidence and argument (the journalists on Lawson). But the nature of the account itself is straightforward – it is the truth. Falsity, on the other hand, calls for a different *kind* of explanation. An infinity of falsities is possible, so we need to account for why particular ones are produced. (It is our own argument, of course, that truthful descriptions can also be indefinitely elaborated.) So, Dean's vanity led to his presenting himself favourably; Lawson's cavalier self-confidence and arrogance led him to think he could contradict blatant truths, and escape the consequences.

This problem is faced just as much by Lawson as by the journalists. That is, he has to account for why the journalists got it wrong about the content of the briefing. Lawson offers an error account in the course of the parliamentary debate on 7 November; however, it is perhaps significant that the newspapers we studied chose not to quote this passage which contains a rather different account which is perhaps more threatening to the newspaper versions:

> *Mr Lawson:* . . . the statements that appeared in the press on Sunday bore no relation whatever to what I in fact said. What I have said to them is that, while we were absolutely, totally committed to maintaining –
>
> *Ms Clare Short* (Birmingham, Ladywood): They will have their shorthand notes.
>
> *Mr Lawson:* Oh yes, they will have their shorthand notes and they will know it, and they will know they went behind afterwards and *they thought there was not a good enough story and so they produced that.* (*Hansard*, 7 November: 26; emphasis added)

Rather than give an account of the error in terms of psychological dispositions, which anyway would be rather more difficult to accomplish for ten individuals simultaneously, Lawson provides an account stressing the institutional pressures on reporters to provide good stories. Lawson's version here attends both to the unanimity of the reporter's accounts (they were the same because they were contrived together) and the differences from what he was intending (because that was not a good enough story). The notion of unanimity or consensus figures strongly in theories of 'attribution', and we shall return to its discursive construction in Chapter 5.

We have argued against the notion of a singular, objective truth that is independent of any particular version of it, or of the constructive work necessary in formulating it. Neisser, Dean, Lawson and the journalists all take pains to establish the credibility of their versions of truth against possible refutation. In doing so, they each present the truth of what happened as definitive, singular and objective – as what should be obvious to any rational person who is apprised of the evidence – while presenting dispositional accounts of the other participants' errors. As we noted earlier, this is a classic move made in the practice and rhetoric of science (Gilbert and Mulkay, 1984; Potter, 1984), where true knowledge requires no contingent explanation, since it is the outcome of the objective scientific method. In contrast, 'false' knowledge is accounted for as being due to some other process, some personal quirk or bias, social influence, false reasoning or whatever.

The problem with these speculative dispositional accounts of error is not so much with their own intrinsic validity, but rather, with the obverse upon which they depend for contrast: the notion of a singular, objective truth, independent of guile or rhetoric, of construction and justification, or of any alternative construction. In the case of cognitive studies of memory, truth is equivalent to the psychologist's direct access to the input. But we have argued that in the study of discourse, this notion of direct, unconstructive access to a singularly meaningful input is illusory, an artefact of experimental design that avoids rather than usefully pins down the epistemological issues of everyday remembering. We would argue that researchers into remembering need to take a more symmetrical (neutral) approach to matters which participants treat as truth and falsity. This is important if we want to examine the methodical procedures by which fact, inference and error are defined as such by the participants (cf. Bloor, 1976; Heritage, 1984).

Memory, truth and discourse

Let us summarize the argument so far. In Chapter 2, we suggested that Neisser's three kinds of truthful remembering – verbatim, gist and repisodic – are each subject to critique. They all depend upon the existence, actual or potential, of a definitive discursive record of events. Neisser's analysis of Dean's testimony ignores important features of its organization *as discourse*, especially the rhetorical and 'occasioned' nature of versions, and preserves the notion of a cognitively abstracted, essential truth that is liable to contamination by errors whose origins are dispositional, rooted in Dean's motivations and personality.

In this chapter we have extended our argument by taking a situation which was comparable to Watergate, but where details of disputation were still readily available. We showed, first, that formulations of where the truth lies are not merely the academic concern of psychologists, but are of practical interest to different parties engaged in a dispute about what went on. Our key point was that these different versions need to be understood as organized rhetorically. Participant's versions of events, and their selection of criteria for truth, could not be disentangled from the pragmatic deployment of these formulations. Secondly, we have shown the way that reasoning about the true nature of the disputed briefing was carried out in a public, accountable manner; and, furthermore, that this reasoning was at its most elaborate when the dispute was at its most acute. Prior to this overt disputation, and again subsequent to it, versions of what happened were 'black boxed' (cf. Latour, 1987 and Box 4), treated as straightforward or even self-evident. Finally, we showed the way that both 'sides' in the dispute maintained the coherence of their positions by the use of error accounting, and we pointed out the parallel with the similar form of accounting engaged in by Neisser with respect to Dean's purported errors.

What we have argued, therefore, is that if we are properly to comprehend what Dean, Lawson and the journalists were doing we need to understand the way notions of accuracy, veridicality, memory, truth and so on occur in discourse as pragmatically occasioned accomplishments. Neisser's interest in Dean is consistent with his reading of Gibson: perception is to be treated as essentially veridical, and memory is to be studied for how accurate it is, against criteria of truth and error. Verbatim recall, gist and 'repisodic memory' are different sorts of accuracy. But when it comes to contentious claims to knowledge, such as we find in the ecology of ordinary talk, the cognitive psychology of memory runs into trouble. It is not only that *we* face the difficulty of knowing the true nature of experienced events, as distinct from, and as a criterion for measuring, how our participants know it. It is also that such knowledge is deceptive, since it is not part of those participants' psychology. It distracts us from the business of examining discourse for what it reveals about how participants themselves deal with knowing things.

All three of Neisser's types of truth, or of accurate recall, featured problematically as to-be-constructed outcomes of the journalists' discourse. The possibility of an objective, *verbatim* record which would solve all problems of what really happened was addressed, but lost itself in the disputation about the tape recording, about the journalists' notes and about the independence of other sources of information. It is clear that even the existence of a 'verbatim transcript' would not have changed things because both Lawson and the journalists concentrated their efforts not upon what was actually said, which was soon conceded, but upon what it was reasonable to interpret was meant (cf. Emmison, 1989). The *gist* of what was said turns out to be precisely the contentious matter to be resolved concerning what was 'meant', the object of all the journalists' work on detailed situational descriptions, discourse context, common knowledge (what 'we all know' the British government to mean by 'targeting'), and the appeal to plausible inference ('logic'). The *repisodic* truth was equivalent to the consensual upshot: like Nixon, Lawson was finally represented as having 'said it', and as having plainly tried to 'cover up' what he said.

'What really happened', the truth of the matter, is intrinsically a major issue to be dealt with in any study of remembering, whether it be grounded in everyday accounts or laboratory-based. What we are arguing is, that if it is everyday discourse that we are examining, then what we have to deal with is how such factual reportings are done, and when and for what. We need to examine discourse for what it reveals about participants' own orientations to fact and cognition. The adoption of experimental controls, through which the nature of the 'input' is rendered relatively certain and unambiguous, only serves to disguise or side-step the importance within everyday remembering of the interpretative and constructive work that has to be done with regard to that original truth. Indeed, we might say that everyday conversational remembering often has this as its primary concern – the attempt to construct an *acceptable*, *agreed* or *communicatively successful* version of what happened (Edwards and Middleton, 1986a, refer to this as the 'validation function' in conversational remembering).

Laboratory studies of individual memory neither resolve nor shed light upon that process; they generally remove the issue from the agenda. The psychologist acts authoritatively as validator, knows absolutely what really happened and arbitrates accordingly after the results are gathered in. The participants' rememberings are allowed no part in that process, of arbitrating on what the 'real truth' was, and so they are debarred from what is often, in everyday remembering, their major concern.

In fact, rememberers may routinely have other communicative goals, more important to them than strict accuracy (Edwards and Middleton, 1986a,b; 1987, 1988; Neisser, 1985) and, in any case, 'strict accuracy' itself is related to goals and criteria, as various philosophers and sociologists of science have effectively demonstrated (Chalmers, 1980; Lawson and Apignanasi, 1989; Woolgar, 1988a). We have emphasized how discursive remembering, factual reporting, descriptions of events and so on are socially occasioned phenomena, sensitive to their placing within contexts of communicative action and rhetoric. One way of looking at this is in terms of the kinds of understandings and inferences that such versions are designed to afford. The social psychology of how explanations and inferences are drawn from given factual statements is the domain of attribution theory. In the next chapter we shall examine relations among attribution theory, factual knowledge and the nature of discourse.

4

Texts, Descriptions and Inferences

In this chapter our aim is to develop the reworking of issues of remembering and factual reporting which have been our main topic up to now and start to show how the same sorts of concerns appear in a main strand of social cognition work: the study of people's attributions of causality and responsibility. One of the features we wish to bring out here is that there are important parallels in basic methodological procedures between work on memory and on attributional reasoning. In particular, both kinds of study tend to treat linguistic materials (texts, sentences and so on) as representations of world and/or mind – of what happened, or of what somebody thinks happened – rather than as situated actions. Both areas of work, therefore, systematically underplay the sorts of pragmatic considerations which are the focus of discursive psychology.

First, we shall explore the involvement of attributional issues in classic examples of memory research. Following this, we consider two recent approaches to attribution which have addressed directly the role of language in how people draw causal inferences. While one of these treats causality as something embodied in the semantics of particular verbs, the other sees conversational context as important but, ironically, construes this in an abstract and decontextualized manner. We will suggest important limitations and inadequacies with both of these approaches. The chapter will end by teasing out some of the implicit work that goes into applying attribution models to natural discourse, using Roger Brown's well-known integrative summary as an example, and start to construct an alternative approach based on the study of discourse.

Discourse, vignette and attribution

Although research on textual remembering ranges beyond the role of inferences and schematic 'gap filling' where specifically attributional issues are at stake, such issues are nevertheless a major feature of such studies. Ideas about cause and motivation provide the kinds of narrative and inferential links that are the basis of both memorability (providing coherence that aids recall) and of construction (introducing spurious elements not explicitly contained in the original materials). Furthermore, even those inferences that are not obviously or directly attributional may nevertheless have important attributional implications and upshots. One of the key points of discursive psychology is that causal inferences and implications are often handled indirectly via ostensibly descriptive or factual accounts. So, while studies of memory for texts focus on events and their representation, with inferences playing a significant part as underlying cognitive processes, attribution theory focuses directly on the causal inferences, but also uses textual event representations as inputs.

Psychological studies of comprehension and memory for textual materials typically begin with a set of sentences or a prose passage, generally invented by the experimenter and embodying some features of interest to the investigation. The participants read these materials, and are later tested to see what they have understood or remembered. Sentences that were and were not amongst the original materials may be offered for recognition, or the participants' recall may be probed, measured and otherwise examined for omissions, alterations and intrusions. By examining the relationships and discrepancies between input and output, the psychologist typically draws inferences about underlying mechanisms of comprehension and memory. Here are some examples of textual materials from classic studies.

> One night two young men from Egulac went down to the river to hunt seals, and when they were there it became foggy and calm. Then they heard war cries, and they thought: 'Maybe this is a war party.' They escaped to the shore, and hid behind a log. Now canoes came up, and they heard the noise of paddles, and saw one canoe coming up to them. There were five men in the canoe, and they said: 'What do you think? We wish to take you along. We wish to make war on the people.'
> (Extract from the story 'The War of the Ghosts', from Bartlett, 1932)

> A burning cigarette was carelessly discarded.
> The fire destroyed many acres of virgin forest.
> (Kintsch, 1974)

> (a) John fell. What he wanted to do was to scare Mary.
> (b) John came to the party. The one he expected to meet was Mary.
> (c) John had a suit on. It was Jane he hoped to impress.
> (Clark, 1977)

> Willa was hungry.
> She took out the Michelin guide.
> (Schank and Abelson, 1977)

> The man was worried. His car came to a halt and he was all alone. It was extremely dark and cold. The man took off his overcoat, rolled down the window, and got out of the car as quickly as possible. Then

he used all his strength to move as fast as he could. He was relieved when he finally saw the lights of the city, even though they were far away.
(Bransford and McCarrell, 1974)

The first example is an extract from an American Indian folk tale which was presented to British participants in Bartlett's (1932) influential study of the cultural and cognitive bases of remembering. Bartlett found that in subsequent recall, not only would some information be omitted, but also details were transformed and even added, which served to maintain or introduce coherence and sense to the story. Since the story originated in a culture different from that of the participants, different criteria of sense would prevail, so that features of the original would be transformed to bring them into line. A supernatural myth-related story about Indian warriors, ancestral ghosts and ritual happenings might be transformed, having passed from person to person in a string of successive rememberings, into a more recognizably European boating adventure.

While the cultural emphasis of Bartlett's work, including its use of real-world materials, is untypical of later cognitive work (cf. Edwards and Middleton, 1987), a later generation of cognitive psychologists (for example, Bransford, 1979; Neisser, 1967) have been strongly influenced by its demonstrations of the constructive transforming nature of comprehension and memory. This influence can be seen in the use made of materials in the other examples presented, where the major concern is with the kinds of inferences that participants make when dealing with text.

Kintsch's participants, after being shown sentences such as those presented, were then asked to evaluate the truth of an inferential statement, such as 'The discarded cigarette caused the fire', and their reaction times for doing so were measured. By comparing these reaction times with ones for sentences where the causal connection was already explicit (for example, 'A carelessly discarded burning cigarette started a fire . . .' and so on), Kintsch was able to show that after a short time interval (15 minutes), it no longer mattered whether the causal connection was explicit or implicit in the materials; reaction times for evaluation were the same. People could not distinguish between the texts they had read, and the inferences they had drawn from them.

Clark's study (the third example) is a conceptual analysis of similar sorts of 'bridging' inferences, and draws upon Grice's (1975) work on implicature. Clark was concerned with the mental computations through which people make such inferences, taking account not only of the content of input sentences, but also of 'contractual' understandings between speaker and hearer. A hearer draws inferences concerning 'what bridge . . . the speaker could possibly have expected him to be able to construct and . . . that the speaker could plausibly have intended' (Clark, 1977: 413). Common bridges include 'causes' and 'reasons', those in the example given being 'reasons'.

Event explanations, in the form of causes and reasons, are among the most popular kinds of inferential links that experimental subjects have to make, and this applies also to computer programs that are designed to understand textual materials. The fourth example is from Schank and Abelson's work, which has been influential in both cognitive and social psychology in promoting the importance of mental schemata, and especially 'scripts' for routine social occasions. The possession of schematic knowledge of occasions, such as eating in restaurants, visiting the dentist, engaging in tutorials and so on, enables gap-filling inferences to be made when comprehending reports, descriptions or other references to them. The programmer's task for this example would be to ensure that it invokes a restaurant-seeking script, rather than the inference that Willa was about to eat the Michelin guide. Similarly, in the last example, from an experiment reported by Bransford and McCarrell (1974), participants had difficulty offering explanations for why the man took off his coat and opened the car window, unless they were also provided with the additional information that the car was 'submerged'. In order to start to explain how participants 'achieve a click of comprehension', Bransford and McCarrell suggest that psychologists will have to 'characterize the abstract relational knowledge derived from perceptual experience, and to study how this information places cognitive constraints on one's ability to understand linguistic strings' (1974: 220).

While these kinds of studies may demonstrate important features of the workings of memory, it is not clear how those features should be understood. Are they features of mental representations, of schematic knowledge structures, of processes of comprehension and cognition? Or do they reflect features of the world, to be extracted by realistic perceptual mechanisms? Or are they features of how language represents events? Or are they things people do with words, such that 'memory' *per se* is relevant only because the experimental design chose to explore them that way?

We do not propose to resolve those sorts of issues here. However, a discursive psychology of remembering focuses upon features of the process that these sorts of studies gloss over or obscure, and which prevent questions of discursive pragmatics from arising. Such studies avoid these kinds of issues by concentrating on disembedded, decontextualized texts, on abstracted, invented propositions that have no status as things somebody might have said, somewhere for some reason. Furthermore, the experimental participants who are asked to recall these texts (if that is the case) have no responsibility for them, did not say them, do not stand by them, have no stake in them, did not choose to formulate them in that way. This, of course, is not some kind of oversight among cognitive psychologists – they expend considerable effort in designing this quality into their experiments.

Memories for textual inputs are typically taken to be a person's best effort at neutral, accurate recall. Studies of remembering as a conversational activity, in contrast, argue for the importance of examining remembering in terms of its conversational, communicative nature (Edwards et al., 1992; Edwards and Middleton, 1986a, 1987, 1988; cf. Coulter, 1979, 1985; Harré, 1983), and call attention to the implications of studying memory through written rather than spoken language (Edwards and Middleton, 1986b; cf. Hildyard and Olson, 1982). Furthermore, principles of discourse analysis suggest that any such rememberings (or any other conversational or textual formulations) will be variable in construction, being functionally designed to fit the occasion, for performing whatever interactional work is at hand (Potter and Wetherell, 1987).

The study of how experimental participants draw causal inferences from linguistic materials is also a major concern of attribution theory, and there are some strong similarities of assumption and method between attributional and memory research. As we have noted, in research on attributions, it is the mechanisms of causal reasoning that take centre stage, rather than the content and organization of knowledge. It is not our intention here to enter into a lengthy and comprehensive review of attribution theory, its empirical basis, nor of the various critiques that have been levelled against it. Rather, our aim is to provide an idea of its basic elements, how it approaches everyday causal reasoning and, particularly, the use it makes of textual materials. The point of this is to draw some parallels with the way cognitive psychology more generally has dealt with texts and memory and, specifically, with the relationships among everyday understandings, discourse and inferences of cause, reason and responsibility.

Attribution theory is designed to describe and account for how ordinary people make causal sense of events, and especially of people's actions. For example, any person's action or reaction towards the world might be explained as due to that person's wishes and intentions, or abilities, personal characteristics and so on, or else, as due to the nature of the world that is acted on or reacted to. Roger Brown's (1986) synthesis will serve as our starting point. Brown defines attributional reasoning as an everyday, quasi-scientific form of common sense explanation (cf. Heider, 1958) for actor–action–situation events such as the following:

1 (a) Mr Brown – has trouble starting – his car.
 (b) John – laughs at – the comedian.
 (c) Sue – is afraid of – the dog.

2 (a) Mr Brown – has trouble starting – most cars.
 (b) John – laughs at – most comedians.
 (c) Sue – is afraid of – most dogs.

3 (a) Few people – have trouble starting – this car.
 (b) Few people – laugh at – this comedian.
 (c) Few people – are afraid of – this dog.
(Brown, 1986; examples (b) and (c) are from McArthur, 1972)

Brown elaborates a 'causal calculus' which is designed to represent everyday attributional reasoning, and is derived in turn from classic statements of the approach by Heider (1958), Kelley (1967), McArthur (1972) and others. According to the calculus, people attribute causal responsibility on the basis of the so-called 'information variables' *consensus*, *distinctiveness* and *consistency*. Each variable can have a high or low value, and each applies to one of the three elements: actor (consensus), action (consistency) and situation (distinctiveness).

For example, the attributional task in 1a is to explain why Mr Brown has trouble starting his car. By varying *consensus* information about the actor role (3a: few people / many people), it is possible to manipulate causal inferences. If lots of other people also have trouble starting the car, then the cause is likely to lie in the car. If only Mr Brown has trouble, the cause lies in him. Similarly, causal inferences also move between actor and situation when the situation's *distinctiveness* is varied (2a–c, 3a–c). If Mr Brown has trouble with lots of cars, then the cause of the trouble is more likely to be internal to him, an actor attribution, than if his troubles are restricted to one car in particular. Again, high and low *consistency*, for the action part of the sentence, can be varied using phrases like 'seldom', 'frequently' or 'always', with further actor/situation consequences for causal reasoning.

The prime concern in experimental studies of attribution has been with actor versus situation inferences, and how these inferences can be manipulated by varying the information contained in input sentences. In McArthur's (1972) study, for example, from which the items about Sue and the dog, and John and the comedian (1–3 above) are taken, participants were given the sentence and asked 'Why?', with a choice of options like 'something about John', and 'something about the comedian'. Brown (1986: 142) is careful to note that the terms actor, action and situation should not be taken literally. In 1c Sue does not strictly 'act', but is afraid, and often the situation element will be a person or object. The terms are meant to represent the three principal elements of any event involving some kind of psychological causal relationship, where it is possible to distinguish an internal causal candidate (actor), and an external one (situation). In 'John praises Mary', for example, John is actor and Mary situation.

As we have seen with some major studies of event memory, the materials used as the input and output of attributional reasoning are linguistic ones. While attribution *theory* is all about event perception, and the cognitive inferences that are drawn from given events, the *method* is all about discourse. And, once again, there is the same assumed identity between the two. Event descriptions are treated as equivalent to the events themselves, or at least to events as perceived, prior to inferences being drawn. It is this tension between perceptual–cognitive theory, on the one hand, and the use of textual materials, on the other, that we wish to explore. And, in turn, this forces us to examine the relationship between experimental sentences and everyday talk and text.

In Kelley's (1967) model, events in the world are subjected to a kind of cognitive analysis of covariance (the ANOVA model), which picks out the regularities of experience (defined in terms of consistency, distinctiveness and consensus). The assumed basis of the process, a kind of perceptual abstraction from experience, is also, as we noted in Chapters 1 and 2, the basis of schema theories of other kinds of cognitive structures and processes.

Recent developments and alternatives to the classic attributional model have started to place much more emphasis on the central role of language. In one approach (for example, Au, 1986; Brown and Fish, 1983; Semin and Fiedler, 1988) the process of attribution is studied in terms of categories which are built into the linguistic system itself and, particularly, into the semantics of the different verbs which people use to describe and explain people's actions and states. These studies make the important point that language is by no means a transparent or neutral system for conveying information but, rather, that the words that we use to describe simple, everyday actions and states carry with them powerful implications for the causal explanation of those events. While some theorists emphasize the importance of language in shaping thought (Hoffman and

Tchir, 1990), Brown's view favours the dependence of linguistic structures on cognitive universals (Brown and Fish, 1983).

In the second linguistically orientated approach (for example, Hilton, 1990; Turnbull and Slugoski, 1988), the emphasis is upon the pragmatic and structural features of conversation, which are considered to underlie both the cognitive and linguistic natures of everyday causal attributions. Hilton (1990) terms this the 'conversational model'. A recent review of studies in attribution theory notes that 'the attention now being paid to linguistic factors is long overdue' (Hewstone, 1989: 93). From the perspective of discursive psychology, however, neither of these approaches pays sufficient attention to the nature and dynamics of ordinary discourse.

We shall not provide an exhaustive survey of the attribution field but, rather, focus upon a number of specific studies which give primacy to language from the 'verb semantics' and 'conversational model' approaches, and develop in this and subsequent chapters an alternative derived from discursive psychology. The discursive approach to attributions urges that these be studied *as social acts* performed in discourse, and not merely as cognitions *about* social acts, which happen to be expressed within conversations. A more detailed review of these and other linguistically orientated studies can be found in Edwards and Potter (1992b).

Attributional semantics

An influential study by Brown and Fish (1983) confirmed the existence of two classes of verbs, which describe either behavioural or mental interactions between persons. A series of experiments showed them to carry different implications for attributions of causality. Take the class of behavioural 'action' verbs such as *help* or *cheat*. When they are placed in simple sentences such as 'Ted —— Paul', causality is predominantly assigned to the actor (or agent), Ted, as in 1a in the example below. That is to say, when people were asked 'Why?', they opted for explanations located in Ted. However, when the action verb was replaced by a mental ('state') verb such as *like* or *notice* (1b), perceived causality switched to the situation (or 'stimulus') element, Paul. In a subsequent study, Van Kleeck et al. (1988) showed that this kind of causality, implicit in verb categories, significantly moderated the influence of information about consistency, distinctiveness and consensus.

1 (a) Ted helps Paul   *Verb*: Action   *Attribution*: Ted (agent)
   (b) Ted likes Paul   *Verb*: State   *Attribution*: Paul (stimulus)

2 (a) John telephones Mary *Verb*: Action   *Attribution*: John (agent)
   (b) John thanks Mary   *Verb*: Action   *Attribution*: Mary (patient)
   (c) John admires Mary   *Verb*: Action   *Attribution*: Mary (stimulus)

(The term 'patient' refers to the grammatical object that is acted on, rather like a patient is treated in a hospital. For the purposes of attributional semantics, the main distinction is between agent and any of the other participant roles, variously called situation, patient or stimulus, as appropriate for each verb.)

Au (1986) extended these findings with the demonstration of a sub-class of action verbs which behave more like state verbs (as in 2b). She summarizes her main findings thus: 'adults consistently attributed the cause of an action to the Agent for some action verbs (e.g., *telephone*), and to the Patient for others (e.g., *thank*). They consistently attributed the cause of an experience to the Stimulus rather than to the Experiencer for experiential verbs (e.g., *amaze*, *admire*)' (Au, 1986: 104). Again, rather than offering an overview of this literature, we shall give specific attention here to one major study, Au's, in order to explore in some detail how textual materials are used and interpreted.

From the perspective of discursive psychology, part of the problem with these studies lies in their unexplicated notion of the *cause* of an action or experience. In Au's study, there are at least two possible meanings of cause.

(a) The direct cause of the action or state of affairs labelled by the verb, i.e., something *synonymous with* the verb's grammatical agent.

(b) The person or thing considered responsible for bringing it about in the world, that the action or state labelled by the verb came to happen.

The second meaning is therefore somewhat more implicational, or less direct, than the first.

Au switches, without acknowledging it, between these two senses; that is, between grammatical and situational causes, in order to assign agentive causality to the agent of action verbs (e.g. *threw*), the stimulus of experiential verbs (e.g. *dismayed*), and to the patient for 'interpersonal' action verbs (e.g. *scold*). The meaning in (a) above is what the discussion of action verbs seems to be largely about, though arguably there has to be the possibility of John's telephoning Mary being caused by somebody other than John, in order for its causality to be an interesting issue in the first place (Semin, 1980). The meaning in (b) is what the discussion of

86   *Discursive psychology*

experiential verbs more often seems to be about, though again, not necessarily. Sometimes, causality appears to be definitionally the 'stimulus', which 'causally' gives rise to the experience. As for agent, this is close to definitional tautology (Au's gloss on stimulus is 'the role of giving rise to a certain experience', 1986: 105; cf. Brown and Fish, 1983: 242). However, the second, more 'implicational' interpretation of 'cause' is also problematical. Consider visual experience. In citing the 'cause' of such an experience, we might commonsensically refer either to whatever object happened to bounce some light into our eyes (the stimulus), or else to some other relevant consideration, such as how the seeing person got to be looking in that direction, or got to be in that situation for that experience to come about (for example, 'she was caused to see his death by her early arrival at the scene of the accident').

The important point, then, is that even with the least ambiguous of action verbs, it is possible to draw a clear distinction between the semantic role agent, and situational responsibility for an action. The verb *telephone* (as in 'Betty telephoned John') was one which, in Au's (1986) study, achieved a 100 per cent rating as agent-causal. It is indeed something we know or assume about people who make telephone calls, that they tend to do so intentionally. But let us put the verb into a more complex sentence: 'Having got a message on her answering machine to call him back urgently, Betty telephoned John.' In this case, we are forced to distinguish between the grammatical agent (Betty), and situational responsibility for bringing it about that Betty made a telephone call. Indeed, further considerations and reversals of situational responsibility might arise if we are informed that Betty had instructed John to call her urgently if situation x arose. Of course, it might be argued that by constructing these more complex sentences or scenarios, we are going beyond Au's strict psycholinguistic concerns, overriding the verb's natural or implicit causal structure, and invoking extraneous situational considerations. But situational considerations – non-grammatical causal responsibility of type (b) – are basic to the entire practice of assigning responsibility for scoldings and criticisms, to the scolded and criticized, rather than to the scolder or critic.

Au's definition of causality in 'interpersonal verbs' is taken from Fillmore's (1971) treatment of presupposition in contrasting pairs such as *scold* and *praise*, where *scold* presupposes that the object person was responsible for doing something bad, while *praise* presupposes she did something good: 'the cause of an interpersonal event . . . is attributed to whoever is *presupposed in the verb* to be responsible for the situation that leads to the event' (Au, 1986:

104; emphasis added). As with causality type (a), such presuppositions are *intrinsic to meaning*, part of what anybody would have to understand, in order to be counted as a competent user of these verbs. The claim that attributional causality is part of these verbs' intrinsic presuppositional semantics is basic to Fillmore's analysis. As psycholinguists are wont to do with ideas of this kind, Au questions whether this grammatical structure has an actual psychological reality:

> As compelling as this analysis may seem . . . it remains an open question whether people are as sensitive to the presuppositions of interpersonal verbs as sophisticated linguists like Charles Fillmore. For example, if John scolded Mary, one may think that it was because John was in a bad mood or was an irritable person, that he scolded everyone in sight, and that she did not deserve to be scolded. But one can also imagine that John scolded Mary because she blundered again or because she had been pestering him all day, that anyone in John's position would have scolded her, and that she deserved to be scolded . . . (Au, 1986: 104–5)

Fillmore's linguistic analysis is taken as an empirically testable one, as if it might be possible to discover that people are unaware of, or even disagree with, Fillmore's intuitions. However, it is important to think more carefully about what is being suggested in this. Fillmore's analysis is of the inherent presuppositional semantics of these verbs. If empirical testing could in some sense prove him wrong, then it would prove him not to understand these verbs as others do – in other words, basic linguistic competence is at stake. In fact, however, Au's set of alternative readings for why 'John scolded Mary' have nothing to do with disputing or proving Fillmore's analysis, in that they all assume its correctness. The notion that Mary perhaps 'did not deserve to be scolded', far from disputing the presupposition that 'scold' blames Mary, relies directly upon it. What Au is disputing here is the appropriateness of John's attribution of blame, not Fillmore's analysis of the word's meaning, that it involves such an attribution.

The notion that somebody might scold another person undeservedly draws our attention to how words perform social actions (Austin, 1962; Wieder, 1974; Wittgenstein, 1953). Indeed, it is important to note, that *scold* and *praise* are not merely 'interpersonal' verbs, but *speech act* verbs; they formulate what John did, as well as implying things about Mary. They draw attention to a speaker's action in saying something. Indeed, there are three levels of responsibility at stake here: what Mary did, what John did in scolding or praising her, and what the current speaker (excluded from all of these verb semantics studies) is doing in constructing

John's action as a scolding or a praising, and what he or she is thereby doing with respect to Mary. Our argument is that the social psychology of language and attribution requires a study of the situated deployment of such verbs, in which *all three sorts of responsibility are taken into account*, and in which they are important in reverse order: current talk and speaker first, John second, Mary third. What Mary purportedly did is not the starting point, but the product of such talk.

In all of the verb semantics studies of attribution, inferring the cause of an event takes no account of the speaker's action in describing it as so caused. The event is merely given, taken as true, so that the attribution of responsibility is for the event, not for the sentence. Let us, then, extend our two kinds of responsibility to include a third:

(a)   Agent or stimulus; the verb's grammatical presuppositions.
(b)   Whoever/whatever is held responsible for bringing about the prior conditions for whatever worldly event is labelled by the verb.
(c)   The current speaker's role in constructing it that (a) and (b) obtain.

The importance of the speaker's responsibility for a particular discursive construction of events forces us to rethink the social psychological importance of attributional semantics. It focuses our attention back to methodology.

By limiting the emergence of central features of discourse (its action orientation, its constructed nature) the verb category studies risk becoming circular, merely confirming the verbs' inherent semantics rather than offering anything of wider psychological interest. Indeed, the researchers themselves occasionally note how the findings have extraordinary levels of statistical significance, with perfect or near perfect scores being obtained. Van Kleeck et al. (1988: 91) remark that 'The results obtained . . . confirmed the reality of the experience verb schemas at a level of consistency . . . that makes the significance tests reported supererogatory', and note that, in the related Brown and Fish (1983) study, 'In effect, just about every subject with just about every verb gave the predicted answer' (Van Kleeck et al., 1988: 93).

The claim that these studies merely provide circular confirmations of verb semantics, rather than interesting social psychological findings, is strengthened by examining their use of decontextualized, simple sentences. For example, just as *telephone* received from Au's participants a 100 per cent rating as an agent-caused (agent-action) verb, so *praise* got a 100 per cent rating as a patient-caused (action-patient) verb (Au, 1986: 111). In terms of how language is used in real situated actions, this result is surely unbelievable, and must immediately send us in search of artefacts: *x* praises *y* for no other reason than that *y* deserves it? What of sycophancy, politeness, irony, lies, speaking for third-party audiences, and such. We know that praisers have motives of their own, other than (and even superseding) some desire to tell the world like it is. What we are dealing with here is an artefact of decontextualization. Since the sentence is presented as speakerless, as merely given, it is also presented as motiveless, as unoccasioned. *Participants are invited by the experimental methodology to treat verbal descriptions as unmotivated, unsituated, true depictions of the world.* We suggest that being thus stripped of all but the word's intrinsic semantic and presuppositional content, experimental participants confirm mere meaning: that praising somebody *consists in* saying what a fine person they were for doing something good.

These studies have demonstrated, were it in doubt, that the experimental participants were competent speakers of English. But in the context of situated action, praise can be sycophancy, and faint praise damnation. The point, then, is that we have to look to the *situational deployment* of such terms for their social psychology, taking account of all three bases for causal inference: verb semantics, situational reference and speakers' pragmatics.

The action orientation of description is so clearly established a feature of ordinary talk, that the choice of what are ostensibly more direct descriptions can serve to accomplish an interpretation *as* a description; it can, for example, be an exercise in 'doing neutrality' (Clayman, 1992). What is to count as mere description, and as the objective reality that descriptions merely refer to, are, in other words, participants' concerns and thus matters of potential contention. In Semin and Fiedler's (1988) work on verb semantics and attribution, a category of 'direct action verbs' (DAVs) is distinguished, which purportedly provide 'a neutral description', where 'no interpretation of the action is involved, merely a description of it' (1988: 559). The verb *kick* is provided as an example, contrasted with more 'interpretational' verbs such as *scold* or *help*. The idea is that while the precise actions involved in *scolding* and *helping* are left open, *kick* specifies that action. However, consider the sentence, 'John kicked his opponent', as a description of an event that is claimed to have taken place during a soccer game. Within the laws of the game, their situated application, their definitions of foul play and of sanctions against misconduct, and a dispute about whether a penalty is to be awarded, this sort of description can be read as accomplishing important 'interpretational work': blaming and warranting, categorizing actions, attributing intent, and so on. It is precisely the work of such descriptive words to classify actions so as to make various judgements and understandings (interpretations) relevant – that it was an intentional kick, rather than an accidental foot contacting shin, or whatever.

Within discursive psychology, action descriptions serve as *externalizing devices* (Pomerantz, 1986; Potter and Edwards, 1990; Potter and Wetherell, 1988; Smith, 1978; Wooffitt, 1991, 1992; Woolgar, 1980, 1988a); that is, ways of accomplishing versions, categorizations and explanations such that they appear as simple, uninterpreted and unmotivated descriptions. The significance of this for attribution theory, as for the cognitive psychology of memory, is that it has failed to address how people themselves construct and deploy descriptions; rather, in most studies, reality has entered predefined by the analyst in terms of vignettes, such that a whole dimension of discursive activity is systematically excluded.

While the verb category studies have explored some of the abstracted semantic implications of verbs, studies of natural discourse would, of course, reveal the deployment of a much wider range of linguistic devices for attributing or implying causality (and for avoiding doing so). These would include uses of the passive voice, and of a variety of intransitive, reflexive and truncated forms that deal obliquely with agency (the vase broke / got broken; Mary got fired / got herself fired / got herself pregnant; and so on), as well as the use of terms such as *for*, *on behalf of*, *because* and so on (cf. Fowler, 1986; Kress and Hodge, 1979). Again, however, our interest as psychologists must be not only in the fact that linguistic structures make such attributions discursively possible, but in how, in situated talk, attributions are actually performed, implied, countered or avoided, in ways far more subtle and flexible than their being forced upon us either by an objectively perceived reality, or else by its corresponding, linguistically fixed description.

Ideal conversations

There have as yet been few empirical studies of attribution in ordinary discourse. Those that have appeared do not treat discourse in its relatively raw, transcribed form, where meanings can be examined for their sequential placement and occasioned nature. One approach begins by categorizing talk into classes of utterances, determined by the analyst's interest in, say, how arguments develop in path and branch structures (Antaki and Naji, 1987), or how attributional statements serve a variety of personality functions (Harvey and Weary, 1984), or by an interest in how participants impose different readings on narrative materials (Howard and Allen, 1989). Another approach (Hilton, 1990; Turnbull and Slugoski, 1988) makes little attempt to study naturally occurring discourse at all, but takes certain abstracted features of conversation (such as Grice's maxims: Grice, 1975) as a model for cognitive attribution processes. Through a critique of this work we shall argue for the virtues of studying real discourse in natural contexts.

The opportunity to describe events, and to object to descriptions, rather than merely to explain them as given, comprises a particularly important focus for the field of discursive psychology. When examined in context for the interactional work that they do, what appear to be simple descriptions of actions, events, states of affairs and so on may be revealed as accomplishing important 'attributional work', much as we suggested with regard to *kick*, and with regard to the remembering of events in Chapters 2 and 3. If these action-orientated features of talk are to be revealed, then it is important to examine their precise sequential placement. The crucial point is that event description is not distinct from, nor prior to, attributional work, but rather, attributional work is *accomplished by* descriptions. Discursive psychology takes as a primary focus of concern, the study of actual talk and texts, for the situated reality-producing work that they do. In conventional attributional studies, that interesting descriptive work is masked by research design, through the provision of disembedded sentences and vignettes, which the disinterested participant is *required* to treat as mere truth or as a stand-in for reality.

In contrast to discourse analysis, the so-called 'conversational model' of attributional reasoning remains wedded to experimental methodology and avoids any systematic analysis of real conversations. Rather, the study of conversation is represented by use of Grice (1975), whose widely influential maxims for cooperative conversation are taken as rules which describe and govern ordinary talk (Hilton, 1990; Turnbull and Slugoski, 1988; cf. Fiedler et al., 1989). It is claimed that 'Grice's (1975) model of conversation is essentially one of a contract between cooperating equals who set out to transmit information in the most clear and efficient manner possible' (Turnbull and Slugoski, 1988: 85; cf. Grice, 1975: 47–8). However, there are major difficulties with this use of Grice for a specification of the nature of conversation. Grice's model is not a mere description of ordinary talk, but is, rather, an idealization of some normative principles to which ordinary speakers may hold themselves accountable. Its precise empirical status with regard to ordinary talk remains problematic, such that using it as a substitute for ordinary talk has the effect of prejudging the nature of natural causal reasoning.

More than this, it is what might be termed a consensus model of interaction, as the 'basic cooperative principle' states: 'Make your conversational contribution such as is required, at the stage at which it occurs, by the *accepted purpose* or direction of the talk exchange in which you are engaged' (Grice, 1975: 45; emphasis added). Again, this presupposition of shared goals makes it suitable for some areas of psychological research, but it is far from clear that the social psychology of conversations, or of conversational attributions, is one of them. One of the points we emphasize (and most of our empirical materials reflect this) is that discursive psychology will be concerned with attribution processes in situations of conflict, rhetoric, power and manipulation; that is, situations where people may be struggling for control of definitions, and have competing aims. These are, as many researchers have pointed out, precisely the situations in which blame and accountability are at stake and attributional talk will be prevalent. While Grice's model is properly seen as possessing important psychological significance, it is not sufficient as a stand-in for actual talk.

The basis of the 'conversational model' is one of 'puzzle resolution', where 'the underlying form of puzzle resolution is that of an answer to a question. Accordingly, the basic unit of analysis of everyday explanation is the question–answer pair' (Turnbull and Slugoski, 1988: 66). Taking inspiration from Hart and Honoré's (1985) analysis of causal reasoning in the context of the law, they suggest that 'the covarying factor that is not taken for granted, which is unusual or abnormal in some way, is typically identified as the cause . . . Thus, an abnormal condition conception of causality seems to be the appropriate conception for everyday explanation' (Turnbull and Slugoski, 1988: 69). Grice's maxim of quantity ('Make your contribution as informative as is required . . . do not make your contribution more informative than is required'; Grice, 1975: 45) is then offered as support for the notion that 'In general, when asked why an event occurred, answerers identify as the cause that factor or set of factors from the total causal field that best complements the questioner's presupposed knowledge' (Turnbull and Slugoski, 1988: 69). Thus, if the speaker assumes that the hearer knows all about the situational circumstances of some action, then the offered cause of that action is likely to be internal to the actor, and vice versa.

Despite its ostensible basis in principles of conversation, the general form of this model is close to the sorts of schema-based approaches that we have identified in the cognitive psychology of memory and attribution. It assumes that human thought and action are predicated upon how the world is represented mentally, via schemata, which are essentially perceptually based, being abstracted from the regularities of experience. Events which conform to expectations are processed in an automatic fashion by schemata, while irregularities pose cognitive problems, or puzzles, which call for efforts at solving them:

> A conscious and deliberate attempt at explanation occurs only when there is a failure to understand and when understanding is of some importance . . . Events do not require explanation. Rather, contrasts between observed behaviour and what would have been considered more normal need to be resolved . . . every explanation/resolution is an answer to a 'why' question. (Turnbull and Slugoski, 1988: 67)

The model ignores the nature of ordinary discourse, and focuses instead on the business of rule-governed problem-solving. A whole range of rhetorical and pragmatic elements of talk are then swamped by informative cooperativeness, by a straightforward, robotic question-answering device, which operates according to considerations of mutual knowledge. What is not fully recognized is the *conversational work* done by explanations – these are taken to be merely informative answers to questions – nor of the subtle, yet pervasive relations between description and inference. Furthermore, the question-answerer is unmotivated, disinterested, objective, seeking merely to be cooperatively informative. The 'puzzle' to be resolved is simply given, in the world, or by experience; no scope is allowed for how puzzles might be discursively constructed as such, and resisted, denied, reformulated and so on, rather than merely solved. Ironically, the 'conversational model' is a model not of ordinary conversational attributions, but of the activities of people precisely like the experimental participants in classic McArthur-style studies (McArthur, 1972), whose attributional answers are provided as part of their experimental cooperativeness.

From the perspective of discursive psychology, therefore, there are three major shortcomings of the 'conversational model' of attribution:

1 The lack of attention to the nature of *actual conversation*.
2 The lack of recognition of the *constructive* work of discourse, in producing descriptions of the world which are constitutive of

an understood reality, rather than reflections of reality as given.
3   The lack of concern with the *interestedness* of speakers and
actors, as displayed in their descriptions and explanations.

A discursive psychology of attribution proposes an active,
rhetorical process, which requires at least two participants.
Versions are constructed not only with regard to attributional
issues, but to counter their potential undermining. Rather than
viewing the entire process from the perspective of an inference-
making perceiver, who passively takes versions as given, we have
to examine how versions are constructed and undermined within a
discursive manipulation of fact and implication. Attribution is to
be studied as a public and social process, done interactionally in
talk and text, where fact and attributional inference are
simultaneously and rhetorically addressed.

Attributions in everyday life

Some attributional studies make a virtue of studying real-world
events, or naturally occurring texts or conversations. Sometimes
these studies are concerned with other features of causal explanation, such as how such explanations may serve personality functions and adaptation to life's crises (Harvey et al., 1990), or they
may explicitly develop criticisms of classic attribution theory
(Antaki, 1985; Howard and Allen, 1989). Antaki's work is particularly useful in pointing out how 'ordinary explanations' occur
not as discrete attributions, for the fictional single actions of
unknown people, but as parts of larger social actions and arguments, concerning events in which speakers are personally
involved, and whose description, as well as explicit explanation, is
also important. Howard and Allen (1989) point to the variable
nature of readers' explanations of story materials, and the importance of understanding those texts not as identical stimuli for all
readers, but as resources for indefinitely many 'readings'.

Nevertheless, it is a feature of all these studies that they use
natural (though elicited) talk as a resource, a kind of treasure trove
of ordinary sense-making, from which items of causal reasoning
can be extracted, coded and counted, rather than taking them as
conversational phenomena *per se*, where causal reasoning might be
studied for the situated interactional work that it performs. For
example, Howard and Allen extract from their data on story interpretation a large number of isolated, coded and sorted attributions,
including personal trait attributions such as 'unemotional, cold', 'a
dreamer', 'an escape from her life', and these are subjected to

statistical analysis. From a discursive perspective, the problem here is that once a context is removed in this way, any study of the situated and occasioned nature of such formulations becomes impossible. Indeed, this decontextualization of attributions from the context of their occurrence may even be sufficient to explain the extraordinary (and, for attribution theory, disappointing) finding that trait attributions were heavily preponderant, and causal attributions 'almost totally absent'. Not only were the stories provided to participants ones which they had no part in constructing, and which consisted of fictional events in which they had no stake, but also the analytical method prevents any study of how causal attributions might be accomplished indirectly. For example, it is perfectly possible that trait attributions, like other kinds of descriptions, might serve in context to perform causal explanations. A harsh and punitive parent, thus described, might serve as explanation and excuse (that is, externalizing blame) for the actions of a resentful child (notions of this kind are explored in detail in Chapter 6). In other words, by studying descriptions and explanations in their discursive contexts, it should be possible to understand attributional formulations not as features of how we disinterestedly understand or explain events to ourselves, but rather as direct and indirect hearer-orientated features of conversational rhetoric.

Another use made of more realistic, real world phenomena is the projection of classic attribution theory onto naturally occurring texts and events. Rather than featuring as systematic, 'serious' analyses in journal articles, these tend to be textbook illustrations of the theory, designed more for exposition than for furthering the theory itself. In Brown's (1986) textbook, for example, there are attributional accounts of imaginary everyday events, such as how a student might interpret feedback from faculty teachers, as well as analyses of real events such as what happened at a Who rock concert in Cincinnati in 1979, and an analysis of some dialogue from Eugene O'Neill's celebrated play, *Long Day's Journey into Night*. While recognizing the tuitional, textbook function of these illustrative materials, we also note that Brown's treatment of attribution theory is unusually innovative for a textbook, and that these sorts of real world illustrations of the theory remain the most explicit statements that we have of its claim to represent ordinary people's everyday thinking. Since the discursive approach is itself strongly orientated towards naturally occurring texts and talk, it will be useful to examine how classic attribution theory is located in such naturally occurring (or naturalistic) contexts.

Given our interest in legal settings, and more specifically Drew's

(1990) study of courtroom dialogue in a rape trial on which we commented in Chapter 2, it is also interesting that Brown uses just that kind of setting to illustrate how attributional issues may arise in real life contexts:

> In a criminal trial for rape the defense attorney will usually make an effort to demonstrate that the woman . . . had numerous lovers in the past. What conceivable relevance does such information have to the charge? Strictly speaking, it has none, because rape is forced intercourse and the number of consenting experiences the woman may have had is irrelevant. However, unless they are carefully instructed, jurors are not likely to think so carefully but rather use the causal calculus to reason that a large number of different male partners argues a certain indiscriminateness (low distinctiveness) and, therefore, that the woman probably consented – at least a little bit – to her rapist. (Brown, 1986: 145)

While it is clear how the 'causal calculus' is relevant to this example, it is also important to draw attention to other features of it. Note first that the starting point is not an event, nor a perception of an event, but rather a piece of discourse, a description, or formulation about the woman's sexual behaviour. Indeed, Brown's entire scheme, including the calculus itself, begins with verbal propositions (actor–action–situation formulations) rather than perceived events, as do other attributional studies. As we have argued, the theory is explicitly all about how events are perceived, but *operationally* attributional studies start with verbal descriptions. Second, note that the defence lawyer would have to 'make an effort to demonstrate' the woman's promiscuity. In other words, whatever attributional implications and trial relevance such promiscuity may or may not have, it is not merely a fact or feature of the world, to be noticed and taken account of. It is a potentially contentious description, a version that has to be interactionally *accomplished as* fact; there is *work* involved. As we saw in Drew's example, it was precisely via the introduction of competing descriptions ('sat at our table', 'people go there') that the alleged victim was able to counter any contentious attributional implications. Third, note that the lawyer's introduction of the topic of promiscuity does its attributional work via its situated placing. Promiscuity does not, of itself, imply anything about rape. It is the topic's context of specific rape allegations and counter-allegations, that occasion the jury's supposed inferences.

Brown's rape trial, though a kind of real world illustration, is nevertheless an invented, or at least generalized example, rather than a study of an actual trial. Another illustration is provided in the form of attributional statements that were made in actual newspapers, following an incident at a Who concert in which eleven people died. Again, Brown's treatment of these data provides a useful counterpoint to our own analyses of press reports of controversial events (Chapters 3, 5 and 6), where competing attributional formulations are made. It should be noted, of course, that Brown's aim in using these data is to illustrate attribution theory, rather than to develop a critical perspective of it. However, that suits our purpose admirably, since it is precisely the theory's adequacy in dealing with real discourse that we want to discuss.

The usefulness of the Who concert incident, for Brown's purposes, is that people produced competing attributional inferences about it which fell directly into attribution theory's major divide, between actor attributions (the deaths, due to crowd crushing, were explicable in terms of characteristics of Who fans) and situation attributions (the deaths were due to factors such as stadium design, ticket allocation procedures, and so on). One major contrast with a discursive approach is that the various descriptions of events are taken either as unproblematical pictures of the world (what happened), or as unproblematical reflections of thought (how people saw it). Our use of perceptual imagery here (pictures, reflections) is deliberate, designed to show how a perceptual/cognitive metatheory of attribution is sustained while dealing with textual or conversational materials. Brown (1986: 131) cites the following newspaper account, and then asks, 'How does one begin to work out the cause or causes of a complex event like this?'

> Eleven persons were trampled to death last night in a crowd of 8,000 concertgoers who waited for hours in near-freezing weather outside Riverfront Coliseum in Cincinnati then 'lost all sense of rationality' and stormed the doors. The concert, by the rock group, The Who, went on for three hours with most of the 18,000 fans inside oblivious to what one survivor called 'the nightmare' outside. (Brown, 1986: 131)

The newspaper account is taken as equivalent to a 'complex event' that has to be explained. But clearly, even given its relatively objective tone (many popular newspapers might be less restrained), what we have here is not an event, but a description. Indeed, it is one of indefinitely many possible descriptions (Heritage, 1984; Schegloff, 1972), and one that offers various formulations and positions on the events so described. People were 'trampled to death' (rather than, say, crushed and died as a result of their injuries); they were 'concertgoers' rather than rock fans, or any of a range of other possible categorical descriptions (cf. Jayyusi, 1984; Potter and Wetherell, 1987; Sacks, 1979). The 'near-freezing weather' is not only thus described/constructed, but its inclusion and placement in the text implies a possible explanatory relevance.

The descriptions 'lost all sense of rationality' and 'stormed' are similarly attributionally loaded, the former also being placed in quotation marks to signal its status as a report, while the latter has the writer's own voice, that of straight factual description. Another account is given the warranted status of an experiential account from a 'survivor', and so on. The point is that our analytic starting point is not an event, however complex, but rather a descriptive account. It is a discursive construction, already loaded with causal formulations and attributional concerns. Again, while the causal calculus is clearly relevant to how such matters may be implied and inferred, we are forced to question the perceptual meta-assumption that people begin with a factually neutral input, and then mechanically infer its causes.

As we have noted, one of attribution theory's major concerns is the distinction between external, or situational causal attributions, and causes internal to actors. Brown notes that, for the Who concert incident:

> Causes internal to the actors would include alcohol, drugs, a disposition to violence, and so on. Causes external . . . include everything in the situation when and where they acted: the cold weather, a five-hour wait, the allocation of seating, the number of police present, the manner of admission to the Coliseum, and so on. (Brown, 1986: 133)

Again, we have to note the dependence of this distinction upon event description. The three term relationship actor–action–situation is not simply 'what happened', nor even a stable, once-and-for-all witness's perception of what happened. Rather, it is a proposition about what happened, in which different elements and persons might be categorized and placed as actor or situation. The crushing crowds might show up either as actors whose actions are to be explained, or as situational causes of individual actions, perhaps according to role ('actors' / 'police'). The flexibility of description allows for alternative causal propositions. It is not that any one of these is the correct one, the single truth or the event *per se*, nor the single underlying cognitive representation of the speaker. Rather, talkers and writers may construct and deploy various versions for whatever activity sequences – narratives, accounts, accusations, mitigations, and so forth – their discourse is organized.

Further still, this descriptive flexibility extends to the fundamental notion of internal and external causes. Take 'alcohol, drugs, a disposition to violence', for example. While these make good sense as plausible 'internal' causes, they also make sense as external ones, depending on how they are discursively deployed. Within a discourse of blame and mitigation, for example, the effects of drugs and alcohol may figure as external, situational causes which can be directly contrasted with a person's own intentions and tendencies: 'yeah but you've I mean (.) like that case I said I ran over that car (.) I'd never have done that if I wasn't drunk' (data from Taylor, 1990). The effects of alcohol are indeed routinely offered as causes of violent behaviour, such as in cases of wife beating (Critchlow, 1983). The point is that their status as internal or external causes is a function of their discursive deployment in action sequences such as blaming or mitigating, excusing or accusing. Intention rather than the cause's 'location', may become the operative criterion (as it is for Heider (1958), Jones and Davis (1965) and some other attribution theorists). Even stable personality dispositions, which in the above example are invoked in contrast to the effects of alcohol, can then be 'externalized' for blame reduction, as happens most dramatically in insanity pleas, but also in more mundane contexts, where trait attributions may be constructed as dispositions that can force themselves upon, and override an actor's best intentions. We discuss the attributional work of role and trait descriptions in Chapter 6.

The essential point is that internal and external causes do not figure as singular features of events, to be read off perceptually, or inferred automatically. They are propositional constructions, whose nature and operation are discursive and dependent for their sense upon the activity sequences (blaming, excusing, and so on) that they are part of. We cannot sensibly list, in a decontextualized way, the set of causes which are internal and external.

Brown draws attention to the fact that different people (Who members, the mayor, letters in the press, and so on) offered different explanations of the events at Cincinnati, and demonstrates how these various explanations can be mapped on to the causal calculus. Variability of this kind might have been used to draw attention to the constructed nature of versions, and to the situated actions that versions are designed for. For example, Pollner (1987) uses his well known research on the disjunctures in versions that can occur in traffic courts in this way. Yet Brown retains a perceptual meta-theory. There is a singular event, the truth of which is known in much the same way that the events at issue in John Dean's testimony were known via their supposedly obvious and consensual outcome (see Chapter 2): 'the primary relevant cause *turned out* not be internal . . . but external (something about the Coliseum), which *eventually turned out* to be nonreserved, general admission seating' (Brown, 1986: 140; emphasis added).

The important point is that the successful operation of Brown's

Box 5 *It's just linguistic behaviourism?*

An approach which emphasizes the study of activity through an analysis of records and transcripts, which considers mentalistic concepts such as memory in terms of publicly available social practices, and which has at times been avowedly anti-cognitivist (for example, Edwards and Middleton, 1986a; Potter and Wetherell, 1987) is linguistic behaviourism. Isn't it?

Much of the past 30 years in psychology has been founded upon the slaying of behaviourist dragons and the championing of cognitivist alternatives. It is perhaps easy to see criticisms of cognitivism as a throwback to old thoughts. Nevertheless, the analogy between discursive psychology and behaviourism is a highly misleading one.

First of all, the emphasis on examining available records of interaction rather than inferences about entities and processes 'under the skull' does not derive from a positivistic concern with observation as such, nor is it the result of trying to achieve as close an ontological shave as possible with Occam's razor; rather, it is a theoretically grounded reorientation to focus on social practices conducted primarily through language. Such a focus does not exclude a concern with the mental or cognitive, but this, as we have argued in different ways in the course of this book, is primarily understood in terms of the part it plays in interaction.

Secondly, we can consider the contrast between behaviourism and discursive psychology using the anthropological and linguistic distinction between 'etic' and 'emic' approaches. Behaviourism is pre-eminently an 'etic' approach: it attempts to replace participants' ordinary language of psychology and social interaction with purportedly more objective and scientific language which captures the underlying causal processes that shape behaviour. In contrast to this, discursive psychology is an 'emic' approach: it starts from participants' own concepts and understandings as these are deployed in practices of interaction. For example, analysts are constantly checking their senses of what is happening in an interaction by reference to understandings displayed by the participants themselves (Heritage, 1988; Wootton, 1989). Crucially, then, it is an approach to *action*, not *behaviour*.

Thirdly, although both approaches emphasize function, they conceptualize this in very different ways. While the functions in behaviourism are causally based, and involve various 'laws' relating 'rewards' to 'operants' and so on, in discursive psychology they are understood rhetorically and normatively. Rhetoric has no causal relation to consequence; it can be effective, but it can also be countered. Many devices for fact construction have their opposite numbers designed precisely for fact destruction. Normative relations do not determine outcomes; they simply ensure that unexpected outcomes raise issues of accountability. There is no law that an answer has to follow a question, but the failure to provide an answer can be an accountable matter.

attributional heuristic is dependent on his presupposing one correct version of what happened at the concert: '*the telling facts were* that crowd disturbances occurred in the Coliseum with every sort of fan (high consensus across actors) and did not occur when Who fans gathered in other situations (high distinctiveness of the Coliseum)' (1986: 141; emphasis added). This can only happen, of course, from a position of *post hoc* epistemological privilege. The studies we have developed in this book show that in the course of such debates there is no such neat split between fact and inference. Rather, both fact and inference are contested and rhetorically structured. Brown constructs the entire issue as a kind of detective story, in which the various explanations are like a set of hypotheses, false trails and red herrings, entertained and championed by audience and participants until eventually the facts can be laid out and the causal truth established. Yet this is essentially a bit of Whig history, reworking the past from the supposed privilege of the present.

Brown's way of formulating attribution theory brings us back to our legalistic motif: his 'layman as intuitive scientist' might just as well be 'layman as intuitive lawyer'. But, of course, lawyers do not enjoy the scientist's public reputation (whether or not deserved) as pursuer of truth and objectivity. The lawyer is partisan, committed to prosecution or defence, engaged in argument, the construction and undermining of versions, and in the allocation of blame and mitigation. However, we have to stress again that we are not proposing to substitute lawyers for scientists as a metaphor for lay persons: far from it. Scientists, lawyers and lay persons alike are all people who produce versions, explanations, arguments, accounts, and do so in context-sensitive, action-orientated ways. All are amenable to discursive study (cf. Atkinson and Drew, 1979; Gilbert and Mulkay, 1984), and if any one discourse is likely to have primacy and shed light on the others, it is the study of ordinary, mundane talk. In discursive psychology, insights are to be found not in trying to represent people in general by particular sorts of persons (scientists, lawyers, psychologists) but vice versa.

We are not suggesting that the attributional calculus has no relevance to how people understand everyday events. Indeed, it has important strengths in spelling out an abstracted logic of attributional reasoning. Our argument is that the study of everyday attributions is almost inevitably the study of everyday discourse. And once we take seriously the idea that we are studying discourse, the perceptual/cognitive meta-theory of attributional reasoning, like the cognitive psychology of textual memory, starts to lose explanatory power. The causal calculus looks like having the sort of relevance to everyday explanations that formal arithmetic has to folk mathematics (Lave, 1988), or formal logic to everyday reasoning and rhetoric (Billig, 1987; Wason and Johnson-Laird, 1972), or cognitive plans to situated actions (Suchman, 1987), or formal linguistics and speech act theory to ordinary talk (Levinson, 1983; Schegloff, 1988a). The relevance of these abstracted formalizations to ordinary practices is not that they describe how people think or talk. Their application is not stipulative but normative. They provide an abstracted model of the sorts of principles to which participants may *hold each other accountable*. Their relevance to everyday thought and action is therefore an empirical matter, and can be approached via discursive psychology. As soon as we begin to study situated discourse, abstracted models of rational thought, soon diminish in explanatory significance, as we discover how versions, explanations and inferences are constructed, implied and embedded in talk. It is in the accomplishment of social actions, rather than the display of underlying cognitive representations, that we find orderliness in discourse.

5

Description as Attribution

In Chapter 4 we looked at some of the ways in which studies of both textual remembering and attribution have conceptualized language in their research practice. We developed a number of lines of criticism, but the central point was that this work has failed to articulate a developed theory of language as a conversational and discursive practice. The cognitivist/perceptual model has the attributional reasoner receiving inputs from some scene, discerning patterns in the information and computing attributions on the basis of these patterns. In contrast to this, the discursive model we are arguing for has people constructing versions in their discourse that provide for particular inferences about motive and causation.

Rather than taking the reality of some scene on trust and considering mental operations that follow from it, the discursive model suggests that in natural discourse these two things are bound together: causal relations are constructed as versions are produced. People *do* descriptions and *thereby do* attributions. When the rape trial witness reformulated the counsel's 'he sat with you' as 'he sat at our table' (Chapter 2) this was *both* a description *and* an attribution. The attributional issues of agency and blame were dealt with precisely via the construction of alternative descriptions. Many of the flaws in current attribution theory can be traced to a failure adequately to theorize what 'description' is in the context of natural discourse.

It is important to note at this point that we are not claiming that people do not make direct attributional statements on occasion; 'it was your fault' and similar are hardly unfamiliar speech acts. Yet even here, we suggest, such explicit blamings are rarely unaccompanied by surrounding talk which offers versions that make the blaming credible and sensible. Indeed, we would expect that blunt criticisms of this kind are very often precisely the occasion for extended sequences of competing descriptions as participants formulate the scene to display their moral status.

The discursive model, then, takes attribution and remembering (version production) out from the mental relays of the human biocomputer and places them in talk and writing. This leads to a basic analytical reorientation. We are no longer concerned with the attempt to construct models of putative hidden inference processes, which requires the usual research technology of social and cognitive psychology; we are now concerned to analyse attributions as situated actions, including how descriptions are produced and how they provide for attributions. In one sense this is an anti-cognitivist position for its focus is squarely on social practices rather than cognitive entities. Yet in another it retains a close concern with cognitive phenomena, but deals with them as issues at stake in discourse, rather than as a basis for the analyst's own explanations. So instead of treating memory, say, as information chunks and processes in the mental storage system, we can examine it as an issue for participants to define and resolve: such as, is Dean remembering or confabulating?

The theoretical reorientation of discursive psychology occasions the analytical reorientation. Indeed, this point cannot be stressed too much, as discourse analysis has sometimes been seen as a method that can be plugged in to questions generated within the perceptual-cognitive model. In the light of the arguments we have developed over the first four chapters, the confusions that are likely to result from such a course should be apparent.

In this chapter we further define the discursive approach to attribution. We take the materials related to the disputed press briefing discussed in Chapter 3 and concentrate on a set of extracts which involve notions of consensus and corroboration. The interest in these is that 'consensus information' is one of the three main kinds of information that, according to the perceptual model, the attributional reasoner draws on when making judgements about patterns of causality. Our aim is to show how these texts concerning consensus both provide for attributional inferences and attend to various issues of accountability; this will, of course, show how potentially misleading it would be to take them as simple descriptions, or literal documents of consensus information, as a kind of neutral starting point for the cognitive attributional machinery to work on. Before this, however, we need to develop further our discussion of the nature of descriptions and factual discourse. What is factual discourse?

Discourse and fact construction

Once we start to consider description as an arena for doing attribution we need to address two basic, but closely connected, sorts of issues. The first is how the description is *made to seem* precisely that: a *description* rather than a claim, a speculation or indeed a lie. This is the force of saying that people *do* description. The second is how the description is used to accomplish a range of activities; for example, indicating causal patterns, accounting for the actions of the speaker, attending to the concerns of the recipient. In discourse analytical terms, these can be seen as issues of *construction* and *function*. It very quickly becomes apparent that these issues are at the centre of a whole area of study which has been virtually untouched by psychologists, namely how factual accounts are assembled and what they are used to do.

The *construction* issue concerns the sorts of devices and procedures that are used to make a specific version appear literal, solid and independent of the speaker. In effect, it concerns the way the 'out-there-ness' of a version is constructed, and how that 'out-there-ness' is managed through the course of interaction where it might come under threat. Looked at the other way round, how precisely is a report constructed to avoid it seeming like an artful construction designed to further the speaker's interests? Techniques of fact construction are sometimes referred to as 'externalizing devices' to emphasize this feature.

A variety of discourse analytical studies have shown that two elements are often prominent here: corroboration and interest or motive (for example, Potter and Edwards, 1990; Potter and Wetherell, 1988; Smith, 1978; Wooffitt, 1991, 1992; Woolgar, 1980, 1988a). At its most simple, these elements depend on the commonplace assumption that something claimed by independent witnesses is less likely to be a fabrication than would be the claims of a single witness; and that someone who has a strong personal stake may manufacture their story to fit in with it. Discourse which bolsters or externalizes a version of events will often draw on one or both of these elements. Furthermore, our rhetorical perspective reminds us that these features will also be a focus when *undermining* versions. On the one hand, these may be pillars for claims that a rebuttal will try to topple; on the other, a competing version may be built to display its superior disinterest or greater corroboration.

As we have already seen in Chapter 3, one useful way of conceptualizing this process is in terms of a hierarchy of modalization. Based on his work on fact construction in science and technology, Latour (1987; Latour and Woolgar, 1986) has suggested that rather than attempt a clear-cut distinction between facts and non-facts, it is more useful to consider a process where statements are progressively modalized. This can be understood in the form of a continuum – I *think* that X, I *know* that X, X is a *fact*, X, and so on (see Figure 5.1). At one end of the continuum, statements are made highly contingent on the mental processes and desires of the

Figure 5.1 A hierarchy of modalization (cf. Latour and Woolgar, 1986)

> [. . .]
> X
> X is a fact
> I know that X
> I claim that X
> I believe that X
> I hypothesize that X
> I think that X
> I guess that X
> X is possible

speaker, while at the other they become so commonplace that they do not even need to be formulated; they are simply assumed. Latour suggests that a whole battery of rhetorical resources are brought to bear to ratchet statements up and down through this hierarchy. Thus the first question about the warranting and externalizing of claims as facts can also be conceptualized in terms of this process of progressive modalization.

The *function* issue is concerned with the way the production of a specific version *as* real allows it to serve as an activity. That is, what can factual accounts be used *for*? In practice, this way of formulating the issue rather oversimplifies what is going on, for such accounts rarely perform a single unitary action; rather they attend to a range of issues simultaneously. For example, consider again the following extract from Drew's (1984) work on reports and invitations which we discussed in Chapter 2. E is responding to an invitation to go shopping:

```
E: . . . and I had to have my foot up on a pillow for two days,
   youknow  ⌈ and – ·hhhmhh
N:          ⌊ Yah?
E: But honey it's gonna be alright I'm sure,
N: Oh I'm sure it's gonna be alri:ght,
E: Yeuh,
N: Oh:: do:ggone. I ⌈ thought maybe we could ⌉
E:                  ⌊ I'd like to get       ⌋ some little slippers
   but uh,
(Drew, 1984: 138)
```

At the start of the extract E offers a report or description. However, as conversationalists, we know that this is not an abstract, disinterested observation. The report is embedded in an 'invitation sequence' (Drew, 1984): N is inviting E to go on a shopping trip; and in this context E's report accomplishes a rejection or refusal despite the attractive possibility of 'little slippers'. Yet this refusal is not done explicitly; she does it through a report which allows it to be inferred from her *inability* to go on the shopping trip. That is, E's report of a state of affairs provides an *attribution* for N, that E will not shop because she cannot because she is injured. Note here that a factor *internal* to E (her injury) serves to *externalize* responsibility for her rejection of N's invitation.

As we noted earlier, it is not just the production of a refusal or rejection that is important but how this is accomplished discursively; in this case how it attends to the relationship between E and N. An 'inability' account of this kind is one for which no one should be blamed because it is no one's fault; it was not intended or desired. Indeed, E stresses that she desires the *reverse*: she would like to go shopping. The point is that the report assigns a non-intentional causality (the injury) which does the action (implicitly) of rejecting the invitation, but at the same time makes the action accountable in terms of the continued good relationship between E and N.

It is necessary to make clear precisely what we are claiming here. We accept that the sorts of considerations, formulated by attribution theorists as issues of consensus, distinctiveness and consistency, are the concern of participants when doing different kinds of attributional work. In this extract from Drew there is a sense in which E is providing the material for situational attribution. Where we differ from attribution theory is in how the operation of these considerations should be understood. Instead of seeing these things as neutral, perceptually based, information ready for automatic processing in the cognitive machinery, we see them as normative considerations, and as such we expect that they can be reworked and reconstituted in the course of conversational interaction. As we will illustrate in the rest of the chapter, they do not determine the outcome of attribution but are resources that people drawn on in the rhetorical cut and thrust of activities such as those involving blame.

Consensus as a rhetorical construction

We are going to concentrate on materials that have a central place both in traditional attribution theory and in the discursive approach. We could have focused on any of the basic kinds of information deemed central in perceptually based models of attribution, but we have chosen to concentrate on accounts invoking or displaying consensus in one way or another. As we have indicated, work in the discourse tradition has shown that such accounts play an important part in the construction of factual discourse. However, they are also pivotal in attribution work.

As we outlined in Chapter 4, in the Kelley/McArthur tradition of attribution research the reasoner comes to attributional conclusions on the basis of mental calculations based on three different kinds of information: about distinctiveness (is someone acting how they would in other situations), about consistency (is someone acting in the way they have done in the past in this situation) and consensus (do other people act in this way in this situation). The idea is that by putting the 'incoming information' through the mental equivalent of a statistical computer program the reasoner can draw causal conclusions. For example, they can infer that the action is caused by features of the situation, or from something within the person. All these forms of information are vital to the theory, although some attribution researchers have suggested that consensus has a particular centrality for causal reasoners (Hilton et al., 1988).

There has been a range of conceptual critiques of attribution theory (see, for example, Buss, 1978; Gergen, 1982; Harré, 1981; Locke and Pennington, 1982; Sabini and Silver, 1980). However, our aim here is rather different from these. Following pointers from Billig (1982, 1987) to the importance of rhetoric in the area of attribution, we will use the discursive model to show how in natural settings attribution is part of a richer and more complex set of participants' activities, and uses a divide between fact and inference which is very different from that deployed by attribution theory. Rather than treating consensus as perceptually available information about events, our first move is to define it as a potentially disputable, to-be-achieved *construction*, designed for whatever discursive 'work' is at hand.

We shall address here two of the major types of devices through which consensus is discursively accomplished, or evoked, both of which are important ways of bolstering a version's factuality. The first of these is to claim the *assent* of reliable witnesses. If one witness to a car accident claims that the driver was going too fast she may be discounted; however, if most or all witnesses claim this they are likely to be more convincing. The second form of consensus warranting attends to a potential problem with the first. Witnesses may agree because they all saw the same thing; however, they may agree because they have cooked up a story together or because, more innocently, through interacting with one another, they have developed a common, but flawed, understanding. Thus there is value in finding witnesses who have not communicated or are independent. Their versions can be seen to be uncontaminated through contact. Thus this second form of consensus warranting stresses the *independence* of the holders of the consensual view.

In ethnomethodological terms, these are both members' methods for constructing factuality. This is not to say that there is anything epistemologically flawed about them – clearly, they are central in institutions such as science and the law, for example. However, what it does point up is that consensus and independence are social products which have to be accomplished; and also that they are open to exploitation for various effects (cf. Molotch and Boden, 1985). Furthermore, they can become sites of rhetorical dispute; the very consensus that can be displayed as evidence of the factuality of a version can also stand as a document of collusion and confabulation.

Explicit consensus: what everybody saw

We start with an examination of the way consensus may be constructed to warrant a case, and then proceed to show how it may be subsequently undermined through being recast as collusion. One of the features of the disputed press briefing between the Chancellor and the ten journalists was the way the purported unanimity of the journalists was used as a warrant for the accuracy and factuality of their stories. Each of the following three extracts invokes consensus as a warrant for truth:

> *Mr A. J. Beith* (Berwick-on-Tweed): How on earth did the Chancellor, as a former journalist, manage to mislead so many journalists at once about his intentions? (*Hansard*, 7 November: 23)

> *Mr David Winnick* (Walsall, North): As all the Sunday newspapers carried virtually the same story, is the Chancellor saying that every journalist who came to the briefing – he has not denied that there was one – misunderstood what he said? (*Hansard*, 7 November: 26)

> The reporters, it seemed, had unanimously got it wrong. Could so many messengers really be so much in error? It seems doubtful. (*Guardian*, 8 November)

As we saw in Chapter 4, in attribution studies, the sorts of factual construction offered in these extracts would be replaced by experimenter-constructed vignettes, of the following sort:

> Sally bought something on her visit to the supermarket.
> Almost everyone else bought something on their visits to the supermarket. (Hilton and Slugoski, 1986: 78)

In the context of an attribution experiment there is nothing participants can do about these statements except to take them as given, and make the appropriate inferences. Sally is unreal, and the constructor of the vignette is not in conversation with its recipient. Further, the recipient has no *stake* in what is going on. He or she is not Sally's friend, or enemy, and Sally's behaviour is not part of the moral fabric of their lives. Sally's purchasing (or failure to purchase) has no implications for the world of the participants and is not subject to potential complaint. Schegloff (1988b), for example, explores in detail the pattern of accusation and account in a girl's unproductive shopping trip to bring an 'ice cream sandwich' back to some friends; such an exploration is denied to the participants when faced with vignettes. More generally, Semin (1980) has emphasized that attributions are principally occasioned by some sort of breach or problem; yet this type of context is absent from the Sally vignette and those used in many similar studies.

The abstract and uninvolved nature of the Sally vignette and similar materials used in a plethora of attribution studies is in marked contrast to the extracts given above. They are posed with irony and as questions – indeed, as rhetorical questions. They are also dialogical, with their rhetorical structure inherent in the presentation of the facts of the matter, such that the desired inferences concerning Chancellor Lawson's veracity are rendered unavoidable. Also, because they are taken from contexts of real discourse, we can start to analyse how their construction is contextually occasioned. What we see is that the Sally vignette assumes the attributional epistemology of given reality (given by the experimenter) *followed by* causal inference (on the part of the subject). Crucially, it is an epistemology that is *built into* method, rather than something *empirically discovered* about how people think.

Let us replace our 'vignettes' in their context. In the sequence of events, our extracts follow Lawson's claims that the reporters were wrong (see Figure 3.1 above). That is, he has questioned the factual status of the reports. Using the idea of witnesses corroborating versions, we take the rhetorical force of these accounts to be something like this: it is reasonable to imagine that some of the journalists might be misled in a briefing of this kind but not that they all should. If a number of observers report the same thing, that encourages us to treat the status of that thing as factual. Thus the consensuality of the reporters' accounts is offered as a basis for scepticism about the Chancellor's.

Given that the accomplishment of a consensus across versions is one of the broad rhetorical tasks of the quoted extracts, we can understand some of their detail as flowing from it. That is, the passages do not merely state that consensus is present, but provide the basis for a rhetorical appeal to the reader to construct it herself. For example, the extracts work on the quality or adequacy of the consensus, emphasizing the *large scale* of the consensus and its *unanimity*.

The large size of the consensus is worked up using the description 'so many' journalists, which picks out the number of journalists as exceptional or notable. In the last extract, the effect is further enhanced by the contrast between the number of the 'messengers' and the size of the 'error': 'Could *so many messengers* really be *so much in error*' (*Guardian*, 8 November). In the second extract, unanimity is emphasized with the description 'every journalist' and this is reiterated in the description 'all the Sunday newspapers'. That is, the newspaper reports are descriptively split from the journalists' reports, as if to provide descriptions of two sorts of consensus each of which confirms the other. This device presents consensus on consensus, doubling up as it were to make the most of what is available. A similar reiteration of consensus with a more marked rhetorical format appears in the following extract:

> Mr Lawson held a press conference for ten political journalists.
> (1) →   All ten got the impression that he had floated the idea of abandoning universal benefits for old people irrespective of need.
> (2) →   All ten wrote stories for Sunday newspapers which were not questioned at the time by the Treasury.
> (3) →   But the next day the Chancellor himself told the Commons the ten were all wallies [a colloquial term of abuse].
>
> (*Sun*, 9 November)

In this extract, the consensus is not only reiterated to repeat its effect but the repeated formulations make up the first two parts of a three-part list – a construction which has been shown to be rhetorically important in discourse as varied as political speeches (Atkinson, 1984; Grady and Potter, 1985; Heritage and Greatbatch, 1986), courtroom dialogue (Drew, 1990) and everyday talk (Jefferson, 1990). For example, this is illustrated in the following passage taken from Governor George Wallace's inaugural speech:

> *Wallace:*   (1) →   . . . and I say segregation ↑<u>now</u>
>   (0.2)
>   (2) →   segregation to↑<u>morrow</u>
>   (0.2)
>   (3) →   . . . and segregation for e↓ver.
> *Audience:*   Hoora – [tape-editor's cut]
> (Atkinson, 1984: 60)

We will see this kind of rhetorical structuring used in television interviews in Chapter 6.

In the next extract, the quantity of the observers is emphasized in a different and rather neat way: 'The Government's case now seems to consist of one unlikely tale piled on top of another: first, 10 journalists all fall victim to the same mass-delusion; then . . .' (*Observer*, 13 November). Lawson's claim that the journalists are mistaken is re-characterized as the claim that they all fell victim to a 'mass-delusion'. This description is effective in two ways. First, it presents Lawson as claiming something highly implausible. The description carries connotations of the paranormal, hypnosis and irrationality; so by attributing this description to Lawson his claims are made to appear weak or unlikely. Indeed, it has already been characterized as an 'unlikely tale'. Secondly, the phrase is often used to deal with large numbers of people, as implied by the term 'mass' (one thinks of mass media, mass society, the masses and so on), more apposite for large crowds than a group of ten journalists; so this description again works to heighten the perceived quantity of the observers.

In these extracts, then, the journalistic accounts are formulated as a consensus. The 'mere fact' that this set of observers agreed over what went on is treated as making Lawson's criticisms doubtful. However, consensus is not so straightforward an indication of truth, and neither was it treated as such in our data.

One of the analytical strategies we have been using when dealing with these materials is to identity and explore variability across versions. As we have argued above, such variability can be used as an analytical lever because it is indicative of the action or rhetorical orientation of the versions (see also Potter and Mulkay, 1985; Potter and Wetherell, 1987; Wetherell and Potter, 1988). It is an approach which is particularly valuable when dealing with materials, such as newspaper articles, where the sorts of sequencing information that is used to such effect by conversation analysts (for example, Atkinson and Heritage, 1984a) is limited.

In the materials we have examined there is variability both between Lawson's versions and those of the journalists, as we have shown, and, of course, it is putative variability within Lawson's own talk that the dispute is all about: has he changed his story in the light of criticism of the purported policy? However, it is also possible to identify variability within the accounts of the journalists themselves.

Box 6   *An alternative version of the briefing*

(cartoons from the *Guardian*, 14/15 November 1988)

. . . it is precisely the symbolic separation of humour from the realm of serious action that enables social actors to use humour for serious purposes. (Mulkay, 1988: 1)

From consensus to collusion

We shall start by looking at Lawson's version(s) of events and examine the way in which they both differ from and orientate to the version offered in the extracts quoted above. Clearly, Lawson's integrity is threatened, both as an individual and as a member of the government, if the newspaper version holds sway in the face of his protestations. He provides his own versions in the course of the parliamentary debate.

The following extract is taken from *Hansard*. In sequential terms, it follows the publication of the original article in the Sunday newspapers and criticisms by various politicians on the Sunday, and within the parliamentary debate it follows shortly after the attack on the Chancellor by Alan Beith (see extract above), which specifically used the argument about consensus:

> *Mr Lawson:* [] Let me say that the only announcement I have to make – the only change I have to inform the House of – is the one that I informed the House of today. This is a matter which I hinted to certain journalists on Friday.
> They misunderstood what I was saying –
> [Laughter.]
> There is no
> [Interruption.]
> *Mr Speaker:* Order. This kind of laughter and these interruptions take up a great deal of time. Many hon. Members want to ask questions about this matter.
> *Mr Lawson:* – and as a result went in for a farrago of invention but that is no reason for the hon. Member to take it out.
> (*Hansard*, 7 November: 24)
> [The Speaker is the parliamentary chairperson who calls members to take turns at speaking, attempts to regulate interruptions, and so on.]

This extract is particularly interesting for the sequential unfolding of Lawson's account of the briefing. In the course of the debate Lawson has repeatedly denied having an intention to introduce means-tested benefits and claimed instead to be preparing to introduce an *extra* benefit for pensioners. He reiterates this point at the start of the extract and suggests that it was this latter policy, the extra benefits, that was indicated to journalists.

He then characterizes the journalists as having misunderstood him. This provokes what one report called a 'gale of raucous and incredulous laughter' (*Guardian*, 8 November) and then Lawson is interrupted entirely and the Speaker has to recover order. At this point Lawson produced another gloss on the reporting. Departing from the rather weakly blaming idea of 'misunderstanding', he suggests that the stories are a 'farrago of invention' (the *Oxford English Dictionary*, 2nd edn, defines 'farrago' as a 'medley' or 'confused mixture').

We can help make sense of this sequence by drawing on an analysis of 'idiomatic expressions' developed by Drew and Holt (1989). Drew and Holt suggest that idiomatic expressions – that is, clichéd or proverbial expressions – tend to crop up at specific junctures in conversations: for example, where a speaker is making a complaint of some kind and the recipients are withholding affiliation or support for the complaint. This is illustrated in the following extract:

Ilene: ·hhh We've checked now on all the papers'e has an' Moss'n
   Comp'ny said they were sent through the post we have had n:nothing
   from Moss'n Comp'ny through the post.
   (0.3)
Ilene: Anyway. (.) Tha:t's th– uh you know you can't (.) argue ih it's
   like (.) uh: ⌈ m
Shirley: ⌊ Well
   (.)
Ilene: banging yer head against a brick wa:ll
(Drew and Holt, 1989: 508)

Ilene's complaining about a company is not supported by Shirley
who noticeably avoids agreeing and supporting the complaint at
various junctures where she might have been expected to. Furthermore, her 'well' preface indicates that a 'dispreferred response' –
a disagreement or some other disaffiliative action – is likely to be
delivered soon (Levinson, 1983). It is at this point that Ilene
produces the idiomatic expression. What is the function of this?
Drew and Holt suggest that because these expressions are largely
figurative or formulaic they have a robustness that makes them
hard to challenge with specific facts or information. That means
they are suited to inauspicious environments, where a speaker's
version of events is not being well received.

   Coming back to our current materials, Lawson's environment is
certainly inauspicious. In nearly 15 minutes of debate he has been
asked a number of hostile questions and has been interrupted on
seven occasions during his replies. There is further vociferous interruption following his complaint about the press in the quoted
extract above. It is following this highly disaffiliative response to
his complaint that he offers the idiomatic formulation that the
reporters 'went in for a farrago of invention'.

   There are some interesting complexities with this phrase. *The
Random House Dictionary of the English Language* offers the
idiom: 'a farrago of doubts, fears, hopes and wishes'. Not only is
this idiom, and indeed the term 'farrago' itself, obscure but it is
not precisely quoted by Lawson. However, even if, as is likely, the
majority of the audience would have been unable to define the
term or recall the idiom, this would have only been to exaggerate
the formal properties of idioms that Drew and Holt identify. It
certainly makes any challenge difficult. Furthermore, in this
context, the phrase 'farrago of invention' allows listeners to infer
that some sort of suspect and possibly foreign sounding kind of
invention was underway. In this respect it has properties similar to
'mass-delusion' used in the extract from the *Observer* quoted
above.

   For those present who might possibly have been familiar with the etymology of the term (and we are certainly not wanting to imply that dictionary definition somehow prescribes meaning for participants), it would also have served Lawson perfectly. The *Oxford English Dictionary* cites Canning (1927, *Poetical Works*): 'No longer we want this farrago of cowardice, cunning and cant' which provides a suitably pejorative frame for understanding the reporters' actions. Moreover, the idea of a 'farrago of doubts, fears, hopes and wishes' applied to the journalists presents the image of a confused group which was motivated to forge a single consensus. The mental states that farragoes accompany are all about doubt, uncertainty, wishful thinking and so on – you do not have a farrago of facts.

Although Lawson's talk in the 'farrago' extract provides the basis for an accusation of collusion, this is not made explicitly until later in the debate:

> *Mr Lawson:* I am grateful to my hon. Friend. In fact, the statements, as I said – the statements that appeared in the press on Sunday bore no relation whatever to what I in fact said. What I have said to them [the reporters] is that, while we were absolutely, totally committed to maintaining –
> *Ms Clare Short* (Birmingham, Ladywood): They will have their short-hand notes.
> *Mr Lawson:* Oh yes, they will have their shorthand notes and they will know it, and they will know they went behind afterwards and they thought there was not a good enough story and so they produced that. They will know that I said that, while . . .
> (*Hansard*, 7 November: 26)

This extract reiterates the wrongness of the journalists' story, and this time uses the strong formulation that the press reports 'bore no relation whatever' to what he had said in the briefing. Here, Lawson accounts for the alleged difference between the stories and 'the facts'. The account is that the facts did not make a good enough story so the reporters *colluded* together to produce a better one. It is this collusion that explains the consensus. The stories tally not because that is how the facts were but because the journalists got together and invented a single story which they all used, and the motive offered is that they needed to invent such a story because the real story was not good enough to print.

We can see here Lawson drawing on one of the other central elements in factual accounting that we noted at the start of the chapter: *interest* or *stake*. Lawson undermines the journalists' story by displaying it as one which is a product of their interests. Such undermining accounts are particularly difficult to rebut because any rebuttal can itself be heard as produced by the very same

Box 7 *'They would say that, wouldn't they?'*

Expressions of the form 'they would say that, wouldn't they?' are usually attributed to Mandy Rice-Davies, a witness during the notorious court case in 1963, involving prostitution, leading public figures including British Defence Minister John Profumo, and possible espionage. The story is dramatized in the film *Scandal*, from which the following segment of cross-examination is taken:

> *Counsel:* are you aware that Lord Astor denies any impropriety in his relationship with you
> (.8)
> *Mandy Rice-Davies:* Well he would wouldn't he
> *Jury etc.:* [Prolonged laughter]

The counsel's rebuttal is economically bounced back from whence it came, without having to perform any detailed descriptive and justificatory work. A more recent example comes from Rupert Murdoch following criticism by the British Labour Party of the announced merger of his television station, Sky, with another station. Asked about Labour's (critical) attitude, he said: 'Well they would, wouldn't they?' (*Independent on Sunday*, 4 November 1990). This effectively constructs the criticism as a product of the motivations of the group doing the criticism rather than features of the criticized context.

The general point that these expressions demonstrate is the way that participants attend to the issues of interestedness in constructing their own discourse as factual and defending this against competing versions. Mandy Rice-Davies also *ironizes* the competing version – challenges its literal reference – by depicting it as a product of interests rather than being genuinely factual.

It is useful to speculate on some of the detailed construction features of this phrase. First, note the work done by the modalization *would*; it does not merely record what was said ('they did say that'), which would anyway merely state what people present already knew; it depicts what was said as strategic and motivated. Moreover, the use of *would* to refer to past events can also imply frequency or regularity: 'we *would* go to the beach or pool on a hot day.' Both of these features contribute to the ironizing force of the utterance. The second point to note is the tag question form: *wouldn't they?* This serves to repeat the 'would' which is central to the point. It also invokes an interactional context and signals expected agreement; that is, it is a way of displaying confidence, and of appealing to common knowledge. The audience is invited to treat the disputed claim as one that they already know about, and which is obvious. Interestingly, such tags are also a feature of Bernstein's (1971: 62) depiction of working-class speech, the 'sympathetic circularity' of a context bound and homely 'restricted code'. Without wishing to endorse Bernstein's descriptive scheme, there is also, in Mandy Rice-Davies' case, the sense of an 'ordinary working girl' using ordinary language to deal effectively with the machinations of a sophisticated lawyer and the denials of a member of the aristocracy.

Finally, the phrase now makes a backward reference to this notorious original legal context, as well as many recent reworkings; that is, it serves as a signifier of situations where claims can be discounted because of their interested basis. The context for the following dialogue is discussion during the Gulf War of a report on Baghdad radio of Iraqi President Saddam Hussein talking about a major counter-attack against coalition forces, reporting many tanks destroyed and the coalition being driven back. The exchange takes place between BBC interviewer Brian Redhead and General Sir Anthony Farrah Hockley, a military expert. Chris Lewis is another radio reporter.

> *Redhead:* What do you make of that kind of stuff? We heard Chris Lewis talking about it earlier and saying it was ridiculous.
> *General:* Well that's the Mandy Rice-Davies factor – he would say that, wouldn't he?
> *Redhead:* What [laughs]
> *General:* [laughs]
> *Redhead:* Not Chris Lewis!
> (BBC Radio 4 'News FM', 24 February 1991)

This example not only shows the orientation to the interestedness of accounts, but also the device's flexibility; it was easy to hear the interestedness attribution turned around, applied to Chris Lewis instead of Saddam, which then generated the laughter. It also shows the cultural availability of this as a 'prepackaged' interest attribution technique; not only the phrase cited, but also its celebrated source.

interests that underpinned the original account. That is, rebuttals are always vulnerable to Mandy Rice-Davies' celebrated courtroom rejoinder: 'he would [say that], wouldn't he?'

This extract further illustrates the rhetorical nature of these discursive devices. They do not, in themselves, speak unequivocally for truth or for error; they are available for rhetorical work, for bolstering a case or else for its refutation (Billig et al., 1988). Thus, while consensus is usable as a warrant for truth, as in our earlier quoted extracts, it also offers the basis for an accusation of collusion as in this extract from Lawson.

Our discussion so far has focused on variability between Lawson and the journalists in their versions of the nature and significance of the consensus in press reports. We have shown the way they use consensus both to warrant and undermine a particular version of events. However, as we have already seen, things are both more complicated and more theoretically interesting than that. In Chapter 3 we showed the way that one newspaper, the *Guardian*, moved between using consensus as a sign of the truth of the newspapers' account (extract quoted above) and as a sign of collusion between reporters (Chapter 3, p. 63). This apparent contradiction became understandable when we considered the accounts in their different pragmatic context of criticizing the Chancellor and criticizing the system of lobby journalism, respectively.

Overall, then, by analysing these extracts for their rhetorical organization, and by understanding them in terms of their discursive context, we have shown how these formulations of facts are not merely 'given' and unproblematic bases for inference, but are constructed and dismantled by the participants themselves, a rhetorical process inseparable from the drawing of inferences. Further, this is not just a feature of discourse noticed by analysts. The participants themselves treat the factual accounts in this way as they invoke interests and undermine consensus claims in the course of rebuttals.

As a further demonstration of the interesting and analysable complexity of these discursive constructions, we turn now to one of the critical aspects upon which the consensus versus collusion dichotomy is argued: the notion that matching accounts are produced by independent individuals. Once again, our aim is to reveal the constructed complexity, and the rhetorical organization, in real discourses, of what attribution theorists take to be 'consensus information'.

Corroboration: independent witnesses agree

When a set of different accounts is used to corroborate one another, it is rhetorically valuable to claim their independence. This idea is important in courts of law, where there is the notion of collusion between witnesses. Indeed, it is part of the reason for which witnesses are kept out of the courtroom, so that they remain uncontaminated by the stories of others. Whether there are objectively measurable grounds for preferring independent testimony over collaborative testimony (Stephenson et al., 1983) is not the issue here. We are dealing with how participants in disputations *deploy* such notions as part of their common sense reasoning. As in courtrooms, the issue of dependence is drawn on in Lawson's account of how 'they went behind and produced' their similar stories: the point being that different inferences are available if the consensus is a contrivance rather than being arrived at independently. Consensus becomes a sign of collusion.

On the weekend following the Lawson briefing, the Sunday papers introduced a new reason for doubting Lawson's version and believing their own. The reason was that new information had been obtained by a television news editor which provided independent corroboration. The claimed virtue of this was that it agreed with the reports from the newspaper journalists – it fitted in to the consensus – but it was obtained independently. The value for the newspapers of such an independent account was that it could be used to rebut Lawson's accusations of collusion. And, indeed, it was used in exactly this way. For example, the following extract uses the independence of the television story to cast doubt on Lawson's explanation in terms of misreporting.

> It emerged yesterday that ITN [Independent Television News] – which ran a similar story in its 8.55 p.m. bulletin on Saturday 5 November – based it on separate conversations with Treasury officials. Until now it had been assumed that the ITN report was based on early editions of last Sunday's papers.
>
> According to Michael Brunson, political editor of ITN, he reached the same conclusion by independent means, without attending the briefing. So far, the Chancellor has claimed the only source for the means-testing stories was deliberate misreporting by the journalists he briefed the previous Friday.
>
> Mr Brunson said yesterday that he spoke to the Treasury last Saturday, having already acquired 'a certain amount of information' and 'came away with the even stronger impression that there would be cuts in the Christmas bonus'. (*Observer*, 13 November)

The rhetorical effectiveness of this passage is similar to that of our extract from *Hansard* and the *Guardian* invoking consensus as a warrant for truth. It warrants the original version produced by the journalists by offering a further degree of consensus in reportings, but this time one which is garnered independently of the journalists' lobby. The same argument was used in a rather more compact form on the front page of another paper: 'ITN says the story was obtained and checked independently of the Lawson briefing, which it did not attend, and was written before the first editions of last Sunday's newspapers appeared' (*The Sunday Times*, 13 November). In these two extracts, then, independence is stressed to warrant the factuality of the version. However, following one of the base heuristics of discourse analysis, we can examine the materials for alternative versions. In fact, we do not have to read very closely to find just such variation. Even in the *Observer* extract, Brunson is quoted as saying that he went to the Treasury 'having already acquired a certain amount of information'. This element is elaborated on as follows:

> Shortly after lunchtime last Saturday, Michael Brunson . . . came across a story that was to dominate the week's news.

Robin Cook, Labour's social security spokesman, told him that something was going on in the Treasury over pensioners' benefits. Cook had been alerted by one of the Sunday paper lobby correspondents briefed by Nigel Lawson . . . at 11 Downing Street the day before.

Brunson had not been to the briefing. But his own Treasury contacts soon confirmed what Cook said the lobby correspondents had been told. Brunson knew he had a story to lead last Saturday evening's main ITN News at 8.55. (*The Sunday Times*, 13 November)

This extract departs from the ideal model of independent corroboration in two ways. First, it suggests that the original source of the television editor's information was one of the journalists from the meeting, and that the channel for this information was an Opposition spokesman who was heavily critical of Lawson in the following week's papers. This seems to offer a much weaker idea of independence than is implied in the previous extracts. Instead of Brunson approaching the Treasury naively and finding the same thing as the reporters – the sort of naivety we might expect from independent witnesses to a robbery – in this version he is already approaching the situation with a ready-made and potentially hostile version of it, which could provide a frame for interpreting any claims then made by Treasury spokespersons. Secondly, the reference to the television editor's need for 'a story to lead [the] main ITN news' echoes Lawson's own suggestions concerning journalists' motivations for misreading the facts. In this extract, then, the ITN editor can be read as being directly influenced by the putatively collusive lobby, and party to exactly the same truth-corrosive motivation to produce a 'good enough story' as the newspaper reporters.

What are we to make of this? Why is there this variability in versions of independence in the newspapers? We are certainly not suggesting that this latter version should be taken as the 'truth of events' seeping through the accounts in some way. Instead, we suggest that the presence of these competing versions is again evidence of the pragmatically occasioned nature of description. The pragmatic force is clear enough for the independent corroboration version, this being used to undermine Lawson's accusations of collusion and confabulation. But why should this newspaper then present this detailed description which only weakens the version? We suggest that there are two considerations here.

One clue to the matter is that over this weekend several of the papers published lengthy pieces presenting what purported to be moment-by-moment accounts of the disputed briefing and the events that followed it. These narratives can be seen as a form of 'empiricist warranting' (Gilbert and Mulkay, 1984; Mulkay and

Gilbert, 1983) of the conclusions that had previously been drawn. That is, they presented conclusions as if these were constrained by a neutral and available record of events. The account of the Labour politician's involvement with the television editor is an integral part of this record because it explains how they both became involved at such an early stage. In effect, the narrative form used requires the detail of connections to maintain its coherence (cf. Gergen, 1988; Gergen and Gergen, 1987; Jackson, 1988).

A further feature of these detailed descriptive accounts is that they contained much collateral information. For example:

> Mr Lawson sat in an armchair in one corner, next to a window looking out over the garden of No 11 Downing Street. The Press Secretary, Mr John Gieve, hovered by the door. The rest of us, notebooks on our laps, perched on chairs and sofas in a circle around the Chancellor. It was 10.15 on the morning of Friday, 4 November . . . (*Observer*, 13 November)

As we noted in Chapters 2 and 3, narrative description of this sort creates a graphic, vivid and believable world, described in terms suggesting direct perception or fresh visual memory (Barthes, 1974; Rimon-Kenan, 1983). Indeed, the irony is that it is precisely skills best understood in the realm of literature and fiction which are drawn on here to offer a rhetorical guarantee of veridicality. Atkinson (1990) effectively explores this point in a comparative analysis of the way detailed description like this is drawn on in the opening passage of a short story and a sociological ethnography.

This highly graphic introduction (a stylistic device rhetoricians call *hypotyposis*) provides a contextual warrant for what is said about the briefing. In effect, then, we can map some potential tensions which arise when the same claim – that Lawson's version of events is flawed – is warranted in different ways. The apparent conflict of versions arises from the deployment of two different kinds of warranting: independent witnessing, and narrative-empiricist description, working against each other. The conflict arises from our decontextualizing them, and placing them in opposition. In the contexts in which they occur, they are separate from each other and sensible, each deployed to bolster the press's case, that its story was not confabulation (independence), and that it belonged to a believably graphic, richly detailed experiential narrative (and is thus a valid bit of remembering).

These detailed narrative descriptions demonstrate the inescapably social-pragmatic status of descriptive discourse. It might be assumed that the more detailed a factual description is, the more graphic its picturing of scene and circumstance, the more careful its construction of a fine-grained sequence of events, then, provided no obvious confabulation is being offered, the less scope there would be for pragmatic work to be done in constructing truths about the world. On the contrary, however, the provision of more and more 'facts' may merely provide further warrant for the narrator's status as truth-teller, or accurate rememberer, such that the more contentious part of the story can be camouflaged amidst a mass of 'realistic' detail. Again, one might say it is the novelist's art to create a believable world for the purveyance of fiction. More generally, this once more shows the way consensus information is a rhetorically organized participants' notion, which has to be understood in terms of its deployment in natural settings. In the light of these kinds of analysis we find it hard to sustain the idea that some kind of neutral, perceptually derived 'information' is the basis for cognitive inference.

Attribution management in everyday talk

We have devoted most of this chapter to materials taken from a political dispute in the mass media. In some ways this could be seen as divorced from the everyday realities of face-to-face inter-action and perhaps threaded with special complexities due to the norms of political briefing and the codes of news reporting. However, while it is undoubtedly the case that there are special features of this material, we would not want to overstate this case. For one thing, this discourse is designed for a lay audience of newspaper readers and television viewers interested in political events. Whatever distinctiveness this form of discourse has, it is also dependent on making its suggestions, hints, denials and complaints intelligible to that audience. Moreover, although there are clearly a range of complexities attending the various parties and their institutional positions, in some respects their interests are displayed in a relatively unambiguous manner. The very fact of having to address an anonymous audience with a variety of back-grounds and competences probably leads to a degree of explicitness that is not necessary among familiars (Kreckel, 1981), or when speaker and recipient are engaged in real time interaction where there is a current shared context (Edwards and Mercer, 1987).

Nevertheless, there are good reasons for being concerned that the sorts of issues we have highlighted generalize to other situations and, more interestingly, to show how they are managed interac-tionally. We will try to give a flavour of this kind of study by drawing on work by Pomerantz (1984c) which is focused on the way participants attempt to elicit a particular kind of response in the course of an interaction; how, for example, they may try to induce an offer or an invitation. Although our own concern is rather different, it can helpfully build on Pomerantz's analysis.

We will concentrate on an interaction in which one nurse is trying to persuade another to take on a patient who has suffered a ruptured aneurysm. Pomerantz notes that we need to understand something about the culture of nursing to make sense of the extract, namely that the condition of the patient is crucial for the quality of the nursing job, that generally the worse the damage the more unpleasant the job, and that permanent damage implies a job that will only end with the patient's eventual death. In this context A is trying to convince B to take on the case.

```
15   B:   And uh isn't she quite a young woman? Only in her
16        fifties?
17   A:   Yes, uh huh
18   B:   Oh, how sad.
19   B:   And that went wrong.
20        (1.0)
21   A:   Well, uh–
22   B:   That surgery, I mean.
23   A:   I don't–
24   B:   Isn't she the one who– I think I heard about it–
25        the daughter in law told me– Wasn't she playing
26        golf ⌈ at the Valley Club?
27   A:        ⌊ Yes, that's the– That's the one
28   B:   –and had an aneurysm.
29   A:   Yes
30   B:   –suddenly.
31   A:   Mm hm
32   B:   They thought at first she was hit with a golf (1.0)
33        ball or bat or something, but it wasn't that.
34   A:   ⌈ Uh huh
35   B:   ⌊ It was a–a ruptured aneurysm, and uh–th–they
36        didn't want Dr L. at M. They took her down to UCLA.
37   A:   Yes. Uh huh.
38   B:   And it– and it left her quite permanently
39        damaged I suppose.
40   A:   Apparently. Uh he is still hopeful.
```
(Pomerantz, 1984c: 154, 156–7)

We shall take up four issues arising from this extract which are relevant to our discussion of memory and attribution in the Dean and Lawson materials. The first two issues concern the relationship between fact and rhetoric in the extract; the second two concern the different levels of accountability that the dialogue displays.

The first point to emphasize is that the very presence of factual reporting in the extract is itself an indication of rhetorical concerns being salient for the participants. As Pomerantz puts it: 'Giving the facts or one's basis for an assertion often is done when persons have different versions of events and/or different interests' (Pomerantz, 1984b: 159). Put simply, when there is nothing to argue about there is no need to formulate the facts. Far from factual reporting being a *contrast to* rhetoric, then, it is a *feature of* rhetoric. We saw this clearly in the course of the journalists' accounts of what happened at the briefing with Chancellor Lawson: it was only after the claims were questioned by Lawson that they started to produce vividly detailed factual accounts as seen in the extract quoted above, and similarly at times in Dean's accounts of his conversations with Nixon.

The second point to emphasize is one that we have encountered repeatedly in dealing with the Dean and Lawson materials, and this is that versions are constructed to lend themselves to rhetorical work. In this case, nurse B (who is resisting the invitation to accept the patient) formulates details which emphasize the severe imposition involved in accepting the request to take the patient. For example, she formulates the youth of the patient (lines 15–16) and the permanence of the damage (lines 38–9). Nurse A resists this latter formulation with a more hopeful contrary prognosis. This is not a cognitively abstracted affair, a matter of expressing in speech one's ready-made understanding or memory of events, but, rather, it is a constitutive part of the activity sequence of requesting and (implicitly) refusing.

The third and fourth points focus on the question of accountability. First, we note that this is a story constructed to display the accountability of the actors involved in the events described. It is a story which deals with issues of blame; for example, it attributes the severity of damage to the patient to the family's delay in getting her to treatment (lines 36, 38–9). However, as this level of accountability is developed in the story it cannot be separated from a further level of accountability (and this is the fourth and final point). This relates to the accountability of the speakers themselves. The story about the family's delay and its implications for the severity of the damage provide nurse B with a warrant for resisting accepting the patient. In the course of blaming the family, her story constructs the degree of severity of the harm in a way which underpins the refusal. That is, her management of the *accountability in the story* is a way of constructing *her own accountability* for refusing to take the patient.

This close relation between accountability for the parties *in* the talk (in the events as recounted) and the parties *to* the talk is something that has been virtually ignored in the sorts of attribution studies we described in Chapter 4. Attribution workers have concentrated on people's identification of blame and responsibility without considering the way that such identifications when displayed in talk are themselves related to issues of blame and responsibility. Put simply, what is absent is an understanding of the attributional work done by attribution talk. This will be the theme of our next chapter.

6

World-making and Self-making

In the course of this book so far we have argued the advantages of a discursive approach which considers description production as orientated to action and accountability and shown some of the difficulties that a failure to theorize this relation has generated for psychological research. We have reworked some of the problems of memory research in terms of how and when accounts of events are constructed; and we have reworked some closely related difficulties with attribution theory in terms of the management of versions to assign responsibility and negotiate moral issues of blame, duty and praise. Rather than seeing the study of discourse as a pathway to individuals' inner life, whether it be cognitive processes, motivations or some other mental stuff, we see psychological issues as constructed and deployed in the discourse itself.

One of the features of the discourse model is that it cuts across the conventional disciplinary boundaries of psychology. The situated construction of versions of what went on (discursive remembering) is understood as related, indeed *constitutively* related, to concerns about blame and responsibility (causal attribution). We have not argued for a redrawing of the psychological map because it is more practical or logical (although these might indeed be benefits to emerge); the point is that these traditional boundaries are not respected by participants *in their discourse*.

In relating these fields together, then, we are taking our cue from the way accounts are managed in lay discourse. In this chapter we shall extend this argument and show that similar considerations relate to issues of self and personality. This is not a new topic as such; rather self and personality are a central feature of what might be thought of as attribution-orientated accounts of the past. Indeed, so-called *trait* attribution has been a central concern of traditional attribution theory (for example, Jones and Davis, 1965), even though it is usually distinguished clearly from causal attribution (see Howard and Allen, 1989). Here too we shall see the way versions of self and identity are constructed as factual and fitted in to people's practical activities and interactions. And we shall show the way that these issues in turn are integrally related to the construction of factual versions of events (remembering), and to what would traditionally be thought of as causal attributional concerns: what happened and why. We examined a particular instance of this in Chapters 2 and 3, where discursive constructions of an actor's personality or disposition (Dean's and Lawson's) served as explanatory devices for 'errors' in their reporting of events. In this chapter, we shall extend those observations by examining how 'role' descriptions offer an alternative, rhetorically useful contrast to 'trait' descriptions for accomplishing different causal accounts.

Factual discourse and texts of identity

Reconceptualization of the way 'self' is understood in psychology has been under way for some time. One important argument for reworking has come from semiotic and post-structuralist reconceptualizations (for example, Barthes, 1974; Henriques et al., 1984; Hollway, 1989; Sampson, 1983, 1988), while another has come from approaches to discourse informed by linguistic philosophy, ethnomethodology and conversation analysis (for example, Coulter, 1979, 1989; Davies and Harré, 1990; Halkowski, 1990; Harré, 1983; Widdicomb and Wooffitt, 1992). In both these traditions, although in rather different ways, the focus has moved from a traditional realist understanding of self discourse, as a more or less adequate description of inner entities, to considering what *activities* particular forms of self discourse make possible, and how a subject may be *constituted* on any particular occasion in talk or writing (Gergen and Davis, 1985; Potter and Wetherell, 1987; Shotter and Gergen, 1989; Wetherell, 1986).

For our present purposes we shall extract a particular theme from this work which concerns the way the central models of the person in psychology (personality traits, the humanistic self) and sociology (role) can be understood as *narrative characters* (Potter et al., 1984; Wetherell, 1986; Wetherell and Potter, 1989). In other words, they can be understood as different constructions of personhood, discursively available for placing in different kinds of narrative or to do different kinds of interpretative work.

Take trait theory, for example. People produced in the world of trait theory are 'honest souls' (Trilling, 1974) who are simply the sum of their traits; they are synonymous with their dispositions from which they have no separate identity. In literary constructions they act as ideal minor characters. They provide a consistent backdrop against which the central characters can, for example, demonstrate their alienation from their roles or develop their potential through pain or self-discovery in the manner of humanistic psychology. That is, in novels narrative characters are resources for constructing stable and complex accounts which generate particular effects.

Narrative characters provide much of the same set of possibilities when people construct their social worlds in everyday discourse. For example, in a study of accounts of violent police action during the protests in New Zealand against the 1981 Springbok Tour, Wetherell and Potter looked at the way certain of these narrative characters were drawn on in the construction of mitigations (Potter and Wetherell, 1987; Wetherell and Potter, 1989). This study explored the way certain trait or dispositional accounts could make violent police action appear a natural and universal feature of being human in this context, making criticisms seem unreasonable; and the way role accounts could be used to formulate a distinction between senior officers who formulated policy which resulted in violence, and individual officers who carried it out, again limiting criticism of involved police although directing blame at their seniors and politicians.

The general point, then, is that the detailed language of describing persons is a resource for action. Quite independently of questions about the reality of particular personality theories and types, or mentalistic notions such as motives, we can study their use in discourse (Coulter, 1989). We can explore how particular constructions of self and others are used to stabilize and make factual seeming, particular versions of events in the world which themselves contribute to the organization of current activities.

Motives for resigning

In this chapter we shall illustrate this way of understanding self discourse through focusing on materials related to the resignation of the British Chancellor of the Exchequer, Nigel Lawson, on 26 October 1989. Our general reasons for focusing on this kind of material are the same as we outlined in the Introduction and in Chapter 3, with the added virtue that many readers will already be reasonably familiar with Thatcher and Lawson, the principal actors. Most importantly, however, it offers an arena to explore the management of competing versions; an arena where the construction of motive and event can be studied as an *interactional* accomplishment. Up to now we have focused much of our attention on newspaper accounts, which are certainly rhetorically organized, and cross-refer to each other, but do not have the direct turn-by-turn logic of conversational interaction. Parliamentary debate has more of this element, but is heavily constrained by protocols such as addressing points to the Speaker. A study of more interactional material allows us to watch the deployment and undermining of versions over a series of turns.

In this chapter we shall also be illustrating further the analytical style of discursive psychology and, in particular, its concern with the *detail* of actual interaction sequences. As we noted in the Introduction, psychologists have traditionally seen their work as fundamentally based around abstraction: the inference of *general* laws or processes from behavioural particulars. This is, of course, closely connected to the traditional modelling of psychology on the natural sciences and the widespread adoption of Fisherian statistics and the assumptions about causal relationships that flow from them. One of the central features of discursive psychology is its basis in the explication of specific stretches of discourse and the attempt to account for their individual properties in terms of what they accomplish. We are here exploring the detail of rhetorical construction. Such generalizations that do emerge, concerning the action orientation of description and inference, rhetorical organization, accountability and so on (formulated more systematically in Chapter 7) will need to be closely tied to that detail.

Our interest is specifically in constructions of the Chancellor's motive for resigning; although, as we shall see, this cannot be kept separate from a range of other concerns. We shall examine different versions of the motive, or versions which may be inferentially related to the motive, and consider both the way different versions are stabilized as factual and, also, the purposes which these different versions may serve.

At the time of his resignation Lawson had been in office for six years, making him the longest serving post-war British Chancellor. Despite some previous newspaper reports that he had no ambition to be Prime Minister (the 'logical' promotion), and that he was preparing at some future date to move on to a very highly paid financial job in the City of London (which he eventually did), the Chancellor's resignation was treated as a surprise and a major embarrassment for the ruling Conservative Party and in particular the Prime Minister, Margaret Thatcher. As will become clear, one of the main issues raised in the resignation was the role of a personal adviser to the Prime Minister, Sir Alan Walters, who was variously claimed to 'have the ear' of the Prime Minister on major issues of economic policy and to be at odds with the Chancellor (see Box 8). The Chancellor cited Walters' activities both in his resignation letter and in his first speech to parliament following the resignation.

Box 8 *Who are Brian Walden and Sir Alan Walters?*

Brian Walden

Brian Walden is a man of charismatic charm.

   But put him in a studio with a politician who is in any way shifty, evasive, ill-informed or unfamiliar with the truth, and he's a tiger. No-one, from the resident of No 10 downwards, puts one across Walden. As they troop in to face him, all our leaders regard him with respect, and some, occasionally, with agitation. Some would rather not face him at all.

Walden, a former Labour MP, is careful always to retain his scrupulous neutrality.

. . . if he finds himself dealing with someone who is clearly not going to answer the question, he starts to think of ways to outflank him [!]. 'Shall we try him with a googly?' says Walden, the cricket fan interviewer. 'Shall we pretend not to care, then slip one through his guard? There's usually a way to do it.'

. . . his salary would keep Mrs Thatcher and half the Cabinet.

('Walden . . . The Tiger on Your Telly', *TV Times*, 29 September–5 October 1990)

Sir Alan Walters

Walters's almost mousey manner makes the stubborn persistence of his beliefs come as a surprise. Like Mrs Thatcher, he does not let go easily. His hard edges have not been softened by a decade, on and off, inside Downing Street. Originally he had a charming innocence about him but that has, I think, been a little corroded by the vanity of the long term insider.

What struck me about the article which triggered off this shattering blow to the Government was it boastfulness and lack of self awareness. (*Daily Telegraph*, 27 October 1989)

Innocent arrogance may seem a contradiction in terms but the phrase clings to Sir Alan Walters like a drunk's arm.

He and Mrs Thatcher were until last night [Walters resigned directly after Lawson] a warm mutual admiration society. He is quintessentially 'one of us', her highest accolade . . . She admires the direct simplicity of his economic views, uncluttered with the fumbling equivocation which can make her eyes glitter dangerously.

Neil Kinnock got his appearance about right when he described him this week as a 'newly-ordained Trappist monk'.

A man of disturbing innocence. (*Independent*, 27 October 1989)

[The Chancellor's] successor . . . was in the happy position of not having to deal with this eminence grise. (*Guardian*, 6 November 1989)

In the last analysis, any sociopsychological image of the self . . . is inextricably dependent on the linguistic practices used in everyday life to make sense of our own and others' actions. (Potter and Wetherell, 1987: 95)

The resignation fell on a Thursday and the Prime Minister was already engaged to give a 50 minute interview to Brian Walden, one of British television's foremost political interviewers, on the following Sunday (see Box 8). In the event, most of this interview focused on the resignation (and specifically the role of Sir Alan Walters), its significance and its relation to the government's handling of the economy and the Prime Minister's controversial management of the Cabinet (the inner circle of government ministers). This interview with Mrs Thatcher provides us with a forum for exploring the way factual discourse, and particularly factual discourse about persons and 'inner states' like motives, is managed interactionally.

Before considering these materials there is one final point that it is important to make. Although we are dealing here with the transcribed utterances of two individuals, we are not assuming that these utterances were the unique creation of Thatcher and Walden. Quite apart from post-structuralist and deconstructionist arguments about the parasitism of forms of talk on established forms of sense-making and the decentring of the individual, there is the more prosaic point that both Thatcher's answers and Walden's questions were undoubtedly developed by more than one person. It is well known that statements made in political interviews, and indeed in courts of law, tend to be prepared in advance. Our concern, however, is in the construction and function of these utterances as part of a piece of social interaction; precisely how they came to this form is the topic of another kind of study.

We shall start by examining the initial exchange from the Prime Minister's interview which includes the framing of the interview by Brian Walden before and after the credit sequence, his first question to the Prime Minister, and her response to that question. (The number after the speaker's name indicates the number of turns after the start of the interview.)

Pre-credit sequence

> *Walden* 1: Nigel Lawson's shock resignation from the Chancellorship has plunged the Prime Minister (.) into the most serious political crisis of her career (.) it has also confronted her with a full-scale economic crisis (.) can she resolve (.) her political and economic problems (.) the Prime Minister is with me here today

Credit sequence

> *Walden* 1: Prime Ministe:r many people including many of your own supporters blame you for the resignation of Nigel Lawson from the Chancellorship and he blames you (.) .hh er this is what he wrote (.2) dear Margaret, the successful conduct of economic policy is possible

(.) only if there is and is seen to be (.) full agreement between the Prime Minister and the Chancellor of the Exchequer (.) .hh recent events have confirmed (.) that this essential requirement cannot be satisfied (.) so long as Alan Walters remains your personal economic adviser (.) I have therefore regretfully concluded that it is in the best interests of the government for me to resign my office (.) without further ado (.4) now Prime Minister (.2) how you res↑po::nd (.) to this claim of blame (.) may be of crucial significance for you personally and to your government so I put it to you (.) are you to blame for Nigel Lawson's resignation (.)

Thatcher 1: well we have done very well together (.) for the last six years and very well for Britain (.) and I think the results are clear to see (.) .hh to me the Chancellor's position was unassailable (.) I always supported him and said quite clearly (.) advisers are there to advise (.) ministers are there to decide (.) and that was the way we did business (.) and we did it very successfully .hh I tried very hard to dissuade the Chancellor from going (.2) .hh but he had made up his mind (.) .h and in the end I had to accept his resignation and appoint someone else.

Making resignation accountable

Let us first take the resignation letter, read out by Brian Walden. As is typical of resignation letters, it accounts for the resignation: it provides a reason or motive for the action. The resignation is presented as occasioned by problems in the relationship between Prime Minister and Chancellor caused by the economic adviser Sir Alan Walters; however, these problems are given not as merely psychological or interpersonal ones, but rather as having direct structural effects on economic policy. That is, Lawson's letter draws on the narrative character of the role actor. Such a character's motives are not 'psychological' in the same way as those of the humanistic self or the trait person; instead, they are embedded in the requirements of role. The Chancellor has duties to make economic policy work and support the government. If these duties cannot be met then the role becomes untenable and resignation is the proper and indeed required course of action.

In Chapter 5 we suggested that it is helpful to approach an understanding of factual discourse with two fundamental questions in mind. These are basically the question of *construction* (how is the account constructed to seem factual and external to the author) and *function* (what is this particular account designed to accomplish). Let us start with the second question. As we have indicated, the Chancellor's use of role discourse provides an account for what is potentially a disruptive and politically destabilizing action. However, not just any explanation for action will be satisfactory in the moral/political realm in which the Chancellor is acting.

For example, to leave for a better-paid job may be an understandable, but hardly a laudable action. Likewise, a 'personal' psychological account, which constructed his actions in the narrative character of developing potential (boredom, new challenges, possibility to exercise new skills), ignores the responsibilities of office and duties to country, as would an account based on some sort of clash or incompatibility of personalities. By constructing himself in the narrative character of role-following, the Chancellor provides a motive which is accountable; it is a way of characterizing his actions as being the 'right thing', proper and correct (rather than, say, trivial, unworthy, avoidable or capricious).

The art here, then, is to produce a *version of events* that supports this role-following account, and to make that version seem to be factual and 'out-there', something existing independently of Lawson and his own desires and concerns. There are at least three elements of this discourse which contribute to producing this effect.

First, the use of role discourse itself not only provides a motivational account, but an attributional one; it situates the relevant motives *outside* of the Chancellor and in features of his situation. That is, the offered motivation for resigning provides no basis for him to have fabricated or exaggerated his version of events; indeed, it presents him as acting selflessly. The effect is reinforced by his use of the familiar resignation letter construction '*I have regretfully concluded* that it is in the best interests of the government for me to resign'. This contrasts his own, personal, *desires* (or interests) with the *duties* of office; the personal and role motivations working rhetorically via their being placed in opposition. In effect, his version of events is offered not merely as a disinterested one, but as actively counter to his personal interests. What we see here, then, as we have seen before with the John Dean materials, and with Lawson's disputed press briefing (in Chapters 2 and 3), is that stake, interest or motivation is crucial to constructing factuality. Versions of events can be warranted by constructing them as disinterested or, even better, as *anti*-interested, as going *against* the speaker's interests as is the case with Lawson's resignation letter.

A second type of externalizing device can be seen at work in the style of descriptive language that is used in the resignation letter.

Walden 1: the successful conduct of economic policy is possible (.) only if there is and is seen to be (.) full agreement between the Prime Minister and the Chancellor of the Exchequer (.) ·hh recent events have confirmed (.) that this essential requirement cannot be satisfied

(.) so long as Alan Walters remains your personal economic adviser (.)

The first part of the letter (as read by Walden) takes an impersonal form. A law-like relationship exists in the world, and 'recent events' are doing the work of 'confirming' without the assistance of any human agent to interpret, marshal or order them. This form of 'empiricist' discourse has been found in studies of scientists' talk and writing which typically draws on a relatively coherent set of terms, grammatical styles, metaphors and figures of speech (Gilbert and Mulkay, 1984; McKinlay and Potter, 1987; Myers, 1990). Characteristically, and in a manner similar to the Chancellor's letter, in this form of discourse, data are depicted as 'doing confirming' and 'concluding' independently of the actions of scientists.

A third type of externalizing device in the letter is the use of what can be called the 'rhetoric of argumentation' (cf. Antaki and Leudar, 1990; Potter and Wetherell, 1988). Events are constructed in almost syllogistic form: if and only if p then q; not p therefore not q. The truth or validity of this argument in some abstract realm is beside the point – our concern is not at that level. It is that this form of construction will have a rhetorical pay-off merely by virtue of its argumentative form. The conclusion is presented as warranted by the impersonal operation of logic rather than the motivated inferences of humans (cf. McCloskey, 1985; Potter et al., 1991; Rorty, 1980).

There is a further notable feature contributing to this effect. The inferences are strengthened by what Pomerantz (1986) calls 'extreme case formulations'. Thus policy is successful *only* if there is *full* agreement which is *essential*; by using the extreme points of dimensions the Chancellor's case is made clear-cut and non-negotiable. Again, looked at rhetorically, one can consider the Chancellor's case as limiting the sorts of opportunities for undermining that would be afforded by less extreme expressions such as: policy is successful *usually* if there is *broad* agreement which is *helpful*.

Overall, then, we have suggested that the resignation letter can be read as accomplishing accountability for the Chancellor's resignation, and as warranting its own factuality in a number of ways; and we have noted some devices that promote these ends. It is important to emphasize at this point that this type of analysis of accountability and warranting is focused on discursive construction and functional orientation; we are not addressing the 'success' or 'effects' of these procedures. Indeed, from a rhetorical perspective the idea of 'success' or 'effects' as discrete, consensual categories becomes problematic (Billig, 1987).

At this point it may be useful to make a general comment on the analytical approach underlying discursive psychology. So far we have discussed the Chancellor's resignation letter as a relatively self-contained document. However, as we have indicated, it is only one part of a complex of disputes. The discourse analytical approach often benefits from focusing on one element in a complex – in this case the Chancellor's motive – and exploring how it is variously constructed in different texts. We have discussed in detail the heuristic value of exploring variation in accounts elsewhere (Potter and Mulkay, 1985; Potter and Wetherell, 1987; Wetherell and Potter, 1988). It provides two major benefits when, dealing with the current materials.

First, documenting variability provides a counter to the type of simple realist interpretations regularly found in memory and attribution research which treat the structuring of discourse as following from the nature of the events and actions that are described. Although the discourse model drawn on throughout this book offers good and plentiful *theoretical* reasons for rejecting such a view, the existence of this kind of variability is a particularly graphic and *practical* demonstration of its problems.

Secondly, and more usefully in the current context, a comparison of different versions provides important clues as to their rhetorical organizations. These versions are often designed not with their relation to events and actions as an overriding consideration; what counts most is their relation to alternatives, their capacity to undermine and frustrate competing versions (Billig, 1988a). Thus up to now we have dealt with the resignation letter, in part, by considering potential problems of accountability which arise with any action of this kind. There is some point to this as it is, in certain respects, the first document in a series. However, we shall need to pay increasing attention to the way versions of the Chancellor's resignation are designed in the light of alternatives as parts of arguments. This is immediately relevant because of the very specific manner in which the resignation letter is framed in the interview.

Formulating and rebutting a blaming

The interviewer's formulation of the letter has two noteworthy and quite characteristic features, which are somewhat in tension with one another. First, he uses Lawson's resignation letter as 'footing' (cf. Goffman, 1981; Levinson, 1988; and Box 2 above). That is, although Walden is what Goffman calls the *animator* of the letter (he speaks its words) he is not wanting to be taken as its *composer*, or as the *origin* of its viewpoint. In this way, the interviewer attends to the institutional requirement of neutrality in television interviews (Clayman, 1988, 1992; Heritage et al., 1988) – he is a mouthpiece rather than an interested party.

Secondly, although Brian Walden, the interviewer, uses this very explicit footing to display his neutrality, he nevertheless provides a very strong gloss on the resignation letter. Despite the absence of an open and explicitly formulated blaming of the Prime Minister in the Chancellor's letter, Walden glosses it unequivocally, before *and* after, as a claim of blame. Furthermore, he reads out only those sections of the letter that provide most basis for criticizing Thatcher, failing to report the rather different closing sentences:

> I am extremely grateful to you for the opportunity you have given me to serve in the Government, particularly in the last six and a half years as Chancellor; and I am proud of what we have achieved together. I shall, of course, continue to support the Government from the back-benches. (*Daily Telegraph*, 27 October 1989)

Here, then, we can see Walden attending to the twin tasks of displaying neutrality, while nevertheless putting searching and potentially confrontational points. He sets up the Prime Minister's first turn as a response to a blaming, but not one from himself.

The Prime Minister's response has a range of elements which deal with the blaming in different ways. She constructs a version which stresses a long, previously good relationship, so that although current disputes are not denied (which would be difficult to do in the context of discussing such a controversial resignation which has just been glossed as 'the most serious crisis of her career'), they are made secondary to what went before. She constructs her own psychological disposition as wanting him to stay rather than go, rebutting the further potential cause that she invoked his resignation because she wanted him to go, or that he went because she simply did not care about his advice.

Despite these intriguing complexities, the thing most interesting to us in the present discussion is the way that she too uses *role discourse* in the shape of the formulation 'advisers are there to advise, ministers are there to decide', and the implication of this for the Chancellor's motivation. This is a formulation which had some prominence in the dispute: she repeated it on six more occasions during the interview, and she used it in the parliamentary debating chamber, both immediately before the resignation became public and also on at least five occasions after that.

Again, we can consider this in terms of its construction and function, starting with function. First, it makes a general rhetorical contrast to the Chancellor's version, which has his resignation as a requirement of problems with the role, by asserting that the protagonists were acting in an entirely role or category *appropriate* manner. In this way it works to remove, or at least undermine, the Chancellor's espoused role-based motivation for his resignation. Secondly, it has a reflexive (Garfinkel, 1967; Heritage, 1984) element. By offering it as a counter to the Chancellor's version Mrs Thatcher implies that his version in some way misunderstands or contradicts this virtually self-evident formulation; by asserting *not* *x* she implies he has asserted *x*. It thus reflexively formulates Lawson as going against something commonplace, or definitionally true.

There is a further relevant element here. The Prime Minister can be seen as caught in a rhetorical dilemma (cf. Billig et al., 1988). While defending herself against (the interviewer's formulation of) the Chancellor's accusations, the kind of counter-blaming that might be expected in such a dispute has to be very carefully managed. This is because the Chancellor has been so closely associated with the Prime Minister herself; she appointed him and supported him for more than half her term of office. Criticisms of his judgement, say, or his competence could easily reflect back on her own judgement. Her stress on the long and fruitful relationship can be seen as one way of attending to this problem.

Furthermore, it is notable that the Prime Minister provides no *explicit* account of Lawson's motivation, she does not directly replace his version with one of her own. However, by systematically undermining his account she at least raises the possibility that some less laudable motivations were at work than the ones Lawson explicitly offered. It is probably significant that at this point in the controversy the Chancellor had yet to make a parliamentary speech about his resignation and he was due to be interviewed for the same television programme the following week. That is, the Prime Minister would be aware that he had two excellent opportunities to make damaging responses to any strong and explicit accusations that she might make on this occasion.

In terms of fact construction, the Prime Minister's response at the start of the interview works rather differently from those we have discussed up to now in this chapter. One way of approaching it is to consider fact construction in rhetorical terms. When part of an argument, the more effectively constructed a fact is, the harder it will be to rebut or undermine. We have seen in Chapter 5 that vulnerabilities can be generated by the inclusion of certain sorts of detail, for such details can provide a basis for constructing competing versions which attribute interest or question corroboration. Turned on its head, this means that vague formulations of events can, on occasion, be difficult to rebut. In effect, this is the point that Drew and Holt (1989) have made with respect to idiomatic formulations. Such formulations are robust with respect to challenge because of their figurative or formulaic quality.

The formulation 'advisers are there to advise (.) ministers are there to decide' has an abstract, epigrammatic quality shared with idioms. It does not offer any precise clues about how it should be applied to the particular events that are controversial, and it therefore does not provide any easy purchase for a critique in terms of its misapplication. Its present tense allows it to be heard either as a claim about correct practice or as a general maxim. It is not clear where such a critique would start. Furthermore, the formulation is virtually tautological: deciding is a commonplace category-based property of incumbents of the category 'ministers'; while advising is a category-constitutive property of 'advisers' (cf. Jayyusi, 1984; Potter and Halliday, 1990).

Constructing a more blameworthy motive

Before leaving this passage there is one final feature to address. We have already briefly noted that the segment 'I tried very hard to dissuade the Chancellor from going (.2) .hh but he had made up his mind and in the end I had to accept his resignation' is a report which formulates the Prime Minister as positively disposed to the Chancellor. However, there is another interesting element here. Having already undermined the Chancellor's role account of his motivation, it raises a question over the nature of his 'making up his mind': what is his *actual* motive for the decision to resign? Mrs Thatcher presents herself as arguing with him hard and long; if reasoning like this is unsuccessful, then perhaps there is a 'psychological' motive at work? There is a normative expectation that it is people who are 'dogmatic', 'emotionally charged' or 'closed minded' who find it hard to 'see reason'. We do not want to suggest that this passage presents such a strong psychologizing account; yet at the very least it is consistent with this, and opens up some rhetorical space for such a possibility.

Formulations by the Prime Minister later in the interview work in this direction rather more strongly:

Thatcher 6: somehow Nigel had made up his mind that he was going.

Thatcher 12: it was quite clear that he had made up his mind ·hh and there was <u>nothing</u> I could do to dissuade him (.4) quite clear (.2) er it was that was just (.) a fact of life and I had to accept it.

Here the 'somehow' suggests an ineffability about the Chancellor's decision-making process, something personal and capricious perhaps, rather than rational and explicable. Indeed, this effect is heightened by the contrast between the detailed, specific and elaborate rejections of the Chancellor's own account of why he resigned (at least, as developed by the interviewer), and the absence of any explicit account from the Prime Minister of why the Chancellor actually decided to go.

The second passage conveys the impression that his decision was based upon a strong prior commitment, in a way that reasoning would not be able to move. Moreover, it is visible ('quite clear', objectively there) from the Chancellor's demeanour despite not being explicable. Again, we do not want to over-interpret these passages. Our point is that there are elements in Mrs Thatcher's discourse, albeit weak or implicit ones, which direct attention to the Chancellor's psychology. Furthermore, this is once again an area where she can blame the Chancellor without raising the serious questions about her own judgement that, say, criticizing his policies or competence would inevitably do.

We can see this process of blaming continued in a more explicit manner after Lawson had delivered his parliamentary speech in the debate on the economy and after his own interview with Brian Walden. The following passage is taken from the regular parliamentary 'Prime Minister's question time' two days after the Lawson–Walden interview. Prime Minister Thatcher is here answering questions from the Leader of the Opposition (Mr Kinnock) which takes up the issue of whether she had lied in her interview when she claimed not to know whether sacking her economic adviser (Sir Alan Walters) would have prevented the resignation.

Mr Kinnock: When the Prime Minister was asked why the Chancellor resigned, why did she not tell the truth?
The Prime Minister: If my right hon. Friend had wanted to resign on a point of policy, I could have understood that. Policy is a matter for ministers. I find it totally incomprehensible that someone who has held the office of Chancellor with high standing, for six years, should want to resign over personality – [Interruption]
Mr Speaker: Order.
The Prime Minister: Over personality, with such suddenness and haste. [. . .] I tried to persuade my right hon. Friend not to go but it was clear that he was determined to go and go that day. (*Hansard*, 31 October 1989: 831–2)

Again, there are a number of subtle elements in this interchange.

The principal point of interest in this chapter is the way that Thatcher is now much more explicitly blaming than in her earlier interview. Of course, 'personality' could be used to mean many things. However, in the context, it appears to mark a contrast between the Chancellor's version, that it was his *duty* to resign because of the destabilizing effects of the adviser Walters, and the alternative version that he did not get on, *personally*, with Walters, or alternatively that he found Walters a *threat* to his position and credibility, such that his demand for Walters' sacking was a consequence of these more personal, less principled motivations. We can note here that the analysis concurs with the noisy jeers which erupt from the Opposition benches immediately on Thatcher's utterance of the word 'personality'. As before, the vagueness or lack of specificity of Thatcher's discourse can also be seen as a design feature contributing to its rhetorical effect; implications are less open to rebuttal than explicit statements.

The self is dependent on the world

So far we have discussed some of the ways in which a version of self can be established to do particular kinds of accounting. Specifically, we have examined the way Lawson developed his account in the narrative of the role player, pushed and pulled by the exigencies of context. In attribution terms, this situates the cause of his resignation outside his psychology and outside his sphere of control more generally; if he is going to act in a manner credible to the role he has no alternative but to resign. In parallel to this, we have examined the way Thatcher develops an alternative, at first in an indirect and hedged manner but later, after Lawson has made his major public pronouncements, in a more explicit and forceful manner. This alternative discounts Lawson's 'situational' version and offers instead a much more blaming account which has the resignation motivated by 'petty' concerns of troubled personal relationships and professional rivalry. The rhetorical force here, of course, is not merely to direct blame onto Lawson, but to direct it away from herself.

One of the lessons of Wittgensteinian linguistic philosophy and more recent ethnomethodological developments is that motive talk of this kind does not have a simple inner referent but is a performative speech act in a complex language game. Mills' famous epigram that 'the different reasons that men give for their actions are not themselves without reasons' (1940: 904) expresses this point very effectively. Motive espousal or attribution is itself a move in a moral universe. A corollary of this is that no single 'first person' avowal is likely to be taken as sufficient to warrant the use of such motive talk; its logic depends on its place in the entire language game.

In terms of our example, neither Lawson claiming that his motive was role based, nor Thatcher claiming that it was based in personality dynamics, is likely to be convincing *on its own* to a sceptical audience. In particular, these speakers will need to develop an account of the *circumstances*, in the form of *event descriptions*, such that these specific psychological attributions can be sensible and warranted. In effect, to stabilize a convincing version of what is going on in Lawson's mind it is necessary for both him and Thatcher to produce convincing versions of his context of action. Put simply, *to build his mind each of them has to build a version of his world.*

Despite its simplicity, this point cannot be emphasized too strongly, for it is at the heart of many of the problems that we have diagnosed in the perceptual-cognitive tradition within psychology. What it does is break down the idea that there are certain classes of utterances whose interest is primarily in their relation to some putative reality, and other classes of ascriptive, confessional or revelatory utterances whose interest is in what they reveal about self, motivation and cognition. The point is that in natural discourse the former sorts of utterances may be offered, and designed in their specifics, precisely to allow inferences about mental life and cognition. And moreover, as we shall show, the converse is also true; the establishment of versions of the world may depend on public depictions of mind and motivation.

The controversy over Lawson's resignation was conducted largely through fact constructions, or event descriptions, all bearing an inferential relationship to Lawson's mental state (his motives, intentions, intransigence, understandings). We shall concentrate on a section of the Thatcher–Walden interview to illustrate this process at work. As we have seen, one of the key issues relating to Lawson's motive for resignation is whether it was a principled one responding to economic and political problems due to visible conflicts between Chancellor and Prime Minister in the form of her adviser, Walters, or whether it was a result of less laudable 'personal' motivations.

The credibility of each of the contrasting versions of Lawson's motive depends on the actual circumstances of the resignation – yet there is no neutral independent record of those circumstances; indeed, it is not clear that such a record is even conceivable. One of the crucial issues at stake, then, is *what happened*; what were those circumstances? In the Thatcher–Walden interview we can see both parties manufacturing versions of events and circumstances that carry implications for Lawson's motive, and for competing causal explanations. The next extract follows directly after the opening section of the Thatcher interview:

> *Walden* 2: ·tch let's ↑look though at what he sa:ys you see (.) he: is making the (.) claim (.) here (.) that (.) >successful conduct of economic policy is possible only if there is <u>seen</u> to be full agreement between the Prime Minister and the Chancellor of the Exchequer< .hh now he's right about that isn't he
>
> *Thatcher* 2: yes ·hh and I am right about the successful six ye:ars he's had in the Treasury (.) <u>very</u> successful the economy of Britain has made <u>great</u> strides under his Chancellorship ·h (.) and we have worked together those are the ↑facts (*W:* But y–) and no one can get round them ·hh it has been ex<u>treme</u>ly successful
>
> *Walden* 3: but you are not claiming Prime Minister (.) it may or may not have been extremely successful (.) but you are not claiming that there <u>was</u> seen to be full agreement between yourself and the Chancellor are ↑you
>
> *Thatcher* 3: ·hhh I am claiming that I <u>fully</u> backed and supported the Chancellor (.) of course we discuss things >we discuss things in Cabinet we discuss things in the economic committee .hh we discuss things with <u>many</u> advisers< there is not only one adviser there are many advisers in the Treasury ·hh we have <u>many</u> advisers and we hammered out a policy and on that policy and on that policy we were <u>totally</u> agreed (*W:* Tch–) totally and it was implemented and it was implemented <u>very</u> successfully and the success <u>matters</u>

Walden starts with what can be considered a response pursuit (Pomerantz, 1984c) by treating Thatcher's first turn as not an adequate response to his question about blame. He focuses in on the issue about perceived disagreement. In her second turn she starts with a brief token of agreement and then reiterates her account of economic success. Again, Walden pursues the blame issue, and this time his formulation seems to leave Thatcher with the choice of either agreeing that there was not seen to be full agreement between her and Lawson, or else to disagree, and thereby directly contradict a central point in Lawson's resignation letter, which could be seen as self-refuting.

Although it appears that Thatcher is on the horns of a dilemma here, either of which will wound her, she deals with it in a rather neat way in turn three. Rather than agreeing or disagreeing with Walden she produces a version which attends to the issue but reworks it. Specifically, she produces an alternative version of *disagreement* in terms of *discussion*. Discussion can involve disagreement; it is not a contradictory version, and yet it suggests a constructive and cooperative process.

If it were just this basic re-wording, swapping 'discussion' for 'disagreement', this example would be very similar to Drew's courtroom example where 'sit with you' is replaced with 'sat at our table' (see Chapter 2). However, here there is considerably more rhetorical work going on. First of all, arguments with Lawson are not only formulated as 'discussion' rather than entrenched disagreement, but they are then developed into an elaborated alternative version:

>   Of course we discuss things
> (1) →   >we discuss things in Cabinet
> (2) →   we discuss things in the economic committee ·hh
> (3) →   we discuss things with <u>many</u> advisers<

As we noted in Chapter 5, listings of this kind have a number of rhetorical uses in persuasive discourse. Here the listing seems to suggest that discussion is going on continually and routinely, with nothing amiss, in a number of different settings; and, although Thatcher never formulates it in this way, it provides a way of making sense of the disagreement interpretation: so *much* discussion and such *varied* discussion could easily be mistaken for disagreement.

A second feature to note is how the *number* of advisers is emphasized:

> there is not only one adviser
> there are many advisers in the Treasury ·hh
> we have <u>many</u> advisers

This contrast works to downgrade the significance of Alan Walters who becomes just one adviser among many (for more on 'quantification rhetoric' of this kind, see Potter et al., 1991). This in turn weakens Lawson's efforts at externalized attribution. Walters becomes implausible as a *situational* cause for the resignation, being thus constructed as less *distinctive* (using the terminology of attribution theory: see Chapter 4). So we are pushed back to Lawson's psychology (an actor attribution) for an explanation. But, as with consensus (Chapter 5), distinctiveness occurs here as no mere feature of the world, or of events, to be merely perceived, but as a *construction* of events done in discourse and organized rhetorically.

Another notable aspect of Thatcher's response is her use of a form of words to describe the policy process that attends to both horns of the dilemma in Walden's previous turn:

> *Thatcher* 3: we <u>hamm</u>ered out a policy
>   and on that <u>policy</u>
>   and on that policy we were <u>tot</u>ally agreed

Walden 3: tch–
Thatcher 3: totally

'Hammering out' a policy invokes the possibility of disagreement, indeed strong disagreement. It suggests hard bargaining and potential dispute. However, the product of this is a single policy on which there was agreement. Thus this account allows for disagreement, indeed requires it for there to be any need to hammer out policy, and yet the account has agreement as the end result. Note also that 'hammered' is another idiomatic formulation, and as such does not lend itself to easy critical decomposition. So without at any point explicitly agreeing or disagreeing with Walden's and Lawson's formulations, Thatcher's alternative draws on a number of their features in a manner which suggests that things are working routinely, and that there is nothing fundamentally awry in the processes of government. This, of course, undermines Lawson's role-based motivational account, which depends on precisely that notion of an unresolved conflict with Thatcher.

The world (in its versions) is rhetorically constructed

Having illustrated the dependence of versions of psychological phenomena such as beliefs and motives on versions of the world, we can start to see how dispute over such versions, and especially the fine detail of the dispute, can be made sense of as a dispute over the social and psychological inferences that they make available. This insight into the inferential work performed by ostensibly descriptive discourse drives us back to details, to the particularities and sequential placing of descriptive terms.

The following exchange takes place about a third of the way through the interview and follows Thatcher questioning the idea that a controversial article written by Walters could have led to the resignation: 'it is not possible that this small particular thing could result in this particular resignation.' She suggests that they move away from discussing the resignation itself and concentrate on general economic matters. Walden responds:

Walden 8: >well I want to ask you about that of course Prime Minister but let's come back to Professor Alan Walters< you see it isn't just (.) this article that he wrote eighteen months ago and that got recent publicity (.2) it's very well known (.) and you must know it (.) er that Professor Alan Walters has been going round the City (.) he's been attending <u>lunches</u> he's been giving <u>jour</u>nalists (.) his <u>views</u> on matters and he's been expressing disagreements with Law↑son (.) Lawson wouldn't just have <u>ob</u>jected about an ancient art↓icle (.) what he objected to is the <u>whole</u> <u>basis</u> of Alan Walters' activities (.) now <u>isn't</u> <u>that</u> <u>the</u> <u>case</u>

Thatcher 8: ·hhh many people in departments at the top of Civil Service departments <u>go</u> <u>out</u> and have lunches in the city (.) they have to keep in contact particularly if they are in <u>economic</u> depart↑ments that is <u>not</u> <u>unknown</u> <u>at</u> <u>all</u> but Bri↑an I am not going to get involved in this tittle tattle (.2) I have had a very competent adviser (.2) ·hh Nigel also had very competent advisers they worked together (.) Alan and his advisers (.) I am not going to get involved in this (.2) there are far bigger things to consider (.) the economy has been run extremely successfully (.) we have created more wealth than ever before (.) and spread it more widely than ever before (.) a standard of living that people have never <u>had</u> before and a reputation of Britain overseas (.) that is second to <u>none</u> <u>these</u> are the achievements and I am not concerned with the tittle tattle (.) I am concerned with getting on with the job (.) and that I shall do

There is a great deal of complexity in this exchange. Let us look first at Walden's turn. This starts by orientating to, but rejecting, Thatcher's proposed topic shift and bringing the discussion back to Alan Walters and his activities. Walden constructs a contrast between Thatcher's minimizing focus on one article (the 'small particular things') and the actual significance of Walters' other activities. This contrast (A/B) is rhetorically formatted such that the emphasized part is made up of a formulation (F) that unpacks into a three-part list:

(A) →   it isn't just (.) this article that he wrote eighteen months ago and that got recent publicity (.2)

(B) →   it's very well known (.) and you must know it (.) er that

(F) →   Professor Alan Walters has been going round the City (.)

(1) →   he's been attending <u>lunches</u>

(2) →   he's been giving <u>journalists</u> (.) his <u>views</u> on matters

(3) →   and he's been expressing <u>disagreements</u> with Law↑son

Walden here builds the second half of the contrast by first prefacing it in implicit consensus terms as common knowledge: 'very well known'. This is neat as it invokes a wide range of consensual knowers without giving any particulars about who they are that could potentially be contested. The formulation that follows – 'Walters has been going round the City' – suggests that Walters has been conducting a systematic campaign, an impression bolstered by the unpacking of the formulation into a three-part list of more specific activities. These provide grounds for the citation of Walters as a crucial and legitimate reason for the resignation. We can see here, then, Walden still pursuing the response to his/Lawson's blame accusation introduced in his very first turn.

As Pomerantz (1984c) notes, pursuing a response may involve

attempting to establish 'common ground'; Walden's version here can be understood as an attempt to warrant the common ground that there were indeed some problems with Alan Walters' activities. The turn ends with yet another contrast between Thatcher's citation of a specific article and the rest of Walters' activities. This time the contrast is heightened by using the extreme case formulations (A/B) 'ancient' and 'whole basis' (cf. Pomerantz, 1986) for each part:

(A) →   Lawson wouldn't just have <u>obj</u>ected about an ancient article↓
         (.)
(B) →   what he objected to is the <u>whole</u> <u>basis</u> of Alan Walters'
         activities

At this point, then, Thatcher is faced with a version which provides a basis for Lawson's own resignation account, and therefore potentially a basis for blame to be directed at herself. Some of the rhetorical difficulty this created for her may perhaps be indicated by the notably long and audible intake of breath at the start of her response. We will concentrate on two features of her response to round off this chapter's discussion of the rhetorical construction of versions in the interview.

The first approach that Mrs Thatcher uses is similar to the one that she drew on in turn three discussed above. She builds a version in the form of a 'script'-like construction of routine social events (Schank and Abelson, 1977). This shares features with the potentially problematic one but offers different inferences about Lawson's motives. In particular, she picks on one of the activities mentioned – attending lunches in the City – and characterizes this as scripted: a commonplace and entirely acceptable activity which is a necessary part of government work:

·hhh many people in departments at the top of Civil Service departments <u>go</u> <u>out</u> and have lunches in the city (.) they have to keep in contact particularly if they are in eco<u>no</u>mic depart↑ments that is <u>not</u> <u>unknown</u> <u>at</u> <u>all</u>

The construction of this extract is similar to that found in defendants' courtroom talk. Atkinson and Drew (1979) have noted that in legal settings defendants recurrently attend to two issues: on the one hand, they attempt to produce accounts that mitigate or soften the blamings that are developed by counsel; on the other, they attempt to minimize disagreement between their versions and those of counsel. Here Thatcher's version both undermines the blaming and at the same time maintains major features of Walden's version in a reworked form. She does not deny that Walters ate in the City; rather she constructs a different sense for this activity: he is not running a systematic campaign against Lawson's view of the economy but conscientiously following the requirement of his economic post. Again, the role construction provides accountability.

Our invocation of 'script' theory here illustrates once again the difference between cognitive and discursive psychology. Script representations are well-established features of both social cognition theory (Abelson, 1976; Eiser, 1986) and of the study of memory (Bower et al., 1979; Cohen, 1989; Schank, 1982). However, rather than understanding the 'scripted' description of Walters' actions as indicative of Thatcher's underlying mental representation, we can see it here as a contextually occasioned production, a way of discursively *constructing* events that attend to their attributional significance within a sequence involving responsibility and blame.

Note also how script formulations link with the concerns of attribution theory; they construct *consensus*. Routine, scripted activities for government advisers are thereby consensual ones, done generally by such actors, and thus requiring no special explanation internal to actors. Several of the lexical details in the extract ('*many* people', 'they *have* to . . .', '*not unknown at all*') display this relationship between routine scripts, consensus constructions and attributional accountability. And the idea that this is not only routine, but 'not unknown at all' precisely counters and reformulates Walden's earlier 'very well known' observation about what Walters had been doing. Effectively, what Walters was 'very well known' (Walden) to be doing, is 'not unknown at all' (Thatcher) to be the unremarkable, scripted behaviour of a government adviser, acting in role.

Furthermore, this consensual construction of Walters (orientated to explaining his 'going round the City') functions as an embedded part of a further construction by Lawson, in which Walters figures attributionally as the situation element in Lawson's resignation. In Thatcher's discourse, Walters' actions are highly 'consensual', and thereby possess 'low distinctiveness' with regard to Lawson's. The important point here is that the sorts of sentence propositions that attribution theory takes as decontextualized representations of events or of perceptions, may be seen in context as flexibly constructible versions. The character of Walters' actions, and their relevance to Lawson's, are neither out there in the world, nor forced upon us by their linguistic expression. Rather, words construct those actions as such, as part of a rhetorically embedded sequence of formulation and counter-formulation, trait and role, blame and innocence.

The extract from Thatcher is similar to Atkinson and Drew's material in another way too, and again note how the work is done in the detail. They note that defendants often *select* areas of blame to defend themselves on, which are weaker or where they have a stronger line of defence. Here we see Thatcher focusing on the elements of Walden's version which have Walters in contact with the City; however, she ignores the elements which involve Walters talking to journalists and expressing explicit disagreements.

The other feature of Mrs Thatcher's response is much less typical of courtrooms, however, although it does appear frequently in political and everyday arguments. It involves dealing with an argumentative point by changing levels: instead of responding directly to the point, the response is directed at the form of argument that the point is couched in, or to some feature of its delivery; the speaker 'goes meta' (Simons, 1989b; cf. Billig, 1989a; Edwards, 1989). We can see this in the following, where Thatcher formulates Walden's version of Walters' activities as 'tittle tattle':

[. . .]
Brițan I am not going to get involved in this tittle tattle
[. . .]
I am not concerned with the tittle tattle (.) I am concerned with getting on with the job (.) and that I shall do

With her first point about 'tittle tattle' (the *Concise Oxford Dictionary* definition is simply 'gossip'), Thatcher ceases to argue about the details of events and attempts to undermine the legitimacy of the whole case. The description of Walden's version as 'tittle tattle' does a number of things. It is a negative evaluation which *suggests* the story is unreliable but does not claim this outright; gossip is often treated as a bad thing but not always as false, merely suspect. This makes it difficult to rebut straightforwardly. Furthermore, it is a formulation with idiomatic features, and therefore has the rhetorical benefits that we have repeatedly seen accrue to this form of discourse. Finally, it presents a well-grounded opportunity for Thatcher to shift topic ('there are far bigger things to consider') and focus her talk on her economic record.

There is an interesting tension between this latest move by Mrs Thatcher, and that of establishing a common ground but reinterpreting it, that was seen slightly earlier in the same turn of talk. Tensions of this kind are perfectly understandable if we see the task here as a pragmatic one, however; both of Thatcher's responses to the criticism implied in the question serve to rebut its blaming force. Again, similar variation is well documented in Atkinson and Drew's (1979) study of courtroom interaction.

This by no means marks the end of this particular dispute, which Walden pursues for several more turns. However, it serves to give a flavour of some of the complexities of the rhetorical construction of factual versions. As the issue of blame is pursued across a number of turns, different versions of the facts are marshalled. Their significance does not derive from their accuracy in the abstract, but from their resilience to immediate rebuttal (and, presumably, their perceived adequacy for an overhearing audience) as well as their implications for the nature of Lawson's motivation for resigning. This motive itself is important specifically because of the implications of blame that it has in the current interaction for the Prime Minister's own responsibility; just as the interviewer Walden's competence and neutrality are threatened if Thatcher can accomplish him as relentlessly pursuing tittle tattle, in favour of Lawson, and in preference to more important matters.

Role, face and discursive psychology

One response that we have met on several occasions when arguing for discursive psychology is that a new name is being used for a theoretical perspective that has a long pedigree in psychology, as self-presentation or impression management. The basis for this claim seems to be in noting some general shared features. For example, both concentrate on interaction as a process occurring between people rather than focusing on individual cognitive processes, and both have come to emphasize variability in human actions; self-presentation studies have repeatedly shown the way people modify their behaviour in accordance with the exigencies of different social contexts (Baumeister, 1982). Also, the emphasis on accountability in discursive psychology is shared by Goffman, undoubtedly the best known of the self-presentation researchers.

In fact, there are considerable complexities here because of the wide disparities between the way self-presentation is understood in the context of social cognition research (Tetlock and Manstead, 1985), as part of symbolic interactionist theories (Hewitt, 1979), as part of Goffman's system of concepts for understanding social life (1971), and in its more linguistic instantiations, such as Brown and Levinson's (1987) research on the notion of politeness as a cultural universal. Without trying to disentangle the various areas of theoretical overlap and disagreement (cf. Schegloff, 1988b, on Goffman) we will concentrate on just two points.

First, face-saving, or impression management, when understood as a global motivation for activity, can easily become entirely empty. For example, we could perhaps understand the subtle discursive techniques drawn on to construct a blaming by a barrister in court as part of her self-presentation; yet this does not account for the detail of what is going on, and raises as many questions as it answers. Secondly, and more importantly, rather than attempting to use self-presentation as a definitive version or theory of how people act, we can make precisely the same move as we have with the notions of role and script. That is, we can consider the way participants themselves draw on the notion and the sorts of interactional work that they can use it to perform.

We can illustrate this with further material on the Lawson resignation. The following extract is a contribution to a parliamentary debate on the economy held a few days after the resignation. Here a backbench Labour MP takes the opportunity to criticize both Lawson and government policies.

> *Allen:* There has been some speculation that the former Chancellor of the Exchequer resigned because of the actions of the Prime Minister or Sir Alan Walters. That is not my view. The former Chancellor of the Exchequer resigned having read the Treasury's economic forecast for next year. It is one thing for a Chancellor to carry the economic can when he is in charge of economic policy and another to be the fall guy for someone else's economic policy. The Treasury forecasts that were prepared for the Autumn Statement were available for the Chancellor to see. There was no need for a crystal-ball – he read the book and got out from under. Much of the forecast information was probably available in the Summer recess: all that was needed was the opportunity artificially to up the stakes on his excuse – Walters – and get out with as much political kudos as he could muster.

(*Hansard*, 31 October 1989: 243)

What is fascinating about this extract is it accomplishes a blaming of Lawson and government economic policy using a complex self-presentation account. It characterizes government economic policy as having been such a disaster that it threatened to ruin Lawson's reputation. So Lawson contrived some circumstances where he could resign, but be seen to be doing so for principled reasons rather than out of self-interest. Indeed, there is a double level of self-presentation going on here; for not only is Lawson presenting himself as resigning on grounds of principle, but Thatcher is presenting events as though the Chancellor is running the economy, when really she is. In pragmatic terms this two-fold split between the display and the real motivations allows the speaker to blame Lawson, for acting in a self-interested and deceitful manner, and also to blame Thatcher, for being responsible for the putative economic ills. The central point, then, is that self-presentation, like the notion of role itself, provides a considerable flexibility because it distinguishes action from motivation; whatever the action, different motives and strategies can be depicted as underlying it. Many stories are possible in a world were the reality differs from the appearance (Potter, 1987).

This example illustrates again the main themes of this chapter, which concerns the complex manner in which versions of the world and versions of mind and self are mutually dependent. The speaker's construction of Lawson's motives is part of his establishment of problems with the economy; they must be that bad because Lawson is trying to disassociate himself. Equally, the so-described forthcoming problems with the economy provide much of the grounds for the sense of this version of Lawson's motivation. Impression management features here not as an analyst's explanatory schema, but as a participants' category, a construction of what Lawson was doing and why, that serves to undermine both Lawson's and Thatcher's positions on the affair.

This chapter has also shown again the value of considering factual discourse as attending to two fundamental issues. On the one hand, it is constructed to contribute to particular actions (here to blame and mitigate). The longer the dispute continues the more 'reports' of events and contexts are generated. This is what we expect, of course, in the light of Pomerantz's (1984b) point that giving claims a basis is a sign of dispute rather than harmony; warranting is an occasioned phenomenon, done when it is considered to be needed, and shaped for its occasion. Furthermore, as we noted in Chapter 4, this involvement of factual reports with stake and rhetoric is precisely one of the features missed by much traditional research (Edwards and Potter, 1992b). On the other hand, factual discourse is constructed to be apparently factual and resilient to rhetorical onslaught. In the course of this chapter and previous ones we have documented a broad range of such resources that can be used in the establishment of 'out-there-ness' of versions or, in Latour's (1987) terms, to ratchet statements up and down through a hierarchy of modalization.

7

Discursive Psychology

Much of the discourse-orientated research and theorizing that has been carried out in psychology up to now has been organized around critiques of existing theoretical concepts, perspectives or analytical practices. This tendency has had the important benefit of showing the relevance of such work to issues of psychological concern and helping prevent it being marginalized as relevant only to linguistics or sociology or whatever. However, as a byproduct, this has led to discourse work being, at times, too structured around the traditional disciplinary concerns of psychology. Indeed, the theoretical coherence of discourse work has not always been apparent, and it has sometimes even been construed as merely an alternative analytical strategy for dealing with traditional research questions; a strategy, perhaps, for those who have taken seriously the critiques of traditional psychological methods that were developed in the 1970s (for example, Armistead, 1974; Brenner et al., 1985; Gergen, 1978; Harré, 1979).

In this book we have also taken as our starting point traditional psychological perspectives: memory and attribution, used as representatives of the cognitive and social cognition perspectives in psychology more generally. However, we have been concerned to develop, in our exploration of the limitations of these perspectives, a coherent discourse-orientated alternative; an alternative that we call 'discursive psychology' to underline the fact that it is a viable perspective on psychological life rather than just a mode of empirical analysis.

For the greater part of this final chapter our goal is tentatively to formulate some of the features of a discursive psychological alternative to the traditional concepts of memory and attribution. This is by no means intended to be a complete account of what discursive psychology might consist of. For example, we do not explore some of the ideological and critical concerns that have been developed in detail elsewhere (Billig, 1991; Billig et al., 1988; Wetherell et al., 1987; Wetherell and Potter, forthcoming). Nevertheless, it pulls together themes and concepts that have been developed in different chapters of this book, and other work, and starts to map out some of the ways in which they relate together.

To emphasize this growing coherence, we have referred to this as the 'discursive action model' (DAM), but readers should be alerted to the fact that this is not a model in the more usual psychological sense of the term; it is perhaps better understood (see Box 9) as a conceptual scheme that captures some of the features of participants' discursive practices that we have found it necessary to distinguish, and illustrates some of the relationships between them. These features are not meant to be seen as independent, although some provide particular focuses for research.

The discursive action model comes in three sections, each of which can itself be broken down into three elements. We will start with a bald listing of the basic elements of the model and then go on to flesh out some of the details using examples from earlier chapters and other discourse-orientated work.

DISCURSIVE ACTION MODEL

Action
1 The focus is on action, not cognition.
2 Remembering and attribution become, operationally, reportings (and accounts, description, formulations, versions and so on) and the inferences that they make available.
3 Reportings are situated in activity sequences such as those involving invitation refusals, blamings and defences.

Fact and interest
4 There is a dilemma of stake or interest, which is often managed by doing attribution via reports.
5 Reports are therefore constructed/displayed *as* factual by way of a variety of discursive techniques.
6 Reports are rhetorically organized to undermine alternatives.

Accountability
7 Reports attend to the agency and accountability in the reported events.
8 Reports attend to the accountability of the current speaker's action, including those done in reporting.
9 The latter two concerns are often related, such that 7 is deployed for 8, and 8 is deployed for 7.

Action

DAM is a model of action, not a model of cognition. This is a major departure from the perceptually and cognitively based approaches of both cognitive psychology and social cognition. As

Box 9 *DAM the model*

Derek: DAM.

Jonathan: What's the matter?

Derek: No, the discursive action model. People are going to say it's not a proper model. I mean, it doesn't really tell you how things work. It's not very specific.

Jonathan: You mean it's not a psychological process model? That's the point, isn't it?

Derek: Well, yes, but why call it that? It's just going to annoy everybody. The cognitivists will object that it's not a proper model because it doesn't specify mental processes, nor even a series of actions. And the discursive and constructionist people won't like it because they don't like models anyway, and they'll think we're giving too much away calling it one.

Jonathan: OK, maybe we could say it's a higher level kind of model. Not a process model, whatever that is, but a set of higher order principles that orientate any psychologist to important features of everyday reports and explanations, that might then provide a basis for generating a series of lower level, more specific models for actual occasions.

Derek: That wasn't very specific, was it?

Jonathan: Why do we have to be specific all of a sudden?

Derek: It's a matter of our own rhetoric, who we are trying to convince, and avoid alienating. We could just call it a 'set of policies and recommendations for discursive enquiry . . .'

Jonathan: 'SOPARFDE'?

Derek: Hmm. So we lose DAM's neat memorability. It makes a nice little TLA.

Jonathan: What's a . . . oh yes. Three letter acronym.

Derek: What if we make a virtue of the idea that it's going to be objectionable. It draws attention to the issue of cognition and rhetoric, to different kinds of explanations of talk and action.

Jonathan: Yes, that's more like it. And, anyway, it's not just recommendations for enquiry, is it? It does try to spell out what participants, rather than analysts, are doing.

Derek: And while we're being whimsical, we could say that its own textual form, as a so-called model, and as a neat little acronym, is yet another reflexive reminder of the constructiveness and rhetoric of description, and the argumentative nature of any explanatory formulation.

Jonathan: DAM the TLA.

Derek: QED.

we argued in Chapter 1, traditionally memories and attributions are perceptually derived cognitive phenomena. That is, they are conceptualized in terms of mental constructs, representations or processes. Within DAM they are recast as things that people and groups do. Discursive psychology generally is concerned with people's practices: communication, interaction, argument; and the organization of those practices in different kinds of settings.

This recasting is on both a theoretical and an operational level. In theoretical terms it is designed to alleviate some of the reductive and individualist tendencies of cognitivism and to take a much more functional, naturalistic approach to traditional concerns. Thus its starting point is curiosity about what remembering is, and is for, in everyday settings; what is the nature and role of attributions of causal responsibility in ordinary life? This theoretical reorientation leads to an entirely different analytical grounding of the phenomena of interest. For studying natural interaction in this way confronts the researcher with discourse: actions performed through talk, texts and various forms of writing. In discourse, memories and remembering can be treated as the giving of reports of 'what went on', the offering of accounts, the deployment of versions, descriptions and formulations. Likewise, attributions can be treated as either the explicit upshots and conclusions about causal relations that are offered in these reports, or else the upshots that they are organized to make available.

In everyday life, these discursive actions do not occur in isolation but as part of activity sequences. Typically, such sequences involve interpersonal or intergroup issues involving blame, responsibility, reward, compliment, invitation and so on. It is these activity sequences, we suggest, that are the primary stuff of lived human life; and it is they that give sense to the individual discursive acts which make them up. Thus one of the central objects of discursive psychology can best be described as the nature of discursive action as part of an activity sequence.

All of the various analyses that we have developed in different chapters of this book illustrate this changed perspective. Take our reworking of Neisser's study of John Dean's memory, for example. Instead of following Neisser's ecological cognitivism and attempting to use Dean's testimony as a pathway to the nature of the cognitive processes that allow him to remember correctly, we took Dean's testimony, and the various reports of events in the Oval Office it contained, as discursive acts which were part of broader activity sequences involving blame, responsibility and mitigation. That is, we tried to make sense of the nature of Dean's reports – their selection of terms, style of delivery and so on – by considering what they could contribute to the activity sequence at hand, most importantly, of course, mitigating his own guilt through building on attempts to support him by 'sympathetic' examiners and deflecting attempts to focus blame on him by 'hostile' examiners.

Other discourse studies have developed similar lines of argument, reworking cognitivist conceptualizations and replacing them with analyses of action situated within a discursive and rhetorical context. The most sustained work of this kind has been on the notions of attitude and belief (Billig, 1987, 1991; Potter and Wetherell, 1987, 1988; Smith 1987); categorization and schematization (Billig, 1985, 1987; Condor, 1988; Edwards, 1991; Potter, 1988b; Potter and Halliday, 1990; Potter and Reicher, 1987; Potter and Wetherell, 1987; Widdicomb and Wooffitt, 1990, 1992); social representations (Billig, 1988b, 1992b; Litton and Potter, 1985; McKinlay et al., 1992; Potter and Litton, 1985; Potter and Wetherell, 1987); conversational remembering (Edwards and Middleton, 1986a,b, 1987, 1988; Goodwin, 1987) and conceptual learning in children (Edwards, 1992a,b; Edwards and Mercer, 1987; Walkerdine, 1988). We suggest that, taken together, the general coherence and fruitfulness of this work provides a strong warrant for the action emphasis of discursive psychology.

Of course, we recognize that the cognitive psychology of memory and of attribution allows for the idea that when people report events, or perform attributions in talk, they may not simply be revealing their true underlying representations of events or causes. The issue is, what do we do about it. In the cognitive approach, it is recognized that people may lie, distort or misrepresent what they *really* think and know, and it is precisely the purpose of experimental designs to exclude or control for those sorts of interferences, or else to introduce them as variables and study their effects. Further, it can sensibly be argued that whatever people say, they must have some sort of underlying cognitive machinery – they have to *be able* to deal with versions and inferences, even in DAM. However, DAM is not designed to deny *all* sorts of cognitive organization. Rather, it questions some major assumptions and procedures through which particular kinds of underlying cognitions are traditionally defined.

The major issue is the treatment of language, as providing, when properly sanitized and shorn of context and usage, a window upon stable underlying representations of the world. It questions the grounds upon which the very ideas of true, underlying knowledge and reasoning are based. Discursive psychology argues that, if underlying mental structures are what are required, then these must be just the ones that allow people to perform all this social action in talk, all this situated and occasioned version production, rhetoric and accountability, and not some idea of what people abstractedly 'really think' (Edwards, 1992b). The study of situated discourse redefines and relocates the relations between language and understandings, and it does this by placing language as representation (whether of cognition or of reality) in a position subordinate to language as action.

Fact and interest

One of the pervasive features of everyday life that has been most systematically purged from studies of both remembering and attribution is the centrality of participants' stake or interest. As we stressed in Chapter 6, it is not that we, as theorists, are proposing a motivational account or model of what people say. This attention to stake or interest is a feature of the content and organization of discourse. People *treat each other*, and often treat *groups*, as entities with desires, motivations, institutional allegiances and biases, and they display these concerns in their reports and attributional inferences. Anyone who produces a version of something that happened in the past, or who develops a stretch of talk that places blame on someone or some category of persons, does so at the risk of having their claims discounted as the consequence of stake or interest. The Mandy Rice-Davies complaint ('he would, wouldn't he?' – see Box 7) looms into consideration. Because their discourse displays these concerns, we suggest that participants should be thought of as caught in a *dilemma of stake or interest*: how to produce accounts which attend to interests without being undermined as interested.

This dilemma can be managed in a variety of ways. However, one approach which we have explored in detail in this book is to examine how it is managed through the use of reports or versions. That is, people can perform attributional actions such as blamings indirectly or implicitly through providing an ostensibly disinterested factual report which allows others to follow through the upshot or implications of the report. It is here, above all, that we have pulled together the traditionally separate concerns of memory and attribution, of course. For the doing of reports ('remembering') becomes a principal way of accomplishing blamings, mitigations and other inflections on responsibility ('attributions'). This directs our attention to very different features of remembering from the competency (accuracy, capacity and so on) concerns central to cognitive psychology, while at the same time suggesting that attribution research, which has overwhelmingly concentrated on entirely disinterested renderings of explicit responsibility, has bypassed a crucial realm of socially significant activity.

Although the analytical strand of this book has concentrated on extended sequences of political discourse, we have also suggested that courtrooms are a rich arena for the study of remembering and attributional discourse; the *raison d'être* of a court is, after all, the establishment of blame or innocence via establishing what happened. In the light of DAM we can expect such talk to be organized to attend to attributional issues, often through the use of reports or accounts. For example, Watson (1983) has shown how the description of the protagonists in terms of group membership categories ('white men', 'black sisters', and so on) performs *indirect* attributional and motivational work. *Without detectably straying from truth or accuracy*, it deploys descriptive categories which establish an act of killing as representing a group interest, and therefore promotes the actor as less *personally* culpable for it than would be the case with a merely self-motivated act of murder. More subtly and indirectly still, Wowk (1984) examines how a murderer's description of his victim's behaviour and speech before the attack implies relevant category membership (that of a prostitute who approached and abused him) and so provides mitigation for the murder, by implying provocation, involvement and lack of innocence on her part. It spreads accountability by dissolving agency into the social interaction between murderer and victim (cf. Drew, 1990; Wooffitt, 1990).

Another example of an indirect device for attributing blame, which we explored in Chapter 6, is to draw upon role and trait talk, where role acting or acting in line with a particular personality type is discursively deployed as a form of attributional accounting. In an analysis of accounts of violent political protest, Wetherell and Potter (1989) found that excuses and mitigations of police violence were constructed via the use of personality and role talk, such as:

> I think the police acted very well. They're only human. If they lashed out and cracked a skull occasionally, it was, hah, only a very human action I'm sure.

> . . . in a way they didn't have much choice . . . they've got to do their job . . . a lot of people tend to forget that. (Wetherell and Potter, 1989: 213–15)

In the first example, police action is constructed as natural, only human, and therefore excusable – what anybody might have done in the circumstances. In the second, it is role behaviour that removes responsibility: they acted not as universal individuals, but as policemen, legitimately and under orders (see also Halkowski, 1990). The deployment of group membership categories, whether universalizing ('only human') or specific role descriptions ('doing their job'), is an indirect way of performing important attributional work. In these cases, as we have noted in other materials (Chapters 5 and 6), a kind of attributional *consensus* accounting is produced, which works to reduce personal responsibility for actions-as-described. Not only are the actions described as ones done by, or potentially done by, many different actors, but there is the additional vector of a *normative* accountability for actions that are assigned to roles, which reinforces the 'consensus' effect in reducing the responsibility of individual actors.

One of the features of using reports to make inferences is that reports will successfully manage the dilemma of stake only if they are either accepted to be factual or have a rhetorical organization which makes them difficult to rebut or undermine. Indeed, in analytical terms, being accepted and being difficult to rebut will often amount to precisely the same thing. One of the themes of this book has been how much is missed if factual accounts are viewed as simple descriptions, which stand or fall by their relation to some neutral, singular reality. In its place we have argued that they are social accomplishments: factual accounts are *constructed as* factual using a variety of discursive devices. Looked at in terms of the traditional attributional distinction, factual accounts are constructed to appear external to the actor, to be representations of features of an 'out-there' world, rather than reflections of the actor's own desires or concerns.

The study of factual accounting is an important realm of social research in its own right, and we have only addressed it as one theme in the current book. However, it is useful briefly to draw together some of the main findings of this research, and note where they appear in this book and other sources. The following list summarizes the main techniques of fact construction that we have explored, very roughly in the order of appearance in the book.

Category entitlements   Much of the time the veracity of a particular report will be warranted by the entitlements of the category membership of the speaker; people in particular categories – official and unofficial – are expected to know certain things or to have certain epistemological skills (Jayyusi, 1984; cf. Sacks, 1972a, 1974, 1979). For example, the head of security at the Greyhound depot is treated by the emergency switchboard as simply knowing when there is a disturbance, while an 'unofficial' caller may be questioned as to how they know (Whalen and Zimmerman, 1990). This device appears in a number of places in our analysis above, where the category memberships themselves are not given, but will often have to be worked up by the speaker. Thus, John Dean can be seen to be attempting to gain the entitlement of one who has an exceptional memory (Chapter 2), while the newspaper reporters in Chapters 3 and 5 are variously defined as people who have special skills in recording facts ('10 fully trained shorthand-writing *journalists*') or people who might have interests that can lead to distortion ('So *the hacks'* notebooks contain only a sketchy summary . . .').

Vivid description Vivid description, rich in contextual detail and incident can be used to create an impression of perceptual re-experience as well as perhaps indicating that the speaker has particular skills of observation (cf. Tannen, 1989). It can also be used to package contentious or problematic events. We see in Chapter 2 John Dean reporting: 'you know the way there are two chairs at the side of the President's desk . . . on the left-hand chair Mr. Haldeman was sitting . . .', and one of the reporters in Chapter 5: 'Mr Lawson sat in an armchair in one corner, next to a window looking out over the garden of No 11 Downing Street. The Press Secretary, Mr John Gieve, hovered by the door.' Some sorts of 'direct quotation', in the guise of ostensibly verbatim recall (Chapter 2), may also serve this function (cf. Wooffitt, 1992).

Narrative This is closely related to vivid description; however, here the plausibility of a report can be increased by embedding it in a particular narrative sequence in which that event is expected or even necessary. As well as aiding the generation of plausibility, a narrative can also set up a context of deniability (Bogen and Lynch, 1989; and Chapter 2). This is a form of accounting that has, of course, been explored in detail in literary studies as a device for producing particular kinds of reality effects (for example, Barthes, 1974; Rimon-Kenan, 1983), although its study as a warranting device has been less developed in social science (but see Atkinson, 1990; Gergen, 1988; Jackson, 1988). In Chapter 5 we explored some of the narratives produced by reporters as part of the warrant for their version of Lawson's lobby briefing, and in Chapter 6 competing constructions of Lawson's motive are partly organized in terms of different narratives. Narrative offers a useful discursive opportunity for the fusing of memory and attribution, or of event description and causal explanation, in that the events are generally recounted in ways that attend to their causal, intentional and plausible sequential connections (cf. Edwards and Middleton, 1986a).

Systematic vagueness This is the rhetorical converse of vivid detail and narrative. It reflects the fact that while rich detail can warrant, it also provides leverage for initiating a rebuttal. Vague, global formulations can provide a barrier to such easy undermining while at the same time providing just the essentials to found a particular inference. Margaret Thatcher's formulaic utterances concerning the role of ministers and advisers in Chapter 6 is an example of this, as is the idiomatic formulation used by Nigel Lawson (Chapter 5) that the reporters went in for 'a farrago of invention' (see also Drew and Holt, 1989; Edwards and Potter, 1992a).

Empiricist accounting This is a style or repertoire of discourse which is especially characteristic of scientific talk and writing. It treats phenomena themselves as agents in their own right, and either deletes the observer entirely or treats her as a passive recipient. In this discourse, the facts force themselves on the human actors who have an entirely secondary role (Gilbert and Mulkay, 1984; McKinlay and Potter, 1987; Mulkay, 1985), not unlike the perceiver who 'picks up' whatever 'information' the environment offers (Gibson, 1966). Features of everyday empiricist accounting appear in the reporter's detailed narratives (Chapter 5) and Lawson's resignation letter (Chapter 6).

Rhetoric of argument Constructing claims *in the form* of logical, syllogistic or other well-known argument types provides a further way of making them external to the speaker or writer. Apart from any putative validity of such forms, they can be considered as a set of tropes that provide a reassuring sense of rationality. Lawson's resignation letter is constructed using this form. Devices of this kind are particularly important when versions are being mobilized to provide particular attributional inferences, for example of blame, for they present those inferences as required by the events or actions themselves rather than desired by the speaker (see Billig, 1987; Potter and Wetherell, 1988; Wetherell and Potter, forthcoming).

Extreme case formulations Pomerantz (1986) has explored how 'extreme case formulations' can be used to make a report or version more effective by drawing on the extremes of relevant dimensions of judgement. Thus 'everybody carries a gun' provides a version of activities in a particular neighbourhood which makes the speaker's own gun toting entirely unexceptional. This manner of constructing elements of versions is a pervasive one – we might say that people are always using them. They appear regularly in examples discussed in the preceding chapters without explicit note. It is also a device that is often meshed with others. For example, we saw it combined with the rhetoric of argument in Lawson's resignation letter and the example 'everybody carries a gun' itself combines extreme case formulation with consensus accounting.

Consensus and corroboration   As we explored in detail in Chapter 5, a major way of warranting the factuality of a version is to depict it as agreed across witnesses, or as having the assent of independent observers (see also Potter and Edwards, 1990). In Smith's (1978) classic study of an account which attributes mental illness, part of the effectiveness of the account derives from its introduction of a number of witnesses who are constructed as both independent and in agreement about the progressive onset of the illness. At times consensus blends in with normativity, as in Lawson's claim that '*any* Chancellor of the Exchequer would have been in *exactly the same position*', which combines what is appropriate for the category incumbent (norm) with what all incumbents would agree on (consensus); all of which is packaged in an extreme case formulation.

Lists and contrasts   Work on political oratory has attested to the rhetorical effectiveness of lists and contrasts (Atkinson, 1984; Heritage and Greatbatch, 1986). However, Jefferson (1990) has emphasized that lists, particularly three-part lists, can be used to construct descriptions which are treated as complete or representative (see also Drew, 1990; Pinch and Clark, 1986; Wooffitt, 1991). We can see examples of this kind in the materials discussed in Chapters 5 and 6. In the latter case (p. 144), the three-part list is combined with a contrast which formulates the 'factual' version in opposition to a threatening alternative, which is itself formulated in an unconvincing or problematic manner (see also Eglin, 1979; Mulkay, 1985; Pomerantz, 1988–9; Potter, 1987, 1988a; Smith, 1978). Finally, we noted in Chapter 6 that contrasts could be designed to present what in attribution terms would be 'distinctiveness information'.

It is precisely the 'complete and representative' implication of lists that prompts the following reflexive disclaimer. Our own list of nine devices for constructing versions as factual and external by no means exhausts all those found in the materials discussed in this book; and, of course, many others appear in different settings (Potter et al., 1991; Woolgar, 1988a). However, it covers some of the principal ones and gives a flavour of the variety of ways in which a factual effect can be accomplished. In practice, of course, they will not be as discrete as they appear here. Moreover, in laying out these devices and accounting techniques in this way we are not wishing to claim that they are some sort of guarantee of being treated as truthful. In practice, people are skilled at dissecting and undermining them; and the various analyses in the earlier chapters testify to the tenacity and inventiveness which may be involved in this. It is also notable that a number of these devices have a more or less standard mode of reply. We have seen, for example, the way that vivid or narrative detail may provide leverage for a critique, and also that consensus across observers may be grounds for an accusation of collusion. With respect to the discursive action model, it is important to note that the majority of these devices involve some formulation or implication about the *stake* of the speaker; they work to construct disinterest, or external constraints, which inoculate the account against corruption by the actor's interests.

This brings us to the final element of the fact and interest section of DAM, which is the notion that reports are designed *rhetorically*. This emphasizes two closely related features about the construction of reports. The first is that they appear in the contexts of dialogues, disputes and conflicts of one kind or another. The second is that they are designed for their adequacy in undermining alternative versions and, at the same time, resisting attempts (actual or potential) to undermine them as false, partial or interested. In its most basic form, this directs us to the study of competing versions deployed by different parties to a dispute, the kind of thing that happens in an explicit and formalized manner in courtrooms and hearings.

Take the following example from the Iran–Contra hearings where Colonel North is being questioned by committee council, Mr Nields, about his actions before the arrival of people to look at documents relating to the case.

Nields: =And you shredded documents before they got there.
North: I would prefer to say that I shredded documents that day like I did on all other days, but (0.5) perhaps with increased intensity, (.) that is correct.
(Halkowski, 1990: 570)

Here we can see again the concerns of memory and attribution joined together on the terrain of rhetoric. Versions of the past (rememberings) are constructed by both Nields and North; they do not directly conflict but they provide for very different inferences about North's guilt (attributions). Nields' minimal narrative, by including only the fact of the document shredding and its timing, effectively provides only one reason for the shredding – that there was something in the documents that North did not want the investigators to see. North's reformulation does not disagree with any particulars of the Nields version; yet it selects a broader, less incriminating time frame – 'that day' as opposed to 'before they got there' – and provides further information that shredding went on like this 'on all other days'. It thus considerably softens the implied causal link between this particular shredding and the arrival of the officials. Again, in attribution terms it manages distinctiveness, attempting to reduce it with the aim of relieving the potentially damning inference. Both Nields' and North's descriptions are rhetorically designed in their formulation of particulars about how the world is; but they do so in a way that implicates different stories of motive and accountability.

It is important to stress that the rhetorical design of versions is not something confined to face-to-face talk, nor to obviously adversarial contexts such as the Iran–Contra hearings. Social life is riven with disputes and competing interests running from the small-scale interpersonal to the large-scale structural, and these provide a field in which versions are likely to be produced in a rhetorically orientated manner. For example, Billig (1991; Billig et al., 1988) has argued that expressions of attitudes, which have often been treated by psychologists and opinion pollsters as abstract representations of underlying personal positions on issues, are organized rhetorically to work against widely available alternatives. To give a further example on a more institutional level, much work in the sociology of scientific knowledge has shown the way scientific claims which are commonly seen as accurate, neutral representations of nature *par excellence*, are organized to rebut competing theories and claims (Collins, 1985; Gilbert and Mulkay, 1984; Pinch, 1986; Woolgar, 1988a). This means that issues of scientific truth, and the referentiality of descriptions to an objectively real world beyond them, are indistinguishable from that essentially rhetorical process.

Accountability

Speakers routinely deal with issues of agency and responsibility when they offer reports of events. While most memory research deals with these issues only indirectly (if at all), they are, of course, the centrepiece of attribution theory. What neither kind of research has addressed in any detail, however, is a further level of account-ability: that of the current speaker or writer. In natural settings, as ethnomethodologists and others have demonstrated in great detail, the report's author can be held accountable for the veracity of her report, and also for any interactional consequences it may have. Furthermore, in so far as reports are a part of activity sequences – and it is a central thesis of our work that this is overwhelmingly what they are – then they have all the potential accountability associated with such acts.

For example, a report that performs part of a blaming will have precisely the potential requirements of accountability of that act. The act of blaming could itself be inspected for its partial or motivated nature, for instance, or for its adequacy *vis-à-vis* some version of 'the facts'. However, these are just broad types of options for which such an act can fail to be made accountable. One of the analytical tasks of discursive psychology will be to look at the way accountability is constructed and defended in specific contexts, and the way different kinds of activities pose different sorts of accountability concerns (Watson and Sharrock, 1991).

We have illustrated this point about the centrality of account-ability extensively in the different analytical chapters above, with regard to the Watergate, Irangate and the Thatcher–Lawson data, as well as other work on conversation. For example, it figures as a strong feature of the nurses' talk about the case of a ruptured aneurysm (Pomerantz, 1984c; see Chapter 5 above). However, it is interesting also to make the same point by examining one of the very few social psychological studies which has examined attribu-tion in open-ended naturalistic dialogue, and has attempted to look at that dialogue as an activity sequence in its own right rather than a compendium of attributional moves. Burleson (1986) analyses a transcript of a discussion between two junior teaching assistants over a failing student, and tries to show that various kinds of attributional information (for example, consistency and consensus information) are searched as the speakers seek out the motive for the student's repeated failure of a test. The talk is treated as the conversational outcome of their thinking about the event in terms of an underlying cognitive ANOVA model. What is significant to us is that Burleson interprets the material entirely in terms of the accountability of the agent (the student), who is the topic of the talk. What is ignored, and what DAM encourages us to attend to, is the accountability of the current speakers: how, in their construction of the accountability *in the event*, are they attending to *their own* accountability? The following is a section from this transcript.

> *Don:* She has – I gave quizzes which, you know, cover the material. So she's got copies of the quizzes which led up to the midterm, and some of the questions on that midterm are just lifted off the quizzes. Just exactly the same as those quizzes.
> *Bob:* And you did go over those quizzes, right?
> *Don:* Oh yes, yes I did. And she still missin' those that are exact copies of the ones on quizzes that she's got copies of.
> *Don:* [Pause] I just don't see that I can do anything for her. I just have – I know the day has passed for dropping the course, but I just gotta –
> *Bob:* – Does she know she failed it?
> *Don:* No.
> *Bob:* Oh . . . I don't envy you man. What are you gonna say to her?
> *Don:* I'm just gonna say 'you failed it again. This is the last straw. I'm gonna get you out of this class.' I don't know how I'm gonna do it.
> (Burleson, 1986: 82)

This is not the place to embark on a systematic study of the role of accountability in assessment and teacher–student relationships; and, anyway, to do this adequately we would wish to collect other kinds of materials, for example other discussions of failure and other talk amongst student teachers. Nevertheless, there are clear indications of the way the participants are attending to their own problems of accountability, for example Bob's 'I don't envy you, man' (not 'I don't envy *her*' for failing) and Don's 'I don't know how I'm gonna do it.' The concern seems to be focused on whether the failing student will be seen to have been poorly taught (*by them*); and whether she might be seen as having been unfairly treated (*by them*). These are recognizably commonplace worries of novice teachers. More particularly, has Don failed to warn the student by the due date? Deviation from required practice could be a specific focus of accountability. Overall, the student teachers construct a version of available attributional information which, apparently, leads inexorably to a person attribution (she has failed because, as Don later puts it, 'she is plain dumb') and in doing so they provide a developed account for their own lack of responsibility, an account suitable perhaps for dealing with potential complaints from the student or questions from their own supervisors. Again, we should emphasize that these points are not directed at Burleson in particular, but at any attempts to treat discourse as a pathway to cognition without attending to the basic issues of fact construction and accountability which we have highlighted.

As well as distinguishing two levels of accountability – in the events, of the current speaker – we suggest that the latter one, the one least addressed by current psychology, is in many situations primary. Much of the time the main concern when providing a version which attributes agency and responsibility to events, circumstances and persons is that these bear directly on the accountability of the current speaker. Indeed, a great many everyday reportings are of events in which the reporter took part, or at least will be treated as having a clear 'interest', and the accountability at stake is precisely their own. Dean reports events in the White House and North describes his document shredding as part of a current negotiation which is designed to establish their own and others' guilt or innocence, and testimonial credibility; Lawson and the reporters formulate and then reformulate what went on in their lobby briefing to display who is at fault; and he and Thatcher both marshal particulars about what led to his resignation, in such a way as to display who did the 'right thing'. This accountability is relatively formalized in court cases and political controversies, of course, but informally similar issues are the centrepiece of much gossip, anecdote, personal story-telling and argumentation.

It is clear, then, that the construction of accountability for actors and events in a report can be used to develop a version of the current speaker's accountability. Yet this process also works in the opposite direction: attending to one's own current accountability can have implications for that of the persons and events in reports. For example, when Thatcher expresses in a television interview her current regret over Lawson's resignation, this is not merely of contemporaneous significance; it has implications for how the viewers should understand what went on *then*, and in particular that Lawson's resignation was motivated by some peculiarity in him, rather than forced or even wished by her. And, in practice, in many situations a complex of reports of past events, and avowals of various kinds about current issues, can be used to provide suitable accountability for the speaker.

A final feature that DAM brings to the fore is the importance of the notion of 'footing' (Goffman, 1979; Levinson, 1988: see Box 2). Footing highlights the basis upon which an account is offered: does it come from direct experience and involvement, or is it a report based upon the testimony of a reliable witness, or is it a disinterested passing on of possibly contentious information, and so on? Footing plays a central part in accountability. The interactional work performed in reporting events, including attributional issues for speaker and audience, may be accomplished indirectly, through the way in which reported events, and attributional issues in them, are handled. Conversely, establishing footing, or one's personal accountability for the veracity of a report, can work towards claiming causal credit for, or distance from (as with Walden in Chapter 6), the reported events.

A case in point arose just as we were writing this chapter, in February 1991, during a growing controversy concerning Gulf War civilian casualties due to the American and coalition forces' bombing of Baghdad. The following extract is from a radio broadcast concerning an event in which nearly 300 people were killed, and the controversy centred upon the extent of the coalition forces' knowledge and responsibility. Note how neutral footing and blaming are discursively managed by using three different descriptions of one entity, the place where the people died.

> Spain and Italy have expressed reservations about the Allied bombing strategy (.) after the attack on Wednesday on a
> (1) → building in Baghdad
> (2) → which the Iraqis say was a civilian shelter.
> (3) → The Americans say it was a military bunker.
> The Iraqis say they have now recovered more than two hundred and eighty bodies from the wreckage.
> A senior official in Italy's Foreign Affairs Ministry says there should be no more bombing of civilian areas (.) and in a letter to President Bush the Spanish prime minister Mr Phillipe Gonzales has also called for a halt to raids on Baghdad and other cities.
(BBC Radio 4 'Today' programme, 14 February 1991)

The two *quoted* descriptions of the structure imply differences in the culpability of the action: attacking *military bunkers* (3) in wartime is acceptable, but attacking *civilian shelters* (2) is not. And this is not an abstract moral issue, as the continuation of the extract makes clear; how this attack is construed has major and immediate implications for the continuing progress of the war. The newscaster's description *building* (1) is designed in this highly sensitive context to be neutral to the two sorts of attributions, and thereby avoids aligning with the consequences that follow from either. At the same time, we should point out that the same process is continued in our own efforts at neutral footing, displayed by our choice of the 'neutral' terms *structure*, *place* and *entity*.

Now that we have been through the main features of the model there is one general point that is worth emphasizing strongly. This is not the basis for an *individual* psychology. Discursive psychology is concerned with the way psychological entities and processes are constituted in discursive acts, and there are two senses in which these acts are not reducible to individual psychology. First, as we have emphasized in various places above, even where an utterance has an individual speaker, this speaker is not necessarily considered to be in sovereign control of her talk. Simple examples of this occur in the sorts of discourse we have concentrated on where news reports are sifted and edited, and television interviews may be scripted and preplanned and in various ways collaborative and collective products. At a more profound level, post-structuralists have produced searching critiques of the very notion of sovereign control in this way (cf. Sampson, 1988).

Secondly, when the psychology of agents or entities is constructed in talk and texts, these things are not necessarily correlated with the unitary subjects who form the basis of much of psychology. We have been concerned with the construction of a whole variety of actors, sub-agents and collectives. Motivation, for example, may be attributed to some sort of sub-system of self ('a part of me wants to get really angry with you'), to a more or less standard individual ('Shelley wants an ice cream') or to a wide range of collectives ('the Kurds have been wanting autonomy for decades'; 'children from broken homes are looking for security'). For these reasons, we have seen it as very important to eschew the image of the single individual accounting for the actions of another individual; in some ways this most common of psychological paradigms is the least interesting to study.

Discursive action model and war in the Gulf

This is not the place for a full, systematic treatment of Gulf War discourse: the role of event descriptions and accounts, of versions of events, their causal explanations and issues of accountability. Nevertheless, some further examples from this material can serve as an illustration of some of DAM's principles. We shall take two examples from 26 February 1991. The first concerns descriptions of what Saddam Hussein's forces were doing on this 'decisive day' when they were moving north out of Kuwait under heavy fire, and were 'decimated' by allied planes and tanks. The second is a statement made the same day, concerning the fate of Iraq's leader Saddam, by an Israeli government spokesperson.

Competing descriptions of what Saddam's forces were doing hinged on the terms 'withdrawal', 'surrender' and 'retreat':

> . . . not withdrawing . . . simply fleeing [they are] in full retreat (*CNN*, 26 February 1991; quoting the US military)

> Those who did not surrender as demanded by America's president but who withdrew as demanded by theirs died as they went. (*Observer*, 3 March 1991)

> Whether they surrendered or whether they withdrew, Saddam's men

were a terrible sight . . . The concentration of killing was unequalled since Hiroshima . . . An American pilot spoke of a 'turkey shoot', a British officer of 'herding sheep'. (*Observer*, 3 March 1991)

The issue for both sides was not merely how to describe events, but what such descriptions would accomplish. *Retreat* and *surrender* are treated as recognized military terms. *Surrender* was taken to mean give up arms and the war is over; the allies wanted the Iraqis to surrender. *Retreat* is a strategic move made while the war continues; one can properly 'retreat under fire', in order to regroup and continue fighting (General Neal, *CNN*, 26 February). *Withdraw* seemed to have no such clear military definition, and the issue arose that if the Iraqis were 'withdrawing', did that mean that they could still legitimately be bombed and shot at? Given the very high Iraqi casualties, comparisons with Hiroshima and descriptions such as 'turkey shoot' and 'herding sheep', the *warranting* of allied military action was particularly important (note again the careful footing here: the journalist backs up a potentially objectionable comparison with Hiroshima with horse's mouth participants' descriptions). Waging and winning the war is inseparable from the success of each side's efforts at describing it; it is on the grounds that the Iraqi army is 'retreating' that the allies can legitimately continue bombarding it.

Furthermore, we should emphasize again that our own text is in the same position of that of the journalists – it needs to secure a more 'neutral' descriptive footing to achieve its own descriptive rhetoric (and even in acknowledging this, bolsters that rhetoric further). We described earlier the Iraqi troops as 'moving north out of Kuwait', avoiding the immediately problematic formulations 'retreat' and 'withdraw'. But no description is free of its context, free of action. Our own descriptive categories 'Saddam Hussein's army' and 'the Iraqi army' provide bases for attributing group motives and explanations. One of the issues that DAM brings to the fore is the issue of reflexivity: if description production is a rhetorical process orientated to action, what of social science texts? What of the factual discourse of psychologists? (See Box 10.)

The term 'withdraw', while lacking (according to the allied military) a precise meaning in warfare, was nevertheless very precisely occasioned in this context (we are putting aside issues of English–Arabic translation here). First, it accomplishes precisely the business of military imprecision, signalling neither surrender nor a continuation of fighting; it offered no clear grounds for enemy military reaction. Secondly, it could be cited as the term used by the United Nations resolutions that were the very pretext/justification for allied military action:

Box 10 *The reflexive box*

Jonathan: We're going to have to deal with it, aren't we?

Derek: What, now?

Jonathan: There's not much space left. We'll end up in the references if we're not careful.

Derek: We could get Malcolm [Ashmore] to do it, or Margie [Wetherell] [both laugh].

Jonathan: Malcolm would probably go to town on our reflexive contradictions and turn it into another chapter of Ashmore [1989]. And Margie would concentrate too much on the political themes. She and Mick [Billig] probably both think we end up soft on the Tories. Anyway, it's our job.

Derek: Only kidding. I suppose we need to show that our own descriptive discourse is put together to generate all sorts of effects. And make the point that there is no time out from these rhetorical processes.

Jonathan: And we want to make the construction point – that it's all put together, worked up, kind of artful.

Derek: I suppose we could do a multi-voice thing; you know, the usual slightly embarrassing fake conversation like Mike's stuff and the Woolgar book [Mulkay, 1985; Woolgar, 1988b].

Jonathan: Yeah. But let's bung it in near the end; we don't want to put people off, particularly any psychologists who've not been in on any of the relevant debates – they'll probably think it comes straight from Mars.

Derek: Well, I wouldn't want to . . .

Jonathan: [Interrupting] Also, I don't know about these fake dialogues. I know they are meant to show the informal negotiation that lies behind the polished final text; and highlight the way descriptions are sited in rhetorical contexts; and I know they remind readers that formal scientific texts are a particular literary convention, and all that, but they can come over as pretty stilted and artificial.

Derek: [Stifling a yawn] Yeah.

Jonathan: Like, OK I'm having a very long turn here. Also, they can be a way of generating a sham informal identity – you know –

Derek: pretentious

Jonathan: – I meant the opposite. And jokey, on first-name terms with Mick, Mike, Margie, Malcolm and, er, many more. Moreover, the turns of talk get so long that they can turn into mini essays – you just end up sneaking in some more of the main text by the back door.

Derek: But surely that's the point.

Jonathan: What is?

Derek: All of that. It displays it. Even without putting in fake pauses and overlaps and stuff. It raises the reflexive issue. It displays the localized nature of our knowledge production and how dependent we are on our informal contacts. You know, like Harry Collins [1985] and all those sociologists of science emphasize. We wrote about that stuff in Chapter 2.

Jonathan: Mmmm. Well . . .

Derek: Also, the use of dialogue like this is quite neat really because it reverses the asymmetry that runs through the rest of the text where the participants' discourse is displayed as precisely that – as <u>discourse</u> – by using transcription conventions, indenting and so on; while our own surrounding text is just there, neutral and transparent. The textual contrasts in the rest of the book help set the analysis up as unproblematic and the voice of reason.

Jonathan: Umm. Atkinson [1990] makes that point rather nicely in his book on ethnography as a textual form. But what do we want readers to conclude? That our text is made up? Or manipulative? Sneaky?

Derek: [Laughing] So why should it be any different from anybody else's? Anyway, it's not that . . .

Jonathan: How about this. We would like them to see *all* discourse as subject to the sorts of processes that we highlight. But that should not be seen as a reason for discounting that discourse. For one thing there is nothing better. There is no non-discursive discourse for doing proper, accurate, non-action orientated description.

Derek: I like it. So using descriptions to do actions is the most sensible thing in the world. In our case, our text is organized rhetorically to undermine arguments from cognitivism, but that is what making a convincing case *is*. Any response to us will also be rhetorically structured – that is only right and proper.

Jonathan: You think that will do the trick?

Derek: How will we know?

Last Monday [25 February] . . . Baghdad radio broke into its broadcasting to announce that 'orders have been issued to our armed forces to *withdraw* in an organized manner to the positions they held prior to 1 August . . . as practical compliance with resolution 660'. (*Observer*, 3 March 1991; emphasis added)

By using the term *withdraw*, the Iraqi government could effectively claim that it was doing everything that had legitimately been asked of it, thus countering the implications of terms such as 'surrender' or 'retreat', undermining any warrant for the allies to continue shelling and bombing its army, while nevertheless not having to admit defeat, and keeping future options open.

In another fragment of war talk, *CNN International* presented a brief interview with an Israeli spokesperson, who was commenting on the war's likely aftermath, and, particularly, on the fate of Saddam Hussein. Rather than Saddam's defeat signalling a loss of political power, the reverse effect was plausible: '. . . for many Iraqis, for many Arabs, *in this part of the world where we live*, he will be a hero' (*CNN*, 26 February; emphasis added). It is the italicized part to which we wish to draw attention. The Israelis were arguing for the necessity of removing Saddam, and it was important to establish that he was not already, merely by virtue of a military defeat, thus removed. Indeed, his political position might even be strengthened, with further implications of threat to world peace. But there arises the dilemma of interest; is this an objective political analysis, or one that merely reflects Israeli interests, and which risks being discounted on that basis? The regional formulation 'this part of the world' defuses and neutralizes the sorts of nationalistic implications that an alternative expression such as 'in Israel' might carry. We do not otherwise need to be informed, in this most obvious of contexts, that Israelis live nearer to Iraq than Americans do (it was an American news interviewer). Further, the whole of the italicized expression effectively reverses the rhetorically dangerous implications of interest; it is the position not of a politically interested citizen of Israel, but of an inhabitant of the area who thereby possesses local and expert knowledge (cf. Drew, 1978). Interest becomes objectivity, as nationality, and being a government spokesperson at that (further possible formulations), are replaced by geographical fact – membership of a local Middle Eastern part of the world, where these judgements are formulated as *consensual* (and thus further objectified).

There is an additional complexity here, of course. The slightly clumsy seeming formulation 'in this part of the world where we live' directs attention away from the specific issue of Arabs living in Israel, which itself involves the issue of what is classed as Israel itself and what as 'the occupied territories'; that is, while addressing one issue of (so-described) invasion and occupation, this is a formulation which does not bring into focus another (a 'link' which was indeed being made publicly by some Iraqis, Jordanians and Palestinians). Again we see the subtle way in which the construction of versions can manage complex and threatening problems of blame and responsibility. It is not that we wish to impute all of this to the speaker's intentions – rather, that it is possible to analyse how various descriptions accomplish different sorts of implications.

These are fragmentary and condensed comments on some features of Gulf War discourse; they are meant to illustrate the operation of DAM rather than form the basis of a systematic analysis. However, they also underline a further linking that DAM provides for. The construction and objectifying of versions of the world such that particular inferences are supported and others undermined is a main theme in the study of ideology. We have not explored this connection in detail here, yet these points about Gulf

War discourse illustrate some of the directions in which we believe such a study could move. Developments of this kind are taken further elsewhere (Billig, 1990, 1991, 1992a; Billig et al., 1988; Bromley, 1988; Schwartz, 1990; Wetherell and Potter, forthcoming). Ultimately we hope that these developments will, for example, provide a distinctive input into post-structuralist debates about politics and international relations (Der Derian, 1989; Shapiro, 1989; Walker, 1990).

DAM and the fragmentation of psychology

As we indicated at the start of this book, and as we have illustrated in detail with the cases of conversational memory and attribution, discursive psychology is a meta-theory and analytical approach which calls for a major reorganization in the geography of psychological research. In particular, the focus on discourse and its organization in activity sequences and participants' social practices cuts across the fragmented sub-fields that have emerged within psychology, as well as developing coherent links to other social and human science disciplines. So far in this chapter we have concentrated on using DAM to provide some detailed specifications about reports (rememberings) and inferences (attributions). In this final section we will briefly sketch the way DAM can provide a context for relating some of the other major concepts of social and cognitive psychology when they are reworked both theoretically and empirically in discursive terms. We will concentrate on three examples: categorization, personality/self and attitudes. As we noted earlier, all of these have been recently subjected to discursive and rhetorically orientated reworkings; however, our aim here is not to repeat these arguments but to show where they might fit into DAM.

Categorization in the form of various kinds of category discourse enters the model in two places. First, and most importantly, categorizations provide a major way of making inferences available (Element 2). Categories of persons, events and objects possess conventionally understood properties and attributes; weapons can hurt people, babies can cry, and so on. Theories of categories that base themselves on idealized cognitive models (for example, Lakoff, 1987; Rosch et al., 1976) offer useful treatments of the kinds of categorical resources that are deployed in discourse; nevertheless, and in contrast to discursive psychology, these studies say little about how particular categorical formulations are chosen and deployed, in situated and indexical ways, within rhetorically and pragmatically organized activity sequences (see Edwards, 1991, for an extended discussion).

For example, the mobilization of categories in reports can be a very economical, and also implicit, way of accomplishing particular inferences about cause and motivation. Potter and Reicher (1987) showed the way that categorizations of a riot/uprising as a 'community relations problem' provide for inferences about the causes of the event in problems of interpersonal relations and understanding, thus paving the way for policy solutions in terms of 'community policing' rather than addressing structural issues such as that of racism in the police or disproportionate unemployment in minority groups. Similarly, Humphreys (1969) provides an example of discursively embedded categorization, in which various descriptive terms have to be assembled and applied (sex, kicks, handball, adultery) in order to accomplish a denial, the rejection of a potential category for the speaker that his actions might otherwise warrant: that he might be homosexual (cf. Watson and Weinberg, 1982):

> That's not really sex. Sex is something I have with my wife in bed. It's not as if I were committing adultery by getting my rocks off – or going down on some guy – in a tea room. I get a kick out of it. Some of my friends go out for handball. I'd rather cruise the park. (Humphreys, 1969: 119)

Again, we are not merely looking at the speaker's cognitive models, or understandings of the world or of himself. And certainly, it is difficult to accept any suggestion that these categorizations are unconscious or automatic indications of underlying cognitions. The study of real talk, of what words *do*, encourages a much more active, constructive notion of the relation between words and what they describe.

Categorizations also enter into DAM in the area of fact construction (Element 5); this relies on the fact that some features of social categories relate to people's supposed knowledge, experience or skills: scientists may know about experiments, policewomen about rape, and so on. As we noted above, one important way of warranting a report or claim is to draw on social categories which have particular knowledge entitlements: for example 'community leaders' are expected to be knowledgeable about their community, such that characterizing a report as originating from a community leader is a way of providing a warrant for it (Potter and Halliday, 1990).

Instead of considering personality and self as psychological objects to be revealed through research they enter into DAM as discursive resources that people draw on to do particular sorts of interactional work. In particular, role and personological notions provide sets of rights and duties as well as various 'natural' attributes (Hilbert, 1981; Potter et al., 1984; Shotter and Gergen, 1988). We noted in Chapter 6 the way Lawson used a role framework for legitimating his act of resigning; in a complementary study Halkowski (1990) has explored the way an act can be constructed as something informal done by an individual or something formal and legal done by a person in their role as representative of the state. Most crucially, role and personality provide models of motivation which can be drawn on in an occasioned manner to make discriminating attributions of blame and innocence. Lawson *had* to resign because he was unable to do his job; police violence was not accountable as such because police are only human; North's document shredding was not illegal because those requesting the documents were not acting in their official capacity.

Finally, attitude becomes a complex and multifaceted notion for participants in natural interaction. The reason for this is that it can be a way of indicating psychological involvement or stake, and this, as we have seen, can provide participants with a powerful resource for discounting a claim or argument. Attitudes, too, can be understood in terms of the different levels of accountability we have distinguished. Consider the accountability of a speaker who is doing evaluations (expressing attitudes) which assign blame to some group or individual. In such a situation there is the possibility of understanding this as personally motivated in some way. Thus in certain situations people construct their discourse to present their evaluations as things lying 'out there', as features of the world rather than a product of their own desires or needs. That is, they produce a version of the world which has the badness set within it; and they can do this, for example, by using the various devices listed earlier (Potter and Wetherell, 1988).

Despite offering these possible integrations of psychological fields of study, we are not wanting to suggest that DAM is a complete model of discursive psychology, nor that it is satisfactory and finished as it stands. It is a scheme for conceptualizing phenomena and integrating studies but it is likely to undergo considerable development before it is ultimately, no doubt, abandoned for something better or at least different. Beyond a more systematic and thoroughgoing attempt at integrating psychological studies, we see the future as lying in the development of research on fact construction, in studies of situated descriptions of psychological states, in further studies of DAM in everyday, non-institutional contexts, and in further integration with work in other social sciences, particularly social anthropology, sociology and politics.

Appendix
Transcription Conventions and Theory

Some of the data extracts in this book are taken from written texts such as newspapers, or from other published sources, and are cited as they occur in those sources, at least as far as words and punctuation, if not context and typography, are concerned. Other extracts are transcriptions from audio and video tape, and use conventions that are designed to provide a mixture of informativeness and readability. These conventions are taken in turn from a larger and increasing set that have been developed for conversation analysis, mainly by Gail Jefferson (for example, Jefferson, 1985b; Sacks et al., 1974). Useful summaries of the more extended system can be found in Atkinson and Heritage (1984a), Button and Lee (1987), Schenkein (1978). We provide below a restricted list of those transcription features used in this book.

The aim of these symbols is not simply to provide increased *accuracy* over a straight, orthographic written transcript. Ultimate accuracy is impossible; even a video tape recording possesses limitations, and a speech spectrograph of the sounds on it, while achieving plenty of accuracy, would be all but indecipherable. Conversation analysis transcriptions are categorizations of speech which build upon the conventions of written text, retaining normal spelling, sometimes with deviations from this to give an impression of vocal delivery. Some of the ambiguities, or grammatical conventions of normal punctuation are removed or redefined in interactional terms, while further symbols are added (using ones available on most typewriter keyboards) for features of intonation, pronunciation, pauses, overlaps and such. The extra details that would otherwise be omitted using ordinary conventions of written text are ones that are thought to possess analytical relevance, ones that have been developed alongside analyses of how speech performs social actions: 'features of talk that persons have been found to display an orientation to' (Button and Lee, 1987: 10).

The choice of a transcription system clearly depends upon the kind of analysis that is being attempted. The development of transcription and theory go hand in hand. One does not precede the other; one does not work out a 'full' transcription system (were that possible) and then find out what it reveals, any more than one develops a theory or analysis of conversation and then wonders how to transcribe it. Transcription is therefore already a form of analysis (Ochs, 1979), with decisions having been made about such things as whether and how to time pauses, and in what sorts of units, and what kind of speech to take as the norm against which such features as vowel elongations, intonation rises and so on, are marked. Nevertheless, it is useful for researchers to avoid a plethora of systems, and to converge upon some common conventions, even if these are always necessarily provisional. This means that in practice, now that such systems have been developed to a useful degree and many studies have been done, it is possible for most purposes to use a transcription system that is ready made.

Our emphasis here, on the theoretically orientated nature of transcription, reflects an important theme of the book as a whole. There is no such thing as mere accuracy, in any version or representation of the world, short of it being the world itself. The same principle applies to the transcription of talk (cf. Cook, 1990). Indeed, this is evident in the variety of forms of transcription that are cited in the book's main chapters. Note, for example, the contrast between Neisser's presentations of Dean's discourse, taken from the published transcripts, and those of Molotch and Boden (see Chapter 2): also the form of transcription used by Burleson (see Chapter 7). These differences are not merely accidental. The use of conversation analysis conventions reflects an analytical concern with how talk accomplishes actions. The presentation of talk using nothing but the everyday conventions of written text is likely to coincide with a different approach to language, in which differences between text and talk are not considered important, and which perhaps treats versions and explanations as windows upon thought, pictures of cognitive representations, or of the world described. It is not that rhetorical and discursive analyses cannot be done outside a Jefferson system transcript, but rather, that the choice of a transcription system, or any other way of presenting text and talk, inevitably reflects the analyst's theoretical position, even though, in any particular analysis, not all of the transcribed features may be discussed.

The following examples of transcription conventions are taken from extracts used in the main body of the book. The point at which overlapping, or simultaneous, speech begins is marked by the use of double slashes (//) thus:

Dean: that was the– the impression that very//clearly came out.
Gurney: In other words, your – your <u>whole</u> thesis

Alternatively, the start and end of overlapping speech may be marked with extended square brackets thus:

N: <u>Oh</u>:: do:ggone I ⌈ thought maybe we could ⌉ some little slippers
E: ⌊ I'd <u>like</u> to get   ⌋
    but uh,

Numbers in round brackets indicate pauses, timed to tenths of seconds, while the symbol (.) represents a pause which is hearable but too short to measure:

<u>now</u> Prime Minister (.2) how you res↑po::nd (.) to this claim of <u>blame</u>
(.) may be of <u>crucial</u> significance

A break in the voicing of sound is marked by a single slash:

as I reca::ll (1.0) with Mister Ghobanifa/r.

Further features of the extracts above include *colons* which signal elongations of the previous sound (the more colons, the longer the elongation), *underlining* to show added emphasis, and an *arrow* to show intonation. Upward and downward arrows precede marked rises and falls of intonation (pitch), while numbered sideways arrows are not transcription features, but merely draw the reader's attention to parts of the transcript:

(1) →   ... and I say segregation ↑<u>now</u>
        (0.2)
(2) →   segregation to↑<u>morrow</u>
        (0.2)
(3) →   and segregation for e↓ver.

A hyphen indicates an abrupt stop:

... and I have to have my <u>foot</u> up on a <u>pillow</u> for two days, <u>you</u>know
and– ·hhhmhh

The raised dot in front of the string ·hhhmhh indicates an audible intake of breath.

'Less than' and 'greater than' signs mark changes in the rate of speech. In the following example, they enclose talk which is delivered at a noticeably slower pace than the surrounding speech:

he: is making the (.) claim (.) here (.) that (.) >successful conduct of
economic policy is possible only if there is <u>seen</u> to be full agreement
between the Prime Minister and the Chancellor of the Exchequer< ·hh
now he's right about that isn't he

References

Abelson, R.P. (1976) The psychological status of the script concept. *American Psychologist*, 36: 715-29.

Alba, J.W. and Hasher, L. (1983) Is memory schematic? *Psychological Bulletin*, 93: 203-31.

Antaki, C. (1985) Ordinary explanation in conversation: causal structures and their defence. *European Journal of Social Psychology*, 15: 213-30.

Antaki, C. (1988) Explanations, communication and social cognition. In C. Antaki (ed.), *Analysing Everyday Explanation: A casebook of methods*. London: Sage.

Antaki, C. and Leudar, I. (1990) Claim backing and other explanatory genres in talk. *Journal of Language and Social Psychology*, 9: 279-92.

Antaki, C. and Naji, S. (1987) Events explained in conversational 'because' statements. *British Journal of Social Psychology*, 26: 119-26.

Armistead, N. (ed.) (1974) *Reconstructing Social Psychology*. Harmondsworth: Penguin.

Ashmore, M. (1989) *The Reflexive Thesis: Wrighting sociology of scientific knowledge*. Chicago: University of Chicago Press.

Ashmore, M., Mulkay, M. and Pinch, T. (1989) *Health and Efficiency: A sociology of health economics*. Milton Keynes: Open University Press.

Atkinson, J.M. (1978) *Discovering Suicide: Studies in the social organization of sudden death*. London: Macmillan.

Atkinson, J.M. (1984) *Our Masters' Voices: The language and body language of politics*. London: Methuen.

Atkinson, J.M. and Drew, P. (1979) *Order in Court: The organization of verbal interaction in judicial settings*. London: Macmillan.

Atkinson, J.M. and Heritage, J. (eds) (1984a) *Structures of Social Action: Studies in conversation analysis*. Cambridge: Cambridge University Press.

Atkinson, J.M. and Heritage, J. (1984b) Introduction. In J.M. Atkinson and J. Heritage (eds) (1984) *Structures of Social Action: Studies in conversation analysis*. Cambridge: Cambridge University Press.

Atkinson, P. (1990) *The Ethnographic Imagination: The textual construction of reality*. London: Routledge.

Au, T.K. (1986) A verb is worth a thousand words: the causes and consequences of interpersonal events implicit in language. *Journal of Memory and Language*, 25: 104-22.

Austin, J.L. (1962) *How to Do Things with Words*. Oxford: Clarendon Press.

Barker, R.G. (1968) *Ecological Psychology: Concepts and methods for studying the environment of human behaviour*. Stanford, CA.: Stanford University Press.

Barthes, R. (1974) *S/Z*. London: Jonathan Cape.

Barthes, R. (1977) *Images-Music-Text*. London: Fontana.

Bartlett, F.C. (1932) *Remembering: A study in experimental and social psychology*. Cambridge: Cambridge University Press.

Baumeister, R.F. (1982) A self-presentational view of social phenomena. *Psychological Bulletin*, 91: 163–96.

Bekerian, D.A. (1987) Review of Graesser, A.C. and Black, J.B. (eds) (1985) *The Psychology of Questions*. Hillsdale, NJ: Lawrence Erlbaum. In *Quarterly Journal of Experimental Psychology*, 39: 815–17.

Bernstein, B. (1971) *Class, Codes and Control*, vol. 1. London: Routledge.

Billig, M. (1982) *Ideology and Social Psychology*. Oxford: Blackwell.

Billig, M. (1985) Prejudice, categorization and particularization: from a perceptual to a rhetorical approach. *European Journal of Social Psychology*, 15: 79–103.

Billig, M. (1987) *Arguing and Thinking: A rhetorical approach to social psychology*. Cambridge: Cambridge University Press.

Billig, M. (1988a) Rhetorical and historical aspects of attitudes: the case of the British monarchy. *Philosophical Psychology*, 1: 83–104.

Billig, M. (1988b) Social representation, objectification and anchoring: a rhetorical analysis. *Social Behaviour*, 3: 1–16.

Billig, M. (1989a) The argumentative nature of holding strong views: a case study. *European Journal of Social Psychology*, 19: 203–23.

Billig, M. (1989b) Psychology, rhetoric and cognition. *History of the Human Sciences*, 2: 289–307.

Billig, M. (1990) Collective memory, ideology and the British royal family. In D. Middleton and D. Edwards (eds), *Collective Remembering*. London: Sage.

Billig, M. (1991) *Ideologies and Beliefs*. London: Sage.

Billig, M. (1992a) *Talking of the Royal Family*. London: Routledge.

Billig, M. (1992b) Studying the thinking society: social representations, rhetoric and attitudes. In G. Breakwell and D. Canter (eds), *Empirical Approaches to Social Representations*. Oxford: Oxford University Press.

Billig, M., Condor, S., Edwards, D., Gane, M., Middleton, D. and Radley, A. (1988) *Ideological Dilemmas: A social psychology of everyday thinking*. London: Sage.

Bilmes, J. (1987) The concept of preference in conversation analysis. *Language in Society*, 17: 161–81.

Bloor, D. (1976) *Knowledge and Social Imagery*. London: Routledge.

Bogen, D. and Lynch, M. (1989) Taking account of the hostile native: plausible deniability and the production of conventional history in the Iran–Contra hearings. *Social Problems*, 36: 197–224.

Bower, G.H., Black, J.B. and Turner, T.J. (1979) Scripts in text comprehension and memory. *Cognitive Psychology*, 11: 177–220.

Bransford, J.D. (1979) *Human Cognition: Learning, understanding and remembering*. Belmont, CA: Wadsworth.

Bransford, J.D. and Johnson, M.K. (1972) Contextual prerequisites for understanding: some investigations of comprehension and recall. *Journal of Verbal Learning and Verbal Behavior*, 11: 717–26.

Bransford, J.D. and McCarrell, N.S. (1974) A sketch of a cognitive approach to comprehension: some thoughts about understanding what it means to comprehend. In W.B. Weimar and D.S. Palermo (eds), *Cognition and the Symbolic Processes*. Hillsdale, NJ: Lawrence Erlbaum.

Brenner, M., Brown, J. and Canter, D. (eds) (1985) *The Research Interview: Uses and approaches*. London: Academic Press.

Bromley, R. (1988) *Lost Narratives: Popular fictions, politics and recent history*. London: Routledge.

Brown, P. and Levinson, S. (1987) *Politeness: Some universals in language use.* Cambridge: Cambridge University Press.

Brown, R. (1986) *Social Psychology*, 2nd edn. New York: Free Press.

Brown, R. and Fish, D. (1983) The psychological causality implicit in language. *Cognition*, 14: 237–73.

Burleson, B.R. (1986) Attribution schemas and causal inference in natural conversation. In D.G. Ellis and W.A. Donohue (eds), *Contemporary Issues in Language and Discourse Processes*. Hillsdale, NJ: Lawrence Erlbaum.

Buss, A.R. (1978) Causes and reasons in attribution theory: a conceptual critique. *Journal of Personality and Social Psychology*, 36: 1311–21.

Button, G. (1990) Going up a blind alley. In P. Luff, G.N. Gilbert and D. Frohlich (eds), *Computers and Conversation*. London: Academic Press.

Button, G. and Lee, J.R.E. (1987) *Talk and Social Organization*. Clevedon: Multilingual Matters.

Chalmers, A. (1980) *What is this Thing Called Science?* Milton Keynes: Open University Press.

Chomsky, N.A. (1959) A review of 'Verbal Behavior' by B.F. Skinner. *Language*, 35: 26–58.

Clark, H.H. (1977) Bridging. In P.C. Wason and P.N. Johnson-Laird (eds), *Thinking: Readings in cognitive science*. Cambridge: Cambridge University Press.

Clayman, S.E. (1988) Displaying neutrality in television news interviews. *Social Problems*, 35: 474–92.

Clayman, S.E. (1992) Footing in the achievement of neutrality: the case of news interview discourse. In P. Drew and J. Heritage (eds), *Talk at Work*. Cambridge: Cambridge University Press.

Cohen, G. (1989) *Memory in the Real World*. Sussex: Lawrence Erlbaum.

Cole, M. (1988) Cross-cultural research in the sociohistorical tradition. *Human Development*, 31: 137–57.

Cole, M. (1990) Cultural psychology: some general principles and a concrete example. Presented at 2nd International Congress on Activity Theory, Lahti, Finland, May 1990.

Cole, M., Hood, L. and McDermott, R. (1978) Ecological niche picking. Laboratory of Comparative Human Cognition, UCSD. Reprinted in U. Neisser (ed.) (1982) *Memory Observed: Remembering in natural contexts*. Oxford: W.H. Freeman and Co.

Collins, H.M. (1981) What is TRASP? The radical programme as a methodological imperative. *Philosophy of the Social Sciences*, 11: 215–24.

Collins, H.M. (1985) *Changing Order: Replication and induction in scientific practice*. London: Sage.

Condor, S. (1988) 'Race stereotypes' and racist discourse. *Text*, 8: 69–90.

Cook, G. (1990) Transcribing infinity: problems of context presentation. *Journal of Pragmatics*, 14: 1–24.

Costall, A. and Still, A. (1987) *Cognitive Psychology in Question*. Brighton: Harvester.

Coulter, J. (1979) *The Social Construction of Mind*. London: Macmillan.

Coulter, J. (1983) *Rethinking Cognitive Theory*. London: Macmillan.

Coulter, J. (1985) Two concepts of the mental. In K. Gergen and K. Davis (eds), *The Social Construction of the Person*. New York: Springer.

Coulter, J. (1989) *Mind in Action*. Oxford: Polity.

Critchlow, B. (1983) Blaming the booze: the attribution of responsibility for drunken behaviour. *Personality and Social Psychology Bulletin*, 11: 258–74.

D'Andrade, R.G. (1981) The cultural part of cognition. *Cognitive Science*, 5: 179–95.

Davies, B. and Harré, R. (1990) Positioning: the discursive production of selves. *Journal for the Theory of Social Behaviour*, 20: 43–63.

Der Derian, J. (1989) Spy versus spy: the intertextual power of international intrigue. In J. Der Derian and M. Shapiro (eds), *International/Intertextual Relations: Postmodern Readings of World Politics*. Lexington, MA.: Lexington Books.

Derrida, J. (1977a) Signature event context. *Glyph*, 1: 172–97.

Derrida, J. (1977b) Limited inc abc. . . . *Glyph*, 2: 162–254.

Drew, P. (1978) Accusations: the occasioned use of religious geography in describing events. *Sociology*, 12: 1–22.

Drew, P. (1984) Speakers' reportings in invitation sequences. In J.M. Atkinson and J.C. Heritage (eds), *Structures of Social Action: Studies in conversation analysis.* Cambridge: Cambridge University Press.

Drew, P. (1985) Analyzing the use of language in courtroom interaction. In T.A. Van Dijk (ed.), *Handbook of Discourse Analysis*, vol. 3. London: Academic Press.

Drew, P. (1990) Strategies in the contest between lawyer and witness in cross-examination. In J. Levi and A. Walker (eds), *Language in the Judicial Process*. New York: Plenum.

Drew, P. and Holt, E. (1989) Complainable matters: the use of idiomatic expressions in making complaints. *Social Problems*, 35: 501–20.

Edwards, D. (1989) Phase transformations as discursively occasioned phenomena. *Quarterly Newsletter of the Laboratory of Comparative Human Cognition*, 11: 95–104.

Edwards, D. (1991) Categories are for talking: on the cognitive and discursive bases of categorization. *Theory and Psychology*, 1 (4): 515–42.

Edwards, D. (1992a) Concepts, memory and the organization of pedagogic discourse: a case study. *International Journal of Educational Research*, in press.

Edwards, D. (1992b) But what do children really think? Discourse analysis and conceptual content in children's talk. In C. Pontecorvo (ed.), *Social Interaction and Knowledge Acquisition*. Florence: La Nuova Italia.

Edwards, D. and Mercer, N.M. (1987) *Common Knowledge: The development of understanding in the classroom*. London: Methuen.

Edwards, D. and Mercer, N.M. (1989) Reconstructing context: the conventionalization of classroom knowledge. *Discourse Processes*, 12: 91–104.

Edwards, D. and Middleton, D. (1986a) Joint remembering: constructing an account of shared experience through conversational discourse. *Discourse Processes*, 9: 423–59.

Edwards, D. and Middleton, D. (1986b) Text for memory: joint recall with a scribe. *Human Learning*, 5: 125–38.

Edwards, D. and Middleton, D. (1987) Conversation and remembering: Bartlett revisited. *Applied Cognitive Psychology*, 1 (2): 77–92.

Edwards, D. and Middleton, D. (1988) Conversational remembering and family relationships: how children learn to remember. *Journal of Social and Personal Relationships*, 5: 3–25.

Edwards, D., Middleton, D. and Potter, J. (1992) Towards a discursive psychology of remembering. *The Psychologist*, in press.

Edwards, D. and Potter, J. (1992a) The Chancellor's memory: rhetoric and truth in discursive remembering. *Applied Cognitive Psychology*, in press.

Edwards, D. and Potter, J. (1992b) Language and causation: a discursive action model of attribution. Mimeo. Loughborough University.

Eglin, P. (1979) Resolving reality junctures on telegraph avenue: a study of practical reasoning. *Canadian Journal of Sociology*, 4: 359–77.

Eiser, J.R. (1986) *Social Psychology: Attitudes, cognition and social behaviour*. Cambridge: Cambridge University Press.

Emmison, M. (1989) A conversation on trial? The case of the Ananda Marga conspiracy tapes. *Journal of Pragmatics*, 13: 363–80.

Fiedler, K., Semin, G.R. and Bolten, S. (1989) Language use and reification of social information: top-down and bottom-up processing in person cognition. *European Journal of Social Psychology*, 19: 271–95.

Fillmore, C.J. (1971) Verbs of judging: an exercise in semantic description. In C.J. Fillmore and D.T. Langendoen (eds), *Studies in Linguistic Semantics*. New York: Holt, Rinehart and Winston.

Fiske, S.T. and Taylor, S.E. (1984) *Social Cognition*. Reading, MA: Addison-Wesley.

Forgas, J.P. (ed.) (1981) *Social Cognition: Perspectives on everyday understanding*. London: Academic Press.

Fowler, R. (1986) *Linguistic Criticism*. Oxford: Oxford University Press.

Gardner, H. (1985) *The Mind's New Science*, New York: Basic Books.

Garfinkel, H. (1967) *Studies in Ethnomethodology*. Englewood Cliffs, NJ: Prentice Hall.

Gergen, K.J. (1978) Experimentation in social psychology: a reappraisal. *European Journal of Social Psychology*, 8: 507–27.

Gergen, K.J. (1982) *Toward Transformation in Social Knowledge*. New York: Springer-Verlag.

Gergen, K.J. (1985) Social constructionist inquiry: context and implications. In K.J. Gergen, and K.E. Davis (eds), *The Social Construction of the Person*. New York: Springer-Verlag.

Gergen, K.J. and Davis, K.E. (eds) (1985) *The Social Construction of the Person*. New York: Springer-Verlag.

Gergen, K.J. and Gergen, M. (1987) Narratives of relationship. In R. Burnett, P. McGee and D. Clarke (eds), *Accounting for Relationships: Explanation, representation and knowledge*. London: Methuen.

Gergen, M. (1988) Narrative structures and social explanations. In C. Antaki (ed.), *Analysing Everyday Explanation: A casebook of methods*. London: Sage.

Gibson, J.J. (1966) *The Senses Considered as Perceptual Systems*. Boston: Houghton Mifflin.

Gibson, J.J. (1979) *The Ecological Approach to Visual Perception*. Boston: Houghton Mifflin.

Gilbert, G.N. and Mulkay, M. (1984) *Opening Pandora's Box: A sociological analysis of scientists' discourse*. Cambridge: Cambridge University Press.

Goffman, E. (1971) *Relations in Public: Microstudies of the public order*. Harmondsworth: Penguin.

Goffman, E. (1979) Footing. *Semiotica*, 25: 1–29. (Reprinted in Goffman, 1981.)

Goffman, E. (1981) *Forms of Talk*. Oxford: Blackwell.

Goodwin, C. (1987) Forgetfulness as an interactive resource. *Social Psychology Quarterly*, 50: 115–30.

Goodwin, C. and Goodwin, M. (1987) Concurrent operations on talk: notes on the interactive organization of assessments. *Papers in Pragmatics*, 1: 1–55.

Grady, K. and Potter, J. (1985) Speaking and clapping: a comparison of Foot and Thatcher's oratory. *Language and Communication*, 5: 173–83.

Graesser, A.C. and Black, J.B. (eds) (1985) *The Psychology of Questions*. Hillsdale, NJ: Lawrence Erlbaum.

Greatbatch, D. (1986) Aspects of topical organization in news interviews: the use of agenda-shifting procedures by interviewees. *Media, Culture and Society*, 8: 44–56.

Grice, H.P. (1975) Logic and conversation: In P. Cole and J. Morgan (eds), *Syntax and Semantics 3: Speech acts*. New York: Academic Press.

Gruneberg, M.M. and Morris, P.E. (eds) (1979) *Applied Problems in Memory*. New York: Academic Press.

Gruneberg, M.M., Morris, P.E. and Sykes, R.N. (eds) (1978) *Practical Aspects of Memory*. New York: Academic Press.

Halkowski, T. (1990) 'Role' as an interactional device. *Social Problems*, 37: 564–77.

Hamlyn, D.W. (1990) *In and Out of the Black Box: On the philosophy of cognition*. Oxford: Blackwell.

Harré, R. (1979) *Social Being: A theory for social psychology*. Oxford: Blackwell.

Harré, R. (1981) Expressive aspects of descriptions of others. In C. Antaki (ed.), *The Psychology of Ordinary Explanations of Social Behaviour*. London: Academic Press.

Harré, R. (1983) *Personal Being: A theory for individual psychology*. Oxford: Blackwell.

Harris, J.E. and Morris, P.E. (eds) (1984) *Everyday Memory, Actions and Absentmindedness*. New York: Academic Press.

Hart, H.L.A. and Honoré, A.M. (1985) *Causation and the Law*, 2nd edn. Oxford: Clarendon.

Harvey, J. and Weary, G. (1984) Current issues in attribution theory and research. *Annual Review of Psychology*, 35: 427–59.

Harvey, J.H., Weber, A.L. and Orbuch, T.I. (1990) *Interpersonal Accounts: A social psychological perspective*. Oxford: Blackwell.

Heider, F. (1944) Social perception and phenomenal causality. *Psychological Review*, 51: 358–74.

Heider, F. (1958) *The Psychology of Interpersonal Relations*. New York: Wiley.

Henriques, J., Hollway, W., Irwin, C., Couze, V. and Walkerdine, V. (1984) *Changing the Subject: Psychology, social regulation and subjectivity*. London: Methuen.

Heritage, J. (1984) *Garfinkel and Ethnomethodology*. Cambridge: Polity Press.

Heritage, J. (1988) Explanations as accounts: a conversation analytic perspective. In C. Antaki (ed.), *Analysing Everyday Explanation: A casebook of methods*. London: Sage.

Heritage, J., Clayman, S. and Zimmerman, D. (1988) Discourse and message analysis: the micro-structure of mass media messages. In R. Hawkins, S. Pingree and J. Weimann (eds), *Advancing Communication Science*. Beverly Hills, CA: Sage.

Heritage, J. and Greatbatch, D. (1986) Generating applause: a study of rhetoric and response in party political conferences. *American Sociological Review*, 92: 110–57.

Heritage, J. and Watson, R. (1979) Formulations as conversational objects. In

G. Psathas (ed.), *Everyday Language: Studies in Ethnomethodology*. New York: Irvington.

Heritage, J. and Watson, D.R. (1980) Aspects of the properties of formulations in natural conversations: some instances analyzed. *Semiotica*, 30: 245–62.

Hesse, M. (1974) *The Structure of Scientific Inference*. London: Macmillan.

Hewitt, J.P. (1979) *Self and Society*. Boston: Allyn and Bacon.

Hewstone, M. (ed.) (1983) *Attribution Theory: Social and functional extensions*. Oxford: Blackwell.

Hewstone, M. (1989) *Causal Attribution: From cognitive processes to collective beliefs*. Oxford: Blackwell.

Hilbert, R. (1981) Towards an improved understanding of 'role'. *Theory and Society*, 10: 207–26.

Hildyard, A. and Olson, D.R. (1982) On the comprehension and memory of oral versus written discourse. In D. Tannen (ed.), *Spoken and Written Language: Exploring orality and literacy*. Norwood, NJ: Ablex.

Hilton, D.J. (1990) Conversational processes and causal attribution. *Psychological Bulletin*, 107: 65–81.

Hilton, D.J. and Slugoski, B.R. (1986) Knowledge-based causal attribution: the abnormal conditions focus model. *Psychological Review*, 93: 75–88.

Hilton, D.J., Smith, R.H. and Alicke, M.D. (1988) Knowledge-based information acquisition: norms and the functions of consensus information. *Journal of Personality and Social Psychology*, 55: 530–40.

Hoffman, C. and Tchir, M.A. (1990) Interpersonal verbs and dispositional adjectives: the psychology of causality embodied in language. *Journal of Personality and Social Psychology*, 58: 765–78.

Hollway, W. (1989) *Subjectivity and Method in Psychology: Gender, meaning and science*. London: Sage.

Howard, J.A. and Allen, C. (1989) Making meaning: revealing attributions through analyses of readers' responses. *Social Psychology Quarterly*, 52 (4): 280–98.

Humphreys, L. (1969) *Tearoom Trade: Impersonal sex in public places*. Chicago: Aldine.

Jackson, B.S. (1988) *Law, Fact and Narrative Coherence*. Merseyside: Deborah Charles.

Jayyusi, L. (1984) *Categories and the Moral Order*. London: Routledge.

Jefferson, G. (1985a) On the interactional unpackaging of a gloss. *Language and Society*, 15: 435–63.

Jefferson, G. (1985b) An exercise in the transcription and analysis of laughter. In T. Van Dijk (ed.), *Handbook of Discourse Analysis*, vol. 3, London: Academic Press.

Jefferson, G. (1990) List construction as a task and interactional resource. In G. Psathas (ed.), *Interactional Competence*. Washington DC: University Press of America.

Johnson-Laird, P.N. (1988) *The Computer and the Mind: An introduction to cognitive science*. London: Fontana.

Jones, E.E. and Davis, K.E. (1965) From acts to dispositions: the attribution process in social perception. In L. Berkowitz (ed.), *Advances in Experimental Social Psychology*, vol. 2. New York: Academic Press.

Kelley, H.H. (1967) Attribution theory in social psychology. In D. Levine, (ed.), *Nebraska Symposium on Motivation*. Lincoln, Neb.: University of Nebraska Press.

188   *Discursive psychology*

Kintsch, W. (1974) *The Representation of Meaning in Memory*. Hillsdale, NJ: Lawrence Erlbaum.

Kintsch, W. and Van Dijk, T.A. (1978) Toward a model of text comprehension and production. *Psychological Review*, 85 (5): 363–94.

Kreckel, M. (1981) *Communicative Acts and Shared Knowledge in Natural Discourse*. London: Academic Press.

Kress, G. and Hodge, B. (1979) *Language as Ideology*. London: Routledge.

Lakoff, G. (1987) *Women, Fire and Dangerous Things: What categories reveal about the mind*. Chicago: University of Chicago Press.

Latour, B. (1987) *Science in Action*. Milton Keynes: Open University Press.

Latour, B. and Woolgar, S. (1986) *Laboratory Life: The social construction of scientific facts*, 2nd edn. Princeton, NJ: Princeton University Press.

Lave, J. (1988) *Cognition in Practice: Mind, mathematics and culture in everyday life*. Cambridge: Cambridge University Press.

Lave, J. (1990) The culture of acquisition and the practice of understanding. In J.W. Stigler, R.A. Shweder and G. Herdt (eds), *Cultural Psychology*. Cambridge: Cambridge University Press.

Lawson, H. and Apignanasi, L. (1989) *Dismantling Truth: Reality in the post-modern world*. London: Weidenfeld and Nicolson.

LCHC (Laboratory of Comparative Human Cognition) (1983) Culture and cognitive development. In W. Kessen (ed.), *Carmichael's Manual of Child Psychology: History, theories and methods*. New York: Wiley.

Lehnert, W.G. (1978) *The Process of Question-Answering*. Hillsdale, NJ: Lawrence Erlbaum.

Leudar, I. and Antaki, C. (1988) Completion and dynamics in explanation seeking. In C. Antaki (ed.), *Analysing Everyday Explanation: A casebook of methods*. London: Sage.

Levinson, S. (1983) *Pragmatics*. Cambridge: Cambridge University Press.

Levinson, S.C. (1988) Putting linguistics on a proper footing: explorations in Goffman's concepts of participation. In P. Drew and A. Wootton (eds), *Erving Goffman: Studies in the interactional order*. Cambridge, Polity.

Linell, P. and Jönsson, L. (1989) Suspect stories: on perspective setting in an asymmetrical situation. Presented at Conference on Dialogical and Contextual Dominance, Bad Homburg, 23–25 November 1989.

Linton, M. (1982) Transformations of memory in everyday life. In U. Neisser (ed.), *Memory Observed: Remembering in natural contexts*. Oxford: Freeman.

Litton, I. and Potter, J. (1985) Social representations in the ordinary explanation of a 'riot'. *European Journal of Social Psychology*, 15: 371–88.

Lloyd-Bostock, S.M.A. and Clifford, B.R. (eds) (1983) *Evaluating Witness Evidence*. Chichester: Wiley.

Locke, D. and Pennington, D. (1982) Reasons and causes in attribution processes. *Journal of Personality and Social Psychology*, 42: 212–23.

Loftus, E.F. (1975) Leading questions and the eyewitness report. *Cognitive Psychology*, 7: 560–72.

Loftus, E.F. (1979) *Eyewitness Testimony*. London: Harvard University Press.

Loftus, E.F. (1981) Natural and unnatural cognition. *Cognition*, 10: 193–6.

Loftus, E.F. and Ketcham, K.E. (1983) The malleability of eyewitness accounts. In S.M.A. Lloyd-Bostock and B.R. Clifford (eds), *Evaluating Witness Evidence*. Chichester: Wiley.

Loftus, E.F. and Zanni, G. (1975) Eyewitness testimony: the influence of the wording of a question. *Bulletin of the Psychonomic Society*, 5: 86–8.

Luff, P., Gilbert, G.N. and Frohlich, D. (eds) (1990) *Computers and Conversation*. London: Academic Press.

Mandler, J.M. (1979) Categorical and schematic organization in memory. In C.R. Puff (ed.), *Memory Organization and Structure*. New York: Academic Press.

Mandler, J.M. (1984) *Scripts, Stories and Scenes: Aspects of schema theory*. Hillsdale, NJ: Lawrence Erlbaum.

McArthur, L.A. (1972) The how and what of why: some determinants and consequences of causal attribution. *Journal of Personality and Social Psychology*, 2: 171–93.

McKinlay, A. and Potter, J. (1987) Model discourse: interpretative repertoires in scientists' conference talk. *Social Studies of Science*, 17: 443–63.

McKinlay, A., Potter, J. and Wetherell, M. (1992) Discourse analysis and social representations. In G. Breakwell and D. Canter (eds), *Empirical Approaches to Social Representations*. Buckingham: Open University Press.

McCloskey, D. (1985) *The Rhetoric of Economics*. Brighton: Wheatsheaf.

Michotte, A. (1963) *The Perception of Causality*. London: Methuen.

Middleton, D. and Edwards, D. (eds) (1990a) *Collective Remembering*. London: Sage.

Middleton, D. and Edwards, D. (1990b) Conversational remembering: a social psychological approach. In D. Middleton and D. Edwards (eds), *Collective Remembering*. London: Sage.

Mills, C.W. (1940) Situated actions and vocabularies of motive. *American Sociological Review*, 5: 904–13.

Molotch, H.L. and Boden, D. (1985) Talking social structure: discourse domination and the Watergate hearings. *American Sociological Review*, 50: 273–88.

Moscovici, S. (1972) Society and theory in social psychology. In J. Israel and H. Tajfel (eds), *The Context of Social Psychology: A critical assessment*. London: Academic Press.

Moscovici, S. (1984) The phenomenon of social representations. In R.M. Farr and S. Moscovici (eds), *Social Representations*. Cambridge: Cambridge University Press.

Mulkay, M. (1979) *Science and the Sociology of Knowledge*. London: Allen and Unwin.

Mulkay, M. (1985) *The Word and the World: Explorations in the form of sociological analysis*. London: Allen and Unwin.

Mulkay, M. (1988) *On Humour*. Cambridge: Polity.

Mulkay, M. and Gilbert, G.N. (1982) Accounting for error: how scientists construct their social world when they account for correct and incorrect belief. *Sociology*, 16: 165–83.

Mulkay, M. and Gilbert, G.N. (1983) Scientists' theory talk. *Canadian Journal of Sociology*, 8: 179–97.

Myers, G. (1990) *Writing Biology: Texts in the construction of scientific knowledge*. Madison: University of Wisconsin Press.

Neisser, U. (1967) *Cognitive Psychology*. New York: Appleton-Century-Crofts.

Neisser, U. (1976) *Cognition and Reality*. San Francisco: Freeman.

Neisser, U. (1978) Memory: what are the important questions? In M.M. Gruneberg, P.E. Morris and R.N. Sykes (eds), *Practical Aspects of Memory*. New York: Academic Press.

Neisser, U. (1981) John Dean's memory: a case study. *Cognition*, 9: 1–22.

190 *Discursive psychology*

Neisser, U. (ed.) (1982) *Memory Observed: Remembering in natural contexts*. Oxford: Freeman.

Neisser, U. (1985) Toward an ecologically orientated cognitive science. In T.M. Schlechter and M.P. Toglia (eds), *New Directions in Cognitive Science*. Norwood, NJ: Ablex.

Neisser, U. (1988) Five kinds of self-knowledge. *Philosophical Psychology*, 1: 35–59.

Neisser, U. and Winograd, E. (eds) (1988) *Remembering Reconsidered: Ecological and traditional approaches*. Cambridge: Cambridge University Press.

Nelson, K. (ed.) (1986) *Event Knowledge: Structure and function in development*. Hillsdale, NJ: Lawrence Erlbaum.

Norman, D.A. (1988) *The Psychology of Everyday Things*. New York: Basic Books.

Ochs, E. (1979) Transcription as theory. In E. Ochs and B. Schieffelin (eds), *Developmental Pragmatics*. New York: Academic Press.

Ochs, E. and Schieffelin, B. (1984) Language acquisition and socialization: three developmental stories. In R. Shweder and R. Levine (eds), *Culture Theory: Essays on mind, self and emotion*. Cambridge: Cambridge University Press.

Oldman, D. and Drucker, C. (1985) The non-reducibility of ethnomethods: can people and computers form a society? In G.N. Gilbert and C. Heath (eds), *Social Action and Artificial Intelligence*. Aldershot: Gower.

Piaget, J. (1970) Piaget's theory. In P.H. Mussen (ed.), *Carmichael's Manual of Child Psychology*. New York: Wiley.

Pinch, T. (1986) *Confronting Nature*. Dordrecht: Reidel.

Pinch, T. and Clark, C. (1986) The hard sell: patter-merchanting and the strategic (re)production and local management of economic reasoning in the sales routines of market pitchers. *Sociology*, 20: 169–91.

Pollner, M. (1987) *Mundane Reason*. Cambridge: Cambridge University Press.

Pomerantz, A.M. (1978) Compliment responses: notes on the co-operation of multiple constraints. In J. Schenkein (ed.), *Studies in the Organization of Conversational Interaction*. London: Academic Press.

Pomerantz, A.M. (1984a) Agreeing and disagreeing with assessments: some features of preferred/dispreferred turn shapes. In J.M. Atkinson and J. Heritage (eds), *Structures of Social Action: Studies in conversation analysis*. Cambridge: Cambridge University Press.

Pomerantz, A.M. (1984b) Giving a source or basis: the practice in conversation of telling 'how I know'. *Journal of Pragmatics*, 8: 607–25.

Pomerantz, A.M. (1984c) Pursuing a response. In J.M. Atkinson and J. Heritage (eds), *Structures of Social Action: Studies in conversation analysis*. Cambridge: Cambridge University Press.

Pomerantz, A.M. (1986) Extreme case formulations: a new way of legitimating claims. *Human Studies*, 9: 219–30.

Pomerantz, A.M. (1987) Descriptions in legal settings. In G. Button and J.R.E. Lee (eds), *Talk and Social Organization*. Clevedon, Avon: Multilingual Matters.

Pomerantz, A.M. (1988/9) Constructing skepticism: four devices used to engender the audience's skepticism. *Research on Language and Social Interaction*, 22: 293–314.

Pomerantz, A.M. and Atkinson, J.M. (1984) Ethnomethodology, conversation analysis and the study of courtroom interaction. In D.J. Muller, D.E. Blackman and A.J. Chapman (eds), *Topics in Psychology and Law*. Chichester: Wiley.

Potter, J. (1984) Testability, flexibility: Kuhnian values in psychologists' discourse concerning theory choice. *Philosophy of the Social Sciences*, 14: 303–30.

Potter, J. (1987) Reading repertoires: a preliminary study of some techniques that scientists use to construct readings. *Science and Technology Studies*, 5: 112–21.

Potter, J. (1988a) What is reflexive about discourse analysis? – The case of reading readings. In S. Woolgar (ed.), *Knowledge and Reflexivity: New frontiers in the sociology of knowledge*. London: Sage.

Potter, J. (1988b) Cutting cakes: a study of psychologists' social categorizations. *Philosophical Psychology*, 1: 17–33.

Potter, J. and Edwards, D. (1990) Nigel Lawson's tent: discourse analysis, attribution theory and the social psychology of fact. *European Journal of Social Psychology*, 20: 24–40.

Potter, J. and Halliday, Q. (1990) Community leaders as a device for warranting versions of crowd events. *Journal of Pragmatics*, 14: 725–41.

Potter, J. and Litton, I. (1985) Some problems underlying the theory of social representations. *British Journal of Social Psychology*, 24: 81–90.

Potter, J. and Mulkay, M. (1985) Scientists' interview talk: interviews as a technique for revealing participants' interpretative practices. In M. Brenner, J. Brown and D. Canter (eds), *The Research Interview: Uses and approaches*. London: Academic Press.

Potter, J. and Reicher, S. (1987) Discourses of community and conflict: the organization of social categories in accounts of a riot. *British Journal of Social Psychology*, 26: 25–40.

Potter, J., Stringer, P. and Wetherell, M. (1984) *Social Texts and Context: Literature and social psychology*. London: Routledge.

Potter, J. and Wetherell, M. (1987) *Discourse and Social Psychology: Beyond attitudes and behaviour*. London: Sage.

Potter, J. and Wetherell, M. (1988) Accomplishing attitudes: facts and evaluation in racist discourse. *Text*, 8: 51–68.

Potter, J. and Wetherell, M. (1989) Fragmented ideologies: accounts of educational failure and positive discrimination. *Text*, 9: 175–90.

Potter, J. and Wetherell, M. (forthcoming) Analysing discourse. In R. Burgess and A. Bryman (eds), *Analysing Qualitative Data*. London: Routledge.

Potter, J., Wetherell, M. and Chitty, A. (1991) Quantification rhetoric – cancer on television. *Discourse and Society*, 2: 333–65.

Potter, J., Wetherell, M., Gill, R. and Edwards, D. (1990) Discourse: noun, verb or social practice? *Philosophical Psychology*, 3: 205–17.

Rimon-Kenan, S. (1983) *Narrative Fiction: Contemporary poetics*. London: Methuen.

Rogoff, B. and Lave, J. (1984) *Everyday Cognition: Its development in social context*. Cambridge, MA: Harvard University Press.

Rorty, R. (1980) *Philosophy and the Mirror of Nature*. Princeton, NJ: Princeton University Press.

Rosch, E., Mervis, C.B., Gray, W.D., Johnson, D. and Boyes-Braem, P. (1976) Basic objects in natural categories. *Cognitive Psychology*, 8: 382–439.

Rubin, D.C. (1977) Very long-term memory for prose and verse. *Journal of Verbal Learning and Verbal Behavior*, 16: 611–21.

Rubin, D.C. (1982) On the retention function for autobiographical memory. *Journal of Verbal Learning and Verbal Behavior*, 21: 21–38.

Rumelhart, D.E. (1975) Notes on a schema for stories. In D.G. Bobrow and A.M.

Collins (eds), *Representation and Understanding: Studies in cognitive science*. New York: Academic Press.

Sabini, J. and Silver, M. (1980) Baseball and hot sauce: a critique of some attributional treatments of evaluation. *Journal for the Theory of Social Behaviour*, 10: 83–95.

Sacks, H. (1964) Lecture 1: Rules of conversational sequence. Reprinted in *Human Studies*, 12 (1989): 217–27.

Sacks, H. (1972a) An initial investigation of the usability of conversational data for doing sociology. In D. Sudnow (ed.), *Studies in Social Interaction*. New York: Free Press.

Sacks, H. (1972b) Notes on police assessment of moral character. In D. Sudnow (ed.), *Studies in Social Interaction*. New York: Free Press.

Sacks, H. (1974) On the analyzability of stories by children. In R. Turner (ed.), *Ethnomethodology*. Harmondsworth: Penguin.

Sacks, H. (1979) Hotrodder: a revolutionary category. In G. Psathas (ed.), *Everyday Language: Studies in Ethnomethodology*. New York: Irvington.

Sacks, H. (1987) On the preferences for agreement and contiguity in sequences in conversation. In G. Button and J.R.E. Lee (eds), *Talk and Social Organization*. Clevedon: Multilingual Matters.

Sacks, H. and Schegloff, E.A. (1979) Two preferences in the organization of reference to persons in conversation and their interaction. In G. Psathas (ed.), *Everyday Language: Studies in Ethnomethodology*. New York: Irvington.

Sacks, H., Schegloff, E.A. and Jefferson, G. (1974) A simplest systematics for the organization of turn-taking in conversation. *Language*, 50: 596–735.

Sampson, E.E. (1983) Deconstructing psychology's subject. *Journal of Mind and Behaviour*, 4: 135–64.

Sampson, E.E. (1988) The deconstruction of self. In J. Shotter and K. Gergen (eds), *Texts of Identity*. London: Sage.

Schank, R.C. (1982) *Dynamic Memory: A theory of reminding and learning in computers and people*. Cambridge: Cambridge University Press.

Schank, R.C. and Abelson, R. (1977) *Scripts, Plans, Goals and Understanding*. Hillsdale, NJ: Lawrence Erlbaum.

Schegloff, E.A. (1972) Notes on a conversational practice: formulating place. In D. Sudnow (ed.), *Studies in Social Interaction*. Glencoe: Free Press.

Schegloff, E.A. (1988a) Presequences and indirection: applying speech act theory to ordinary conversation. *Journal of Pragmatics*, 12: 55–62.

Schegloff, E.A. (1988b) Goffman and the analysis of conversation. In P. Drew and A. Wootton (eds), *Erving Goffman: Studies in the interactional order*. Cambridge: Polity.

Schegloff, E.A. (1989) Harvey Sacks – Lectures 1964–1965: an introduction/memoir. *Human Studies*, 12: 185–209.

Schenkein, J. (ed.) (1978) *Studies in the Organization of Conversational Interaction*. New York: Academic Press.

Schwartz, B. (1990) The reconstruction of Abraham Lincoln. In D. Middleton and D. Edwards (eds), *Collective Remembering*. London: Sage.

Scribner, S. and Cole, M. (1981) *The Psychology of Literacy*. London: Harvard University Press.

Searle, J.R. (1969) *Speech Acts*. Cambridge: Cambridge University Press.

Semin, G. (1980) A gloss on attribution theory. *British Journal of Social and Clinical Psychology*, 19: 291–300.

Semin, G. and Fiedler, K. (1988) The cognitive functions of linguistic categories in describing persons: social cognition and language. *Journal of Personality and Social Psychology*, 54: 558–68.

Shapiro, M. (1988) *The Politics of Representation: Writing practices in biography, photography and policy analysis*. Madison, WI: University of Wisconsin Press.

Shapiro, M. (1989) Textualizing global politics. In J. Der Derian and M. Shapiro (eds), *International/Intertextual Relations: Postmodern readings of world politics*. Lexington, MA.: Lexington Books.

Shaver, K.G. (1983) *An Introduction to Attribution Processes*. Hillsdale, NJ: Lawrence Erlbaum.

Shaw, R. and Bransford, J. (eds) (1977) *Perceiving, Acting and Knowing*. Hillsdale, NJ: Lawrence Erlbaum.

Shotter, J. (1984) *Social Accountability and Selfhood*. Oxford: Blackwell.

Shotter, J. and Gergen, K. (eds) (1989) *Texts of Identity*. London: Sage.

Silverman, D. and Torode, B. (1979) *Language and Materialism: Some theories of language and its limits*. London: Routledge.

Simons, H. (ed.) (1989a) *Rhetoric in the Human Sciences*. London: Sage.

Simons, H. (1989b) 'Going meta' in political confrontations. In B. Gronbeck (ed.), *Spheres of Argument*. Annandale VA.: SCA.

Smith, D. (1978) K is mentally ill: the anatomy of a factual account. *Sociology*, 12: 23–53.

Smith, J. (1987) Making people offers they can't refuse: a social psychological analysis of attitude change. In J. Hawthorn (ed.), *Propaganda, Persuasion and Power*. London: Edward Arnold.

Stephenson, G.M., Brandstätter, H. and Wagner, W. (1983) An experimental study of social performance and delay on the testimonial validity of story recall. *European Journal of Social Psychology*, 13: 175–91.

Stigler, J.W., Shweder, R.A. and Herdt, G. (eds) (1990) *Cultural Psychology: Essays on comparative human development*. Cambridge: Cambridge University Press.

Suchman, L. (1987) *Plans and Situated Action: The problem of human–machine communication*. Cambridge: Cambridge University Press.

Tannen, D. (1989) *Talking Voices*. Cambridge: Cambridge University Press.

Taylor, C.E. (1990) The 'truth' about alcohol: a discourse analytic approach. Unpublished dissertation, Department of Social Sciences, Loughborough University.

Tetlock, P.E. and Manstead, A.S.R. (1985) Impression management versus intrapsychic explanations in social psychology: a useful dichotomy? *Psychological Review*, 92: 59–77.

Thorndyke, P.W. (1977) Cognitive structures in comprehension and memory of narrative discourse. *Cognitive Psychology*, 9: 77–110.

Todorov, T. (1968) Introduction: le vraisemblable. Cited in P. Atkinson (1990) *The Ethnographic Imagination: The textual construction of reality*. London: Routledge.

Trilling, L. (1974) *Sincerity and Authenticity*. London: Oxford University Press.

Turnbull, W. and Slugoski, B.R. (1988) Conversational and linguistic processes in causal attribution. In D. Hilton (ed.), *Contemporary Science and Natural Explanation*. Brighton: Harvester/Wheatsheaf.

Van Kleeck, M.H., Hillger, L.A. and Brown, R. (1988) Pitting verbal schemas against information variables in attribution. *Social Cognition*, 6: 89–106.

Vygotsky, L.S. (1987) *Thought and Language*. Edited by Alex Kozulin. Cambridge, MA: MIT Press.

Wagenaar, W. (1986) My memory: a study of autobiographical memory over six years. *Cognitive Psychology*, 18: 225–52.

Walker, R.B.J. (1990) Sovereignty, identity, community: reflections on the horizons of contemporary political practice. In R.B.J. Walker and S.H. Mendlovitz (eds), *Contending Sovereignties: Redefining political community*. Boulder: Lynne Reinner.

Walkerdine, V. (1988) *The Mastery of Reason*. London: Routledge.

Wason, P.C. and Johnson-Laird, P.N. (1972) *Psychology of Reasoning: Structure and content*. London: Batsford.

Watson, R. (1978) Categorization, authorization and blame-negotiation in conversation. *Sociology*, 12: 105–13.

Watson, R. (1983) The presentation of victim and motive in discourse: the case of police interrogations and interviews. *Victimology*, 8: 31–52.

Watson, R. and Sharrock, W.W. (1991) Something on accounts. *The Discourse Analysis Research Group Newsletter*, 7: 3–12.

Watson, R. and Weinberg, T. (1982) Interviews and the interactional construction of accounts and homosexual identity. *Social Analysis*, 11: 56–78.

Weisner, M.J. (1991) Mario M. Cuomo decides to run: the construction of a political self. *Discourse and Society*, 2: 85–104.

Wells, C. and Loftus, E. (eds) (1984) *Eyewitness Testimony: Psychological perspectives*. Cambridge: Cambridge University Press.

Wertsch, J.V. (1985) *Vygotsky and the Social Formation of Mind*. Cambridge, MA: Harvard University Press.

Wetherell, M. (1986) Linguistic repertoires and literary criticism: new directions for the social psychology of gender. In S. Wilkinson, (ed.), *Feminist Psychology*. Milton Keynes: Open University Press.

Wetherell, M. and Potter, J. (1988) Discourse analysis and the identification of interpretative repertoires. In C. Antaki (ed.), *Analysing Everyday Explanation: A casebook of methods*. London: Sage.

Wetherell, M. and Potter, J. (1989) Narrative characters and accounting for violence. In J. Shotter and K. Gergen (eds), *Texts of Identity*. London: Sage.

Wetherell, M. and Potter, J. (forthcoming) *Mapping the Language of Racism: Discourse and the legitimation of exploitation*. London: Harvester/Wheatsheaf.

Wetherell, M., Stiven, H. and Potter, J. (1987) Unequal egalitarianism: a preliminary study of discourses concerning gender and employment opportunities. *British Journal of Social Psychology*, 26: 59–71.

Whalen, M.R. and Zimmerman, D.H. (1990) Describing trouble: practical epistemology in citizen calls to the police. *Language in Society*, 19: 465–92.

Widdicomb, S. and Wooffitt, R. (1990) 'Being' versus 'doing' punk (etc.): on achieving authenticity as a member. *Journal of Language and Social Psychology*, 9: 257–77.

Widdicomb, S. and Wooffitt, R. (1992) 'Well what do you expect looking like that?': a study of the use of 'ordinary identity' in the construction of a complaint. Mimeo, University of Edinburgh.

Wieder, L. (1974) *Language and Social Reality*. The Hague: Mouton.

Wilson, J. (1990) *Politically Speaking: The pragmatic analysis of political language*. Oxford: Blackwell.

Winograd, T. (1972) *Understanding Natural Language*. New York: Academic Press.

Winograd, T. (1980) What does it mean to understand language? *Cognitive Science*, 4: 209–41.

Winograd, T. and Flores, F. (1986) *Understanding Computers and Cognition: A new foundation for design*. Norwood, NJ: Addison-Wesley.

Wittgenstein, L. (1921) *Tractatus Logico-Philosophicus*. London: Routledge.

Wittgenstein, L. (1953) *Philosophical Investigations*. Oxford: Blackwell.

Wooffitt, R.C. (1990) On the analysis of interaction: an introduction to conversation analysis. In P. Luff, G.N. Gilbert and D. Frohlich (eds), *Computers and Conversation*. New York: Academic Press.

Wooffitt, R.C. (1991) 'I was just doing X . . . when Y': some inferential properties of a device in accounts of paranormal experiences. *Text*, 11: 267–88.

Wooffitt, R.C. (1992) *Telling Tales of the Unexpected: The organization of factual accounts*. London: Harvester/Wheatsheaf.

Woolgar, S. (1980) Discovery: logic and sequence in a scientific text. In R. Krohn, K. Knorr and R.D. Whitley (eds), *The Social Process of Scientific Investigation*. Dordrecht: Reidel.

Woolgar, S. (1988a) *Science: The very idea*. London: Tavistock.

Woolgar, S. (1988b) *Knowledge and Reflexivity: New frontiers in the sociology of knowledge*. London: Sage.

Wootton, A. (1989) Remarks on the methodology of conversation analysis. In D. Roger and P. Bull (eds), *Conversation*. Clevedon: Multilingual Matters.

Wowk, M. (1984) Blame allocation, sex and gender in a murder interrogation. *Women's Studies International Forum*, 7: 75–82.

Yearley, S. (1984) Proofs and reputations: Sir James Hall and the use of classification devices in scientific arguments. *Earth Sciences History*, 3: 25–43.

Yearley, S. (1985) Vocabularies of freedom and resentment: a Strawsonian perspective on the nature of argumentation in science and the law. *Social Studies of Science*, 15: 99–126.

Yearley, S. (1986) Interactive-orientation and argumentation in scientific texts. In J. Law (ed.), *Power, Action and Belief: A new sociology of knowledge*. London: Routledge.

Yearley, S. (1987) Demotic logic: causal discourse and the structure of explanations. *Text*, 7: 181–203.

Zimmerman, D. and Pollner, M. (1970) The everyday world as a phenomenon. In J. Douglas (ed.), *Understanding Everyday Life*. London: Routledge.

Index